foreword

Now and then Utopians (realists of the long run, that is, rather than of the moment) actually undertake to plan their physical surroundings. Instead of setting loose controls over broad categories of land use, they specify in detail the character and location of this structure, such and such a space, that link between them. Architects enjoy elaborating such plans: Sforzinda, Ville Radieuse, Broadacre City. Great planners like Wren and Burnham dream up whole cities. The moral Utopians—St. Thomas More, Tomaso Campanella, and Lewis Mumford come to mind—likewise lean toward the design of whole environments. But sociologists rarely do. Perhaps they are too cautious, too aware of the complexity of the problem, too worried about seeming goody-goody. Whatever the reason, the very men who have made it their business to examine how men live in cities have refrained from redesigning those cities in the light of their discoveries.

William Michelson, however, is both an accomplished sociologist and a Utopian in disguise. Most of his book contains cool, orderly, and illuminating appraisals of what is known (or unknown) about links between the form of cities and the social life which goes on within them. But once in a while we see Michelson the Utopian pick up his blocks and start to build a new city genuinely fitted to the varied needs and desires of a diverse population. His is an anti-totalitarian Utopia; it maximizes convenience and freedom of choice while guaranteeing at least a minimum of comfort, beauty, and security. It differs from others in substituting, where possible, evidence on the way men behave in existing cities for assumptions about how they would behave in one ideal community or another. In his low-keyed, serious exhortations, Michelson tells us to find out what men want, learn how they respond to different sorts of settings, and then pay attention to both when building cities.

The advocate usually stays out of view. Michelson has done his work well; one could disagree profoundly with his preferences and yet find his analysis exceptionally helpful. For he has had the wit and the patience to break the form of the city down into its components, to analyze variations in social life in a simple, reasonable way, and then to review systematically the evidence concerning the interactions of form and social life within the framework produced by his two schemes.

The analysis of form is deliberately egocentric. It begins with the relations between a single individual and his environment, and builds from there. Michelson proposes to compound four elements—specifically (1) physical distance, (2) "manipulated" or "perceived" distance separating the individual from (3) other persons, and (4) nonresidential land uses—into more complicated characteristics of form: density, for example, or accessibility. His formulation helps us specify the differences between a cityscape mingling stores, factories, dwellings and vest-pocket parks from another in which each of these occupies its own large cluster. Perhaps more important, it makes it much easier to sort out the implications of a particular condition—a widespread demand, let us say, that shops be out of sight of one's front door—for the overall form of the city. Michelson's scheme does not serve all purposes. (It is a long leap, I think, from his egocentric springboard to what Kevin Lynch calls the "focus" of a city.) Nor has Michelson worked out all the permutations of his variables. At present, his scheme works best in the translation of individual preferences into specific arrangements of people and land use on the small scale. That is no mean accomplishment.

The analysis of social life reduces the variations in response to urban form to five dimensions: life style, stage in life cycle, social status, value orientation, and personality. The book deals with the first four systematically, and leaves personality relatively unexplored. Michelson shows great talent as a guide. He leads us through a broken terrain with patience, modesty, and thoroughness. First he reviews how people's responses to different kinds of environment vary with life cycle, then he moves on to change through the cycle of life, and so on through his set of variables. Along the way he makes a good many observations that students and planners of cities need to take seriously. An important part of his evidence, for example, makes it appear rather unlikely that the construction of high-rise apartments downtown will "bring back the middle class," however much mayors and shopkeepers plagued with dwindling revenues may cherish the fantasy. The demand for single-family houses turns out to be extraordinarily widespread and pressing.

Finally Michelson turns to the prickliest question: how much, and how, does the physical form of the city itself shape the social lives of the men within it? His answers are prudent and partial. They stand apart from the brash determinism of the critics of mass-produced suburbs who flourished in the 1950's, or the new determinists of overpopulation and high density who caught the public imagination in the 1960's. His conclusions are likely to last longer, and provide a firmer agenda for the next round of inquiry into the nature of cities. They open the way to a far more effective collaboration among architects, planners, sociologists, politicians, and ordinary city-dwellers in building cities men actually want. This Utopian has respect for the facts, and for the desires of living men.

Charles Tilly

acknowledgments

Although my name may appear as author of this book, this can in no way be construed as a one-man job; I am indebted to many.

Charles Tilly gave stimulating guidance and close review to the entire project. Martin Meyerson first interested me in the general question explored here and encouraged me to pursue it.

Active aid in developing the book was received from Olusola Avoseh, Richard Brause, Samuel Brause, Jonathan Caulfield, Mark Gould, Janet Lytle, Kathleen McDonnell, and Anna-Rose Spina. Among those who read earlier drafts of the manuscript and offered helpful comments are Trudi Bunting, Andrew Effrat, Herbert Gans, Julie Hanson, John Hitchcock, Suzanne Keller, Paul Reed, Norman Shulman, James Simmons, and Barry Wellman.

The Department of Educational Planning of the Ontario Institute for Studies in Education and its Chairman, Cicely Watson, gave encouragement and, when available, assistance, although this undertaking was not an official project. Ruth Colling was especially kind in this regard.

Inevitably, there were many others whose informal comments and reactions to specific elements were extremely thought-provoking. Of course, none of the above-named are responsible for the final product; that responsibility remains the author's alone.

WM

contents

preface

This book is devoted to an examination of relations between man and his urban environment, a huge area of inquiry. That the area is so huge and this volume is so thin is at once a commentary on the fruits of past research and a determinant of the structure of the discussion.

More specifically, the current endeavor is an attempt to present a synthesis of past research efforts linking the social characteristics and activities of people with the home, neighborhood, and other aspects of physical environment in which urbanites live, which have been and can be shaped by planners, architects, engineers, and all other men who modify the landscape. Although I shall establish by necessity broad limits over what aspects of this relationship will be considered here, the literature to be discussed is still diffuse and uncoordinated, and there is little precedent for any single set of grounds for synthesis.

Therefore, the first section of this book is devoted to the specification of a frame of reference through which past studies may be related to one another and future studies undertaken. It is a tree on which discrete items may be arranged so that they stand a chance of forming a larger pattern. Chapter 1 concentrates on the general frame of reference.

Although this frame of reference fills a void, some mention must be made as to how it differs from more orthodox approaches which are concerned, at least nominally, with the same subject matter. Since the field of human ecology is particularly concerned with man and his urban environment, considerable attention is devoted in Chapter 1 to explicating what human ecologists have done and how the present synthesis differs from their valuable contributions.

Chapter 2 then focuses more specifically on the *component parts* of a theoretical scheme including men and urban physical environment. It deals more specifically with the concepts to be used.

Following the groundwork laid in Section I, Section II, comprising Chapters 3 through 8, concentrates on the synthesis of the contributions of assorted research efforts, as grouped according to broad "social" headings. The content of these chapters relies intuitively on the logic of Section I, although it does not meet the rigor of its frame of reference, which of course was devised quite apart from the conduct of the various studies. This section aims to demonstrate not only the richness and extent of studies which tie together social and physical phenomena, but also the glaring weaknesses of this body of knowledge through obvious sins of omission.

In the final section and chapter, an attempt is made to summarize some of the concrete findings, to evaluate them with reference to theoretical and practical needs, and to suggest how knowledge of these phenomena might be advanced in the future.

A bibliography of relevant literature follows the final chapter.

Toronto, Ontario   WM
December 1969

section I
a frame of reference

what human ecology
left behind in the dust

Men are increasingly assuming conscious control over the development of their cities.   As societies group progressively larger
proportions of their populations in urban areas, the construction and
reconstruction necessary to supply their elemental wants enters
a state requiring critical attention. No longer do conscientious
citizens find sufficient the reassurance that every man should have a
roof over his head. They now ask with concern whether housing
provides adequately for the health, safety, and welfare of its
occupants.[1]

Public concern over an updated view of housing adequacy
makes some large assumptions. Central among them is the assumption that man is capable of creating optimal environments. This, in
turn, is dependent on the assumption that, beyond the most
elementary aspects of accommodation, the nature of housing,
neighborhoods, and cities makes a difference in the ways in which
people lead their lives.

---

[1]   These assurances must be at least nominally included in any public act
concerning mass reconstruction of cities.

Can people consciously create an environment that will facilitate achievement of their goals better than some alternative environment? Does an existing arrangement of buildings and spaces make some forms of human activity more difficult or even impossible, while encouraging others? Or, on the other hand, is what people do purely a matter of custom or volition, completely indifferent to the physical components of their setting?

If citizens and designers alike feel that there is something they can do about the *quality* of urban life, then they automatically take a stand on these questions. Is this stand justified?

At the roots of this question lie the considerations of social science. Human behavior has been explained in many ways through many different disciplines. Now the aims of modern urban development assume that human behavior articulates in some systematic way with the physical environment.

The assessment of this complex assumption is a frontier of urban sociology. It is also prerequisite for intelligent physical design and planning. One might logically expect that a multitude of answers on this subject would have emerged from the past 40 years' research in the discipline which calls itself human ecology. Indeed, even a critic of traditional human ecology extends explicit credit to this school for having covered this ground:

> . . . it [i.e., Human Ecology] took a rather simple-minded approach to causality, tending to view ecological factors, *such as building type, site plan,* and community size, as independent variables or causes which had predictable effects on the quality of social life.[2] (italics mine)

I do not believe, however, that the ecologists have provided these answers, and I shall hazard some explanations as to why this is so. I do this not to berate ecologists, whose work is valuable in many other ways, but simply to show the need for a pattern of study markedly different from practice in traditional ecology for studying these phenomena. Then I shall propose a scheme which, whether or not included within the formal bounds of human ecology, represents the union of sociological methodology and theory both to make sense out of an otherwise farflung and disjointed literature and to form the focus of new research which might add to knowledge of the relation of man and his environment.

---

2   Janet Abu-Lughod, "The City is Dead—Long Live the City: Some Thoughts on Urbanity," in Sylvia F. Fava (ed.), *Urbanism in World Perspective,* New York: Thomas Y. Crowell Company, 1968, p. 157.

ECOLOGY: GREAT EXPECTATIONS

Human ecology grew up during the 20th century, hard upon the heels of the development of plant and animal ecology. Both standard definitions of the word "ecology" and analogous work in the other ecological disciplines lead to the expectation that human ecology would have contributed much knowledge on man's relationship to the physical environment which surrounds him.

Webster's Third New International Dictionary defines ecology as follows:

1.   A branch of science concerned with the interrelationship of organisms and their environment . . .

2.   The totality or pattern of relations between organisms and their environment.

The dictionary goes on to define human ecology as "a branch of sociology that studies the relationship between a human community and its environments."[3]

Some commentators on what has recently been called "eco-system science" support this expectation. They urge study of "Relationships to environment—the influence of the entity on the environment as well as the environmental effects on the entity."[4]

The pattern of study suggested would apply equally well to humans and plants. The point of view held by biological ecologists, that all entities are interrelated regardless of species, is transferable to the study of man, unless specifically restricted by additional assumptions. When Robert E. Park first broached the study of human ecology, it was no accident that he cited the nursery rhyme, "The House that Jack Built," which binds together into a single system malt, mice, men, and marriage.[5]

Recent findings by animal ecologists have been particularly provocative. A variety of studies cited by Hall, for example, points to a decided effect of living densities on the health and social

---

3   By permission. From Webster's Third New International Dictionary© 1966 by G. and C. Merriam Co., Publishers of the Merriam-Webster Dictionaries, Springfield, Mass.

4   Dillon Ripley and Helmut K. Buechner, "Ecosystem Science as a Point of Synthesis," *Daedalus*. (Fall 1967): p. 1194.

5   See Robert E. Park, *Human Communities*, Glencoe, Ill.: The Free Press, 1952, pp. 145-158.

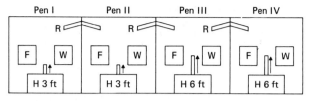

Fig. 1 Diagram of the pens in which Calhoun studied a behavioral sink among rats. (Courtesy of Academic Press, Inc.)

organization of animals.[6] In one longitudinal study of deer, a herd on an uninhabited and lush island built up from five to about 300 over 40 years; then approximately half the deer died the following year, and the herd gradually stabilized at about 80 deer. Examination of the carcasses, before and after the "dieoff," showed only a great drop in the weight of the adrenal glands of the deer that died in great number. It was concluded that physical crowding brings about intense interaction among animals, which in turn lowers adrenal weight, which then lowers the animals' defense mechanisms. Parallel findings were reported for muskrats and for woodchucks. They appear to indicate that a physical condition in the environment brings about a particular social condition among animals which can lead to physical pathology. This situation has been labelled the "behavioral sink."

Calhoun's study of Norway rats shows vividly the social processes involved with the decline of population in the behavioral sink.[7] Calhoun put 80 rats in high densities in four pens located in a row and connected by ramps (Fig. 1). There were two major environmental effects operating. The first was the high density, which affected all the pens. However, the position of the ramps made the nature of the two middle pens different from the two end pens; that the two latter pens had only one ramp instead of two connecting them to other pens allowed a more strict system of social control inside them.

6   Edward T. Hall, *The Hidden Dimension*, Garden City, N.Y.: Doubleday, 1966, Ch. 1.

7   *Ibid.* See also John B. Calhoun, "Population Density and Social Pathology," in Leonard Duhl (ed.), *The Urban Condition*, New York: Basic Books, 1963, pp. 33-43; "The Social Use of Space," in W. Mayer and R. Van Gelder (eds.), *Physiological Mammalogy*, N.Y.: Academic Press, 1964, p. 93.

        Man and his urban environment

Each of these environments led to distinctive distortions of the prevailing pattern of rat activity. The end pens were characterized by the dominance of a single male and homosexuality among most of the other males who remained. The middle pens featured a high rate of infant neglect and mortality, a constant turnover of leadership accompanied by violence, and the occurrence of pansexuality among males.

Thus these rat experiments gave some clue as to the social concomitants of the physical pathologies observed in previous behavioral sinks. Pessimists have had a heyday in making analogies to social conditions in the crowded slums of large cities, while others in reply have stressed the unique ability of man to adapt to changing physical conditions.

With these findings as incentive, one might well imagine a rush of human ecologists to apply this perspective to human life.[8] One of the most respected contemporary human ecologists has written only recently that:

A way of life and its setting comprise an interdependent unity. Either is regarded as extrinsic to the other only at the peril of overlooking the interrelations on which depends the stability of the system as a whole.[9]

Yet, the Midwestern pioneers of ecology have left the study of these crucial phenomena behind them in the dust as they have launched forth in pursuit of other matters. I shall outline briefly what ecologists have studied, if *not* the relationship between man and physical environment. Then I shall turn to some speculation as to *why* they have not treated this subject before turning to the suggested scheme.

---

8   There has been a beginning of work in this area, but it has not been from anyone primarily identified with human ecology. See, for example, Albert D. Biderman, Margot Lourie, and Joan Bacchus, *Historical Incidents of Extreme Overcrowding*, Washington, D.C.: Bureau of Social Science Research, Inc., 1963, and Robert C. Schmitt, "Implications of Density in Hong Kong," *Journal of the American Institute of Planners,* Vol. 29, no. 3 (Aug. 1963): pp. 210-217.

9   Otis Dudley Duncan, "Social Organization and the Ecosystem," in Robert E. L. Faris (ed.), *Handbook of Modern Sociology*, Chicago: Rand McNally, 1964, p. 69.

HUMAN ECOLOGY: WHAT IT HAS DONE

One searches this literature in vain for more than superficial reference to the brute facts that men live in a physical environment and that they employ material technology in adapting to it.[10]

The above criticism was directed by human ecologists *at other* behavioral scientists. But I believe that it fits equally well when trained on human ecology. What, then, has been done in the field?

Human ecology received an impressive formulation in the work of Park. Park saw patterns and forces in the biological sciences that made sense out of many of man's actions. Man, for example, finds himself living in territorially organized communities, inside which everyone contributes to the degree of well-being of everyone else. The process whereby "birds of a feather flock together" is neither rational nor conscious, but it happens to people and their activities just as it happens to plants, according to Park. Inexorable and extra-human forces, including *competition, dominance, invasion,* and *succession,* deeply rooted in classical economic theory, formed and governed the existence of spatially local clusters called *natural areas.*

Park took pains to stress that man had improved over animals and plants and did not stand in a similar state of subjugation to nature. Man can cope with his environment through technological devices, and he has institutions which are deeply rooted through culture. Man's unique superstructure is referred to as "society," so as not to be confused with "community," which accounts for the physical distribution of man in the above-mentioned, unalterable patterns.

Human ecology, however, as Park conceived it, restricted itself to a study of the community groupings of men through time and space, as buffeted by the nonrational, subsocial forces originally suggested by biologists.

Park's students and colleagues devoted themselves to applying his theoretical model to real and often pressing situations in the modern city, which, operationally, meant Chicago in the early days. They typically studied a phenomenon (usually a pathology such as crime or mental illness) at an aggregate level, having divided the city

---

10 Otis Dudley Duncan and Leo F. Schnore, "Cultural, Behavioral, and Ecological Perspectives in the Study of Social Organization," *American Journal of Sociology*, Vol. 65 (1959): p. 134.

into a number of subareas corresponding as much as possible to natural areas. They explained the existence of the phenomenon by referring to the homogeneous social organization to be found within the subarea, which in turn was dependent on the spatial relations of that place to surrounding subareas. Since the people or use of an area often changed, the character of a natural area at any given point in time would be a function of the constant competition for space and a hierarchy of dominance; therefore, the pathologies usually found their explanation in an unalterable cause with strong economic overtones. Social pathologies were explained in this setting by social variables; but the ultimate explanation of both of them, inasmuch as they were found together in a local area, lay in subsocial forces.

For example, according to the Burgess concentric zone theory, the concentration of vice and gambling just outside the Central Business District of cities found its explanation in the land values associated with the growth of the C.B.D. [11] The argument runs as follows: The C.B.D., home of the highest land values in town, is in a constant state of growth, encouraging speculators to purchase property on its periphery in anticipation of eventual incorporation of the property into the C.B.D. So as to minimize expenses and maximize short term profits, the interim landlords retain older buildings without improving them. These they subdivide into a number of rooms, each of which rents for little, but which in aggregate return a handsome rental. Attracted to these accommodations are the newcomers to the city who can afford no other residence and who stay only short periods. The atmosphere of the area is one of short term residence and minimal commitment, with little personal contact among neighbors or between landlord and tenant. Men and women who find it desirable to escape from social scrutiny find this anonymous situation desirable, and it is thus that they are found in such areas. But the ultimate reason lies in economic factors associated with the C.B.D.

Park considered the community a basic unit which would reflect the subsocial forces. Hence, concentration on such aggregates reflected far more than the ready availability of data at the census tract level. Yet much of the work which followed Park's led to a

---

11   Ernest Burgess, "The Growth of the City," in Robert E. Park, Ernest W. Burgess, and Roderick McKenzie, *The City*, Chicago: University of Chicago Press, 1925, Ch. 2.

Fig. 2 Sub-communities based on census tracts of Chicago: schizophrenia average rates 1922-1934 by zones and divisions of the city. (Adapted from Faris and Dunham, *Mental Disorders in Urban Areas,* Chicago: University of Chicago Press, 1939. Used by permission.)

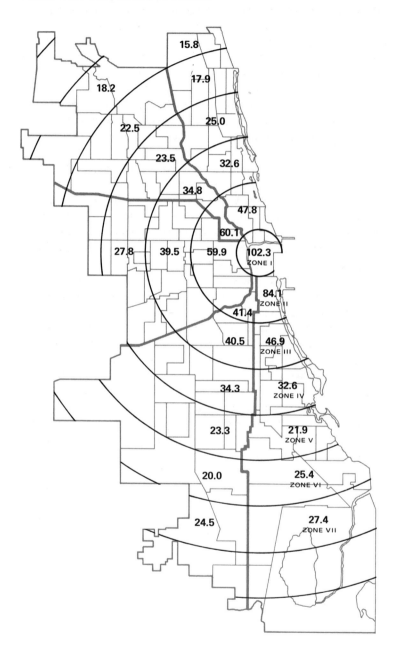

general conception of ecology as a *method*, rather than a *discipline*. Areas of a city would be rated with respect to given social variables, and maps would show the distributions of the variable around the city. Such maps and the statistics based on comparable subunits made possible the search for relationships among variables: the ecological correlation. Ecology thus became one method of establishing and testing the degree of relationship among variables.

For example, Faris and Dunham sought to gather evidence in 1939 on the relation of various types of schizophrenia to measures of probable causes (Fig. 2). To do this, they investigated whether high rates of schizophrenia in census tracts were associated with high scores on such factors as percent home ownership, percent hotel and room residents, and percent foreign born or Negro—and whether low rates were associated with low scores. Many of their correlative scores between such factors were very high.[12]

This method proved very valuable, both because it made the presentation of data simple and clear and because it standardized the search for relationships among variables thought relevant to cities. Critics pointed out quite validly that ecological correlations can be fallacious as methods of proof for theories concerning individuals, since they deal with aggregates rather than with individual cases and thus obscure one-to-one relationships.[13] Nonetheless, the ecological method has been pursued through the years because it suggests relationships in the absence of hypotheses, because it points to higher level, common explanations for variables which show high correlations but which are logically unrelated,[14] and because data is much more readily available for aggregates than for individuals.

When Park's disciples used the ecological method, they returned to orthodox human ecology for *theoretical* explanation of their findings. Others used the method without recourse to orthodox theory. The ecological method became independent of the discipline of human ecology. Later critics could thus attack both the discipline

---

12   Robert E. L. Faris and H. Warren Dunham, *Mental Disorders in Urban Areas,* Chicago: University of Chicago Press, 1939.

13   W. S. Robinson, "Ecological Correlations and the Behavior of Individuals," in George A. Theodorson (ed.), *Studies in Human Ecology,* Evanston, Ill.: Row, Peterson and Company, 1961, pp. 115-120.

14   Herbert Menzel, "Comment on Robinson's Ecological Correlations and the Behavior of Individuals," in Theodorson, *op. cit.,* pp. 121-122.

with its biological analogies and the method with its possible obscurities.[15]

Since the 1930's, human ecology has been much less clearcut. A whole string of authors has offered criticism and correction of the classical position without consolidating into any kind of solid front except on embarrassingly obvious principles such as the existence of evolution and interdependence. A review by Theodorson[16] of "revisionist" writings suggests three camps which typify recent work: neo-orthodox, social area analysis, and socio-cultural.

Those in the neo-orthodox school labored to rid human ecological theory of the image of mindlessness created by careless use of the ecological method. They argued strongly against patterns as the final product of study, and reverted to an insistence on community structure and its underlying forces as the proper form of explanation. This much was pure orthodoxy.

In addition, the neo-orthodox school (as most fully expressed in the work of Hawley[17]) tried to build into human ecology a more accurate representation of its biological counterpart. Although this work elaborated many of Park's basic ideas into a more complete system, it retained the emphasis on the community as the prime unit of analysis, arguing that this was the unit formed by symbiotic processes.

Later writings of Schnore and Duncan,[18] while suggesting that social scientists might want to view social organization as the dependent variable for their own purposes in human ecology studies, go on to state emphatically the basic law in ecology of the interdependence of systems. There are, they claim, four interdependent variables in the ecological complex: population, organi-

---

15 The first broadside against both was by Milla Alihan, *Social Ecology,* New York: Columbia University Press, 1938. While it presented an outline of what human ecology had to answer, it did not provide a replacement for existing theories.

16 Theodorson, *op. cit.*

17 Amos Hawley, *Human Ecology: A Theory of Community Structure,* New York: Ronald Press, 1950.

18 See Duncan and Schnore, *op. cit.,* Schnore, "The Myth of Human Ecology" *Sociological Inquiry,* Vol. 31 (1961): pp. 128-139, and Duncan, "From Social System to Ecosystem," *Sociological Inquiry,* Vol. 31 (1961): pp. 140-149. A critique of this approach is S. M. Willhelm, "Concept of the 'Ecological Complex'," *The American Journal of Economics and Sociology,* Vol. 23 (1964): pp. 241-248.

zation, environment, and technology. Each has its own effects on each of the others, resulting in a mutually explanatory balance of forces. They urge that one never lose sight of the many directions in which forces might act.

Duncan cities the case of explaining smog in Los Angeles. It is almost equally a product of the presence of large numbers of people (population), who live in a bowl-shaped setting (environment), who depend greatly on their industries and automobiles (technology), and who have taken some but not all the steps, through local groupings, to combat smog (organization).[19]

Yet when these theorists have produced studies based predominantly on their discipline of human ecology rather than on the ecological method or within more common sociological frameworks of theory and method, they have centered largely on economic variables as the main explanatory forces.[20] Such an emphasis is by all means valid, but the place of the physical environment in the ecosystem has been left unexplored.

Researchers working with Social Area Analysis have dealt with an explicit methodology, based on ecological theory.[21] They have isolated what they feel are three major characteristics of modern society—social rank, urbanization, and segregation—which can be used to describe subareas of cities with the aid of census data. These subareas, operationally census tracts, can be labeled according to their relationships to the three characteristics. Researchers use these labels as independent variables in hypotheses, with various aspects of social organization as the dependent variable.

For example, Bell chose to study four census tracts in San Francisco which, according to Social Area Analysis, represented the various combinations of high and low on status and urbanization. He

---

19 Otis Dudley Duncan, *loc. cit.*

20 See, for example, Amos Hawley, *The Changing Shape of Metropolitan America*, Glencoe, Ill.: The Free Press, 1956.

21 See Eshref Shevky and Wendell Bell, *Social Area Analysis, Stanford, Cal.*, Stanford University Press, 1955; Shevky and Marilyn Williams, *The Social Areas of Los Angeles,* Los Angeles and Berkeley: University of California Press, 1949; and Bell and Maryanne T. Force, "Urban Neighborhood Types and Participation in Formal Associations," *American Sociological Review,* Vol. 21 (1956): pp. 25-34. For a critique of Social Area Analysis, see Janet L. Abu-Lughod, "Testing the Theory of Social Area Analysis: The Ecology of Cairo, Egypt," *American Sociological Review,* Vol. 34 (1969): pp. 198-212.

a

Fig. 3 Part (a) shows a street scene from the center of Beacon Hill in Boston (Louisburg Square). (Photo by the Boston Chamber of Commerce.) Part (b) is what researchers suggest would have happened to Beacon Hill on the basis of economic forces had particular values not been strong among its residents. The apartment complex pictured was, in fact, erected immediately adjacent to Beacon Hill on the site of the old West End of Boston, whose characteristics are discussed in Chapter 3. (Photo by Northeast Aerial Photos.)

then investigated whether various measures of formal and informal social participation were related to standing on these measures, showing that each type of social area factor was related to at least some type of difference in participation. For example, the areas high in status contained people less isolated from their friends.[22]

The intent of Social Area Analysis is as its name suggests; it is to identify important *social* characteristics of selected sections of metropolitan areas. As such, the locality emphasis of the earlier ecologists is missing, as is any explicit reference to physical

22 Wendell Bell, "The City, the Suburb, and a Theory of Social Choice," in Scott Greer, Dennis L. McElrath, David W. Minar, and Peter Orleans (eds.), *The New Urbanization*, New York: St. Martin's Press, 1968, pp. 132-168.

environment.[23] Thus, in operationalizing their aspects of urbanization, the researchers have used *social* variables for the most part as their measures of urbanization. Of the six substantially different variables used, only one has to do with physical environment: the incidence of single family housing. But before this is used for any empirical purpose, it is averaged with fertility and women in the labor force.

There is nothing wrong with this; it is standard practice in sociology to relate social variables to each other. Indeed, Social Area Analysis has made possible a greater understanding of what social variables tend to cluster in space. It also makes known certain gross characteristics of areas so as to choose among them for future studies. Its practitioners have also thrown off the yoke of earlier ecologists by stressing the voluntaristic components of residential selection.[24] Nonetheless, while valuable for many reasons, Social Area

23 See, for example, the comparison of schools by Peter Orleans, "Robert Park and Social Area Analysis," *Urban Affairs Quarterly*, Vol. 1, no. 4 (June 1966): pp. 5-19.

24 For a full discussion of voluntarism, see Wendell Bell, *loc. cit.*

Analysis says almost nothing about the physical nature of areas and its relationship to social phenomena.

The third "school" of human ecology noted by Theodorson is the sociocultural school. Picking up Alihan's criticism of orthodox theory, Firey in particular started to point to examples of land use and neighborhood character that were determined by people according to cultural goals.[25] He stressed that if the economic forces which normally played such a strong part in determining which aggregate would be located where had been working in Boston, then a historical burial ground would be replaced by commercial buildings, an open green would be covered by a highway, and the atmospheric, old Beacon Hill area would have lost its low-rise, residential character. Instead, he argued that groups of Bostonians valued preservation of the past and organized to guarantee resistance against invasion by any other land use (Fig. 3).

Jonassen used this point of view in explaining the migration of Norwegian-Americans from one part of greater New York City to another.[26] He showed that the original choice of Brooklyn by these people was consistent with their nautical background, but that when Brooklyn became more crowded, they found that the semi-rustic yet nautical setting of North Bergen, New Jersey, on the Palisades, satisfied their cultural needs even more fully. This is one of the few cases in ecology in which a researcher established logical connections between physical and social phenomena. But unfortunately this lead has not been followed in any systematic way.

Indeed, critics of the socio-cultural school have argued that its proponents have merely substituted their own form of determinism for essentially economic determinism. While I believe that what the sociocultural school had to demonstrate is basically healthy and even essential for the field, there is, nonetheless, merit in arguments which stress the interdependence of these variables, with a priori determination by none of them.

To this point, a hasty review of major developments and applications of human ecology has suggested that physical variables and their interrelation with social variables have been very largely

25   Walter Firey, *Land Use in Central Boston*, Cambridge, Mass.: Harvard University Press, 1947, and his "Sentiment and Symbolism as Ecological Variables," *American Sociological Review,* Vol. 10 (1945): pp. 140-148.

26   C. T. Jonassen, "Cultural Variables in the Ecology of an Ethnic Group," *American Sociological Review*, Vol. 14 (1949): pp. 32-41.

neglected by human ecologists who have pursued other interests, albeit with a good measure of success. Why might this have happened?

HUMAN ECOLOGY: WHY IT WASN'T SOMETHING ELSE

I would like to suggest four reasons why the human ecologist never explicitly studied the interrelations of the physical environment and the many variables of social science.

1.   Incomplete Conceptualization of Environment

Space has been utilized as a *medium* in most of human ecology rather than as a *variable* with a potential effect of its own. The environment has been seen as a flat plane, with occasional internal boundaries such as railroads or parks which could set apart natural areas, within which subsocially determined aggregates jockey indefinitely for turf.

When speaking of environment, the human ecologists have referred to *social* environment. By what social groups or activities is a particular territorial aggregate surrounded? What difference do these social surroundings make for an aggregate's internal social structure and hence pathologies?

Quinn, for example, goes so far as to include among his basic assumptions the following:

. . . that human ecology, as a branch of sociology, always studies the relations of man to man, and never the direct relations of man to environment . . .[27]

The incomplete conceptualization of the physical environment in this context was underscored by another recent commentator:

There is only a beginning of a scientific literature on behavior settings. Except in their applied phases, the biological and physical sciences have eschewed ecological units with human behavior as component elements. They have stopped with man-free ponds, glaciers, and lightning flashes; they have left farms, ski-jumps, and passenger trains to others. And psychology and sociology have, for the most part, shied in the other direction: they have avoided whole, unfractionated ecological units with physical objects as well as

---

27   James A. Quinn, "The Nature of Human Ecology: Reexamination and Redefinition," in Theodorson, *op. cit.,* p. 138.

people and behavior as component parts. So behavior-setting-type units have almost completely fallen between the bio-physical and the behavioral sciences and this has been a source of serious trouble for the eco-behavioral problem; there have been no solid empirical ecological units. Unbounded, demi-theoretical, demi-empirical units do not provide the firm base an empirical science must have.[28]

To be fair, mention must be made of housing condition as a factor which has been analyzed. For example, U.S. census information on the condition and equipment of housing by census tract has been utilized, but the difficulty of the ecological method has prevented it from proceeding very far. Housing conditions tend with few exceptions to correlate highly with all indices of socioeconomic status. It is therefore difficult to establish any significant relationship at an aggregate level of housing condition per se to a dependent or interdependent variable, since the latter may simply be a function of class.[29] Indeed, housing condition and even type has been used as a *measure* of status.[30] Furthermore, the amount of information in census materials which actually describes basic elements of the urban physical fabric is quite limited.

Yet there are significant differences within the physical environment (to be discussed in detail in Chapter 2) which have potential relevance for the ways in which men organize and lead their lives. Families, for example, may raise their children differently from a 30th floor base than from a bungalow, just as rats do when faced with one instead of two ramps. Men living two hours from their jobs may well lead different lives (quite willingly) than those living two minutes away.[31]

Refining present conceptions of the environment may be difficult, particularly in making them operational. But that they

---

28   Roger Barker, "On the Nature of the Environment," *Journal of Social Issues*, Vol. 19, no. 4 (1963): p. 26.

29   Faris and Dunham went as far as anyone on this, suggesting a relation of schizophrenia to the anomie of rooming houses and apartment hotels. But they were still restricted in drawing firm conclusions by the pitfalls of the ecological correlation. See R. E. L. Faris and Warren Dunham, *Mental Disorders in Urban Areas*, Chicago: University of Chicago Press, 1939.

30   Lloyd Warner, M. Meeker and Kenneth Eells, *Social Class in America*, Gloucester, Mass.: Peter Smith, 1957.

31   See, for example, Walter T. Martin, "The Structuring of Social Relationships Engendered by Suburban Residence." *American Sociological Review*, Vol. 21 (1956): pp. 446-453.

have not been systematically and satisfactorily refined so as to include significant physical factors has by definition prevented much analysis of the relationship of physical and social variables by human ecologists.

2. Fixation on Aggregates

The focus of human ecology both as a discipline and as a method has been on aggregates. For theoretical and for very practical reasons, people living in subareas of cities have been treated as undifferentiated masses. When concerned with community-level social organization, this focus makes good sense. Park urged concentration on community aggregates because their organizational structure represented a successful functional adaptation to the demands of competing social environments. However, what is functional for one kind of group at one level may be indifferent or even dysfunctional to other groups.

Social groups adapt to much more than the supply of food and shelter. The structure of family groups, for example, may make functional adaptations to varying conditions of ease of access to other people and activities, to unwanted noises, or to dwelling size—all physical conditions. The adaptation represented by community structure to the social environment is clearly but one of many types of structural adaptations to environment. Restriction of study to just certain forms of aggregation may have served to limit the kinds of environment investigated to which structural adaptation has been made, as well as the kinds of adaptation analyzed.

This restriction may be viewed from the perspective of the individual as well as that of group process. An individual's roles, which in combination form the basis of much behavior, come from a variety of intersecting affiliations and differ widely within communities, if for no other reason than that many stages in the life cycle are apt to be found within a single community. Such roles may be expected to articulate differentially with different aspects of the environment. Viewing people largely from the perspective of the community restricts analysis to roles germane to community organization and deprives such analysis of the human, group-centered differences which might be most relevant to the physical environment.

Such a concentration on aggregates poses problems to study of the relationship of physical and social variables not only from the point of view of the latter. Few natural areas are physically undifferentiated. People within an area experience different encounters with the physical environment. They do not all work in the same place. They have varying access to the stores of their choice. And the impingements of person to person inherent in housing are likely to vary from place to place within even a relatively homogeneous neighborhood. Certainly it is too much to expect studies based only on inflexible aggregates not reflecting other possible ways of aggregating the variable traits of its individual members to provide data on such a varying concept as physical environment.

In short, a person's or family's relationship to the physical environment can be a much more microscopic relationship than one involving communities. Its course is influenced by the roles a particular actor plays, and hence by the set of social groups with which he is involved, only some of which may be relevant to community structure. It is, therefore, doubtful that the human ecologists *could* have made a sensitive treatment of the subject even if they had wanted to, given their fixation on community aggregates.

3. Erection of Disciplinary Boundaries

Still another barrier to the study of the interrelations of the physical environment and social variables has been the formalizing of human ecology into a unique discipline. Traditionally, establishing a discipline means erecting disciplinary boundaries, which then determine what researchers will study and what they will leave behind in the dust.

Research in human ecology has for the most part been conducted by sociologists[32] who have heeded well the dictum of Park that:

Human ecology, as the sociologists would like to use the term, is . . . not man, but the community; not man's relation to the earth which he inhabits, but his relations to other men, that concerns us most.[33]

Park justifies this by asserting the independence of man from his local habitat through social cooperation at the community level.

---

32   Biologists have taken a predominantly nonsocial view of human ecology which I am excluding from consideration. See, for example, Jack B. Bresler (ed.), *Human Ecology*, Reading, Mass.: Addison-Wesley, 1966.

33   Park, "The Urban Community as a Spatial Pattern and a Moral Order," in *Human Communities*, New York: The Free Press of Glencoe, 1952, p. 165. Reprinted by permission of Macmillan Co.

Literal acceptance of this view makes possible the treatment of environment in human ecology as only an arrangement of social aggregates in space formed by their competition. Any direct relation of physical environment to human life has been ruled biology, and outside the pale of inquiry to human ecologists.

Yet, whatever articulation the physical environment may have in this case is with man as a member of social groupings, and collective adaptation is as much involved as it is where a group is in confrontation with *social* groups. Sociologists generally study the structure and behavioral consequences of human groups. Nonetheless, the human ecologists left to other disciplines whatever understanding of social structure and consequent behavior might stem from relations with the physical environment. And there is no evidence that biologists among others have rushed in to accept the study of variables that the sociologists themselves are best trained to understand. The geographers have come closer, but even they have not yet bridged the gap.

In short, I claim that in the interests of establishing a neat discipline, the ecologists have eliminated subjects of study which are sorely missed at present. Hawley's treatment of variables in the psychological realm is representative of this process:

Attitudes, sentiments, motivations, and the like are eliminated from consideration not because they are unimportant but because the assumptions and point of view of human ecology are not adapted to their treatment.[34]

This, I believe, is a major explanation of the lack of certain work that might have been expected of human ecologists.

4.   Recent Acceptance of Intervention

A final factor that may help explain all the foregoing is that large-scale, rational intervention in the urban environment is comparatively recent in the United States. When human ecology was formulated, Americans were not consciously remaking large sections of cities, nor were they building cities of over 100,000 residents from scratch on farmland or woods, as they are now. No one demanded answers as to the social concomitants of one collection of urban forms as opposed to another proposed set—all designed to maximize the quality of life.

It is true that the City Beautiful movement gained momentum from the design and siting of building at the Chicago World's Fair of

---

34   Hawley, *Human Ecology*, p. 180.

1893, and that city planning and zoning grew up in the quarter century that followed (very strong in Chicago!). It is also true that public housing became a reality, under the assumption that clean sanitary housing (one definition of the environment, but an exceedingly limited one) would alter the health and lives of slum dwellers. Yet none of these movements dealt explicitly with a sophisticated or systematic inquiry into the interrelations of physical environment and social variables. Many of their early failures come from this lack.

Now, however, a pressing need for such information is generally recognized among those charged with urban design. Federal laws make possible large-scale renewal of cities now requiring improvements in all aspects of the urban condition, both physical and social, and past failures urgently point to the need for new knowledge. Private entrepreneurs in America have started to follow the example of European new-town development, and are forced to consult with social scientists if only because their investment depends in part on the best fit of the environment they create with their particular residents. Many of the cities being built on the fringes of major cities (for example, Reston, Va. and Columbia, Md., outside Washington, D.C.) compete with each other and with smaller subdivisions that can offer lower rentals and carrying charges. To compete successfully, new towns must optimize what their residents deem important, and the market mechanism has already made casualties of entrepreneurs whose assessment of these phenomena was inaccurate.

In short, cities are now created and recreated much less by piecemeal accretion than they once were. Public officials and private entrepreneurs have the power to create an environment intended to satisfy a multitude of explicit goals, not the least of which is the successful accommodation of social units starting at the level of the individual and his family grouping. This recent phenomenon incorporates power not known during the formulation of human ecology and creates a demand for knowledge never as strongly realized as today. In the early days, man at best was thought to have the power to adapt to the environment; now he can intervene to form the entire city environment.

To summarize up to this point: although one might have expected human ecologists to have analyzed the interrelations of the physical environment with social phenomena, their efforts, while valuable in many ways, were largely inconsequential toward that particular end. This is quite understandable given (1) their conceptualization of the environment, (2) their fixation on aggregates, (3) their erection of disciplinary boundaries, and (4) the recent acceptance of intervention with its concomitant pressures for new knowledge.

To get at this information an orientation very different from that of traditional human ecology is required.

A CHANGE OF EMPHASIS

Given the enormous number of variables contained within the terms physical environment and social phenomena, stating all combinations of these variables would be encyclopedic. Rather, I shall confine myself at this point to outlining a frame of reference which I feel can theoretically unify as well as clarify needed research. Its general form, though by no means all its details or applications, is directly influenced by the theoretical work of Talcott Parsons.

Social scientists have commonly conceived of and studied people according to three systems: cultural, social, and personality.[35] Anthropologists have customarily focused on the cultural system, which, roughly, includes the rules and goals by which behavior is guided. Sociologists have concentrated on the social system, roughly the relationship of men to each other in social groups. Psychologists have focused on personality, a more or less permanent set of predispositions to behavior which people internalize as a result of their own unique life experiences.

Each system can be viewed analytically as independent of the others, as within each there exists a multitude of variables which interact primarily with each other. Each of the disciplines spends a major part of its efforts in understanding and demonstrating the relationships of variables within its special system.

Nonetheless, the systems impinge on each other. Someone with a given personality, for example, may be more or less able to participate in a group with a given structure; people who rank high in authoritarianism may totally reject a permissive, loosely structured group while feeling comfortable in one with well defined relationships. All groups, on the other hand, may not attain given

---

35   This is a standard conception from the work of Parsons. See, for example, his essay, "An Outline of the Social System" in Parsons, Edward Shils, Kaspar K. Naegele, and Jesse R. Pitts (eds.), *Theories of Society*, New York: The Free Press of Glencoe, 1961, pp. 30-79.

cultural ends as easily. In other words, a variable taken as given from one system may limit the range of phenomena in another with which it may easily articulate. Some variables are congruent and others are incongruent.

Fields of study have grown up to handle the relations of variables between systems. "Culture and Personality" and "Personality and Social Structure" are standard frames of references from which the study of intersystem relationships may be studied.

Parsons is one who has championed such an approach, adding as an integral part of his recent work a fourth system, the behavioral organism, which has not been adopted by others to the same extent as the other three systems.[36]

A fifth system touched on by Parsons has even more rarely been pursued in this context by social scientists: the environmental system. Aspects included in the environment could potentially be geological environment, topographic environment, climate, and doubtless many more. For present purposes, I should like to restrict my attention to the *man-made physical environment*, as available or potentially available in cities.

I propose that the impingements of phenomena in the man-made physical environment *on* the other systems and *from* them can and should be thoroughly studied. Just as one can now study the interdependence of elements of personality and culture, so one could study the interdependence of physical environment and social structure. Each system can still be viewed as analytically distinct from the others, but the significance of mutual contact and interchange must be noted.

This falls within the framework suggested for other phenomena by Barker:

Until someone is able to subsume the facts of the ecological environment, the organism, and behavior within the same explanatory, conceptual system, we have to seek for some degree of lawfulness in the links between the separate systems. The question arises of how the elements of one level may possibly enter upon their own terms, yet in a systematic, derivable way, into the structure and processes of another level. Are there theories which can account for some of the consequences of the interaction of

---

36 Talcott Parsons, *Societies: Evolutionary and Comparative Perspectives*, Englewood Cliffs, N.J.: Prentice-Hall, 1966, Ch. 2.

conceptually unrelated phenomena, while these phenomena continue to operate according to their own incommensurate laws?[37]

The nature of articulation I see between systems has been described in passing by Schnore:

... the environment is viewed as a set of limiting conditions, which may be narrow or broad, depending upon the technological devices and modes of organization that prevail in a given population.[38]

Research can proceed from the point of view that a particular physical environment sets broad limits as to the range of phenomena from other systems which can be found there. Some social systems, personalities, or cultural goals (possibly only a few) may be impossible in given settings. Beyond this limit, an environment may make some phenomena in other systems either easier or more difficult to maintain, so that, all else equal, these phenomena will tend to be found successfully maintaining themselves more in some types of settings than in others.

This notion of physical environment as a potential limiting factor with respect to human behavior was indeed inherent in Wirth's writing:

... physical factors ... are at best conditioning factors offering the possibilities and setting the limits for social and psychological existence and development.[*]

Conversely, seen from the point of view of another system in this interdependent model, people rationally seeking to best match a specific social, cultural, or personality variable with a planned setting will find their range of possible environments narrowed. They may still have a choice of urban forms, but the choice is not one of total indifference. Within these limits there is obviously much variation, and perception of environment is a major explanatory factor at this level, *given* the implications of the physical environment per se.

---

37   Barker, "Ecology and Motivation," in *Current Theory and Research in Motivation* (University of Nebraska), Vol. 8 (1960): p. 12.

38   Schnore, "Social Morphology and Human Ecology," *American Journal of Sociology,* Vol. 63 (1958): p. 628.

*   Louis Wirth, "Human Ecology," in Richard Sennett (ed.), *Classic Essays on the Culture of Cities,* New York: Appleton-Century-Crofts, 1969, p. 177.

Thus the model I suggest is not of determinism or the dominance of one system over another,[39] but rather one of *congruence—* of states of variables in one system coexisting better with states of variables in another system than with other alternative states. It is an *intersystem congruence model.*

An applied physical statement of this approach was put forward by Studer:

As I have been discussing it, the designed environment can be seen as a complex **prosthetic** system which impinges in two interdependent modes: (1) it **supports** certain behavioral goals through maintenance of appropriate physiological states, and (2) it **elicits**, or exerts stimulus control over certain behavioral topographies. Human behavior occurs via an intricate biological system. When critical physiological states are not properly accommodated, intended behavior is modified, or even suppressed. This goal of physiological optimization is one which has been fairly well understood in design, but a more systematic linking to behavioral consequences may reveal unexplored possibilities.[40]

Congruence, however, carries with it the opposite, incongruence, and the latter may be found in real life situations linking the environmental system with the others. Mismatches are possible, and they may even be frequent due to the exigencies of economics and politics. Witness the complaints of families with small children who live high off the ground in public housing projects. Mothers are not always free to follow their children to ground level, where great numbers of them frequently roam without supervision. Getting to and from the ground requires elevators, which the children often adopt as play toys, putting them out of commission. The smaller children often are set upon by older bullies, who can find hiding places in areas such as stairwells where authorities are hard pressed

---

39 I would maintain that this does not argue for strict environmentalism, a now-discredited branch of geography. The environmentalists argued that such phenomena as weather and soil conditions dictated certain forms of social organization. The present conception stresses variables from several systems interacting so as to present broad limits to combinations of variables. As such, it resembles more the conception of interdependence that replaced environmentalism. See Robert S. Platt, "Environmentalism vs. Geography," *American Journal of Sociology*, Vol. 53 (1947-1948): pp. 351-358.

40 Raymond G. Studer, "Environmental Fit and the Dynamics of Living Systems: Some Methodological Issues," paper presented to the B.A.C. Conference on Design Methodology, Boston, May 6, 1967.

to control them.[41] But mismatches may even be maintained through time despite their dysfunctional nature largely because they may be the result of other, more functional relationships. For example, some families may prefer living in public housing even if high rise, because it is usually easier on the budget than lower-rise alternatives they might have to accept instead on the private market. And, too, it may provide some degree of aid and solace to people like husbandless mothers, who can find others with similar problems.[42] Nonetheless, the existence of mismatches is accompanied by some degree of additional cost or pain which could be minimized through a change in the nature of one of the variables.

Models of intra-urban migration have emphasized the occurrence of *stress* between the needs and expectations of households, on the one hand, and their housing, on the other. According to this model, stress alone does not cause migration because one or another factor in the stress-creating situation may be modified either in nature or in the importance attributed to it. However, if the members of a household are unable to counteract stress due to particular household characteristics, stress may escalate into *strain*, which then leads to a change in residence.[43] In the above example, the mismatched family *without* compensating factors would be the one desiring to move, *if they could.*

This is not to say that variables might not intervene between the environmental system and the others to produce the final degree of congruence or incongruence. The fact of interdependence would have us expect it. But this does not subtract from the value of asking whether, despite a chain of intermediate variables, phenomena from one system do in fact articulate systematically and for good reason with a limited range of variables in another.[44]

---

41   See Lee Rainwater, "Fear and the House-as-Haven in the Lower Class," *Journal of the American Institute of Planners,* Vol. 32 (1966): pp. 23-31.

42   Louis Kriesberg, "Neighborhood Setting and the Relocation of Public Housing Tenants." *Journal of the American Institute of Planners,* Vol. 34 (1968): pp. 43-49.

43   Julian Wolpert, "Migration as an Adjustment to Environmental Stress," *Journal of Social Issues,* Vol. 22, no. 4 (Oct. 1966): pp. 92-102.

44   Space may itself be an intermediate variable between others, but this is another possible area of study. We can also view these phenomena without reference to the nature of specific environmental factors. One writer, for example, suggests that any notion of optimal environment must include some degree of built-in *change* leading to a situation of variety for each individual. See J. D. Kendrick, "Human Factors Affecting Design of Physical Environments in Buildings," *The Medical Journal of Australia,* Vol. 2 (1967): pp. 267-269.

This represents a departure from the way Parsons handles similar concepts. He emphasizes a hierarchy of control between systems with intersystem consistencies explained by the cybernetic dominance of generalized normative factors.[45] The cultural system ranks highest in this hierarchy, followed by the social, personality, organismic, and environmental systems. In the intersystem congruence model, however, variables in each system are taken *on their own terms*, without a priori determination of the direction of their influence on variables in other systems. This model focuses on the fact of congruence rather than on any brand of determinism.

The intersystem congruence model is exemplified by studies which show that areas of cities with a high proportion of multiple dwellings and often scattered commercial enterprises are successful in accommodating people who wish to maintain relatively wide kinship networks. These studies, which will be discussed individually in Chapter 3, characteristically note the fact that working class families living in older, more crowded sections of town depend on a wide range of relatives for recreation, assistance, and just plain companionship. They have followed people from these areas who were subsequently forced to relocate in locations with far different physical characteristics (i.e., "typical" suburbs), and they then noted an unanticipated, undesired, and unfortunate lessening of extended family activities which could only be explained by environmental factors. In this case, one could suggest that intense family interaction is *congruent* with the physical factors of the former setting and incongruent with that of the latter.

Some researchers who emphasize the study of perception continually deflate the most hardnosed positivists who try to link physical design and social phenomena. Just when the positivists have come up with what they think is a design that is congruent with a specified social variable (e.g., chairs spaced around a hotel lobby just well enough to let people talk if they want or ignore others if they want), perceptionists will provide the knockout blow. It won't always work, they say, because people from different backgrounds learn on the basis of their culture to give different meanings to the separations involved. As a result, they *perceive* them differently and hence act differently in the same objective spatial situation.

Hall, for example, suggests that people carry around with them a series of invisible bubbles. Entry within each successive layer of

---

45   Parsons *et al., Theories of Society*, p. 38.

bubble connotes increasing intimacy, or, when undesired, invasion. Depending on his cultural background, a man's bubble will vary in size. For example, such differences in perception of space create misunderstandings when diplomats merely try to talk to each other, regardless even of what they are trying to say; one diplomat advances to get what he thinks is close enough to talk while the other backs away in disgust.[46]

Fried and Gleicher have pointed out quite rightly that different kinds of people will use the same spatial patterns in quite different ways depending on their orientations. For example, working classes will use a street as living and congregating space, while the middle classes will use it as a corridor to travel elsewhere. The walls of homes are perceived as much stronger by middle class people, since less of their everyday living is carried out into streets.[47]

Barker and his colleagues have studied what they call behavior settings.[48] They have studied the amount of time people in different countries spend in common settings such as drug stores, taverns, homes and the like. They find that certain kinds of behavior are localized in certain types of settings. People have *learned* that they act specific ways in specific places, and hence to understand behavior, one must understand this aspect of physical environment.

All these types of argument would imply in common that any relations that exist between environment and people are a function of perceptions that are learned in given cultures. But I believe that they do not confront our basic issue. We wish to investigate the broad limits within which variables representing different systems articulate with each other. What is the "path of least resistance" that differential perceptions must contravene? Is there such a path?

---

46   Edward T. Hall, *The Hidden Dimension*, Garden City, N.Y.: Doubleday, 1966. See also his book, *The Silent Language*, Greenwich, Conn.: Premier Books, 1959, Ch. 10.

47   Marc Fried and Peggy Gleicher, "Some Sources of Residential Satisfaction in an Urban Slum," *Journal of the American Institute of Planners*, Vol. 27 (1961): pp. 305-315.

48   See, for example, Roger Barker, *Ecological Psychology,* Stanford, Cal.: Stanford University Press, 1968. See also "On the Nature of the Environment," *Journal of Social Issues,* Vol. 19, no. 4 (1963): pp. 17-38, Barker and Herbert F. Wright, *Midwest and its Children,* New York: Harper and Row, 1955, and Barker and Louise Barker, "The Psychological Ecology of Old People in Midwest, Kansas, and Yoredale, Yorkshire,"*Journal of Gerontology*, Vol. 16 (1961): pp. 144-149.

Within these limits, there exists a wide range of human variability and choice which is undoubtedly based on perception, learning, and the like. These phenomena are certainly crucial to understanding behavior in particular environmental settings. But they do not rule out the basic relationships between systems.

Does the particular type of environment inevitably limit certain social phenomena despite what people want to happen? Do some settings accommodate certain activities better than others despite varying perceptions which would mitigate but not destroy the advantages they provide? These questions must be pursued hand in hand with perceptual questions. I shall maintain a strict concentration on space as a variable and not as an indeterminate medium to which people give meanings, even though study of the latter is of undoubted value. But in so doing, I shall not ignore human rationality when forming or reacting to patterns in the physical environment.

Man, as a thinking being, relates to his spatial environment both in his mind and in his actual presence. This gives rise to two approaches to research in this area; both necessary: mental congruence and experiential congruence between people and their environment. While fundamentally different, they complement each other.

Mental congruence exists if an individual thinks that particular spatial patterns will successfully accommodate his personal characteristics, values, and style of life. If a great number of people in a society believes that families can best be raised in suburban space, for example, then there is a state of mental congruence between "familism" and "suburbanism";[49] this relationship between a physical phenomenon and a social end is a social fact[50] worth noting, even if the relationship is not empirically substantiated as necessary.

All studies that set out to discover what people want and why they want it are concerned with mental congruence. If people regularly expect the same social situation to result from the creation

---

49 Wendell Bell, "Social Choice, Life Styles, and Suburban Residence," in William M. Dobriner (ed.), *The Suburban Community*, New York: G. P. Putnam's Sons, 1958, pp. 225-247.

50 A classic discussion of social facts as a phenomenon is Emile Durkheim's, *The Rules of the Sociological Method*, New York: The Free Press of Glencoe, 1958, orig. ed. 1938.

or maintenance of a particular physical environment, then a state of mental congruence between the two can be said to exist.

People cannot be expected to be consistently rational in their preferences. Even though their feelings about environment are usually based to some degree on observation and experience, most people haven't seen or lived in various types of physical environments. Therefore, what is involved in mental congruence is in the nature of hearsay evidence. Yet it is important evidence, since people's beliefs about these relationships affect the objectives they demand. For example, an urban renewal proposal meets with considerable opposition if people feel that the replacement housing will not accommodate them appropriately.[51] Another phenomenon is the so-called self-fulfilling prophecy,[52] whereby the belief in the existence of something often makes it come true. If a man believes that handyman activities are impossible in high density residential situations, for example, then he probably won't undertake this kind of activity while living in such housing.

Experiential congruence, on the other hand, deals with how well the environment actually accommodates the characteristics and behavior of people. Thus studies of experiential congruence would not ask a person his preference for environment; they focus on people living in a specific environment. Although people may not be aware of the existence of experiential congruence, their daily experience can point out the constraining or enabling power of their environment. Thus, in the case of the apartment-bound handyman, we could demonstrate the experiential incongruence of handyman activities and dwellings that feature minimal separations between individuals, if it could be shown how formerly active handymen unexpectedly find it impossible to continue this pastime after their move to a multiple dwelling.

Experiential congruence of people and environment is the most fundamental approach pursued in the following chapters. Nonetheless, a knowledge of mental congruence is necessary to assess the

51   An appropriate example from Cambridge, Mass., was described by Ronald Nuttal, Erwin K. Scheuch, and Chad Gordon, "On the Structure of Influence," in Terry N. Clark (ed.), *Community Structure and Decision-making: Comparative Analyses,* San Francisco: Chandler, 1968, pp. 349-380.

52   For a full discussion of the self-fulfilling prophecy, see Robert K. Merton, *Social Theory and Social Structure,* New York: The Free Press of Glencoe, 1957, pp. 179-195.

public's predisposition to accept and make successful proposed physical plans.

Pursuit of phenomena according to this scheme, however, requires good conceptualization of the man-made environment and the empirical specification of the nature and amount of relation of these concepts to variables in the more traditional systems. But the way is clear to attempting it. The intersystem congruence model is not traditional human ecology; neither is it pure Parsonian theory. But it amalgamates the general concerns of ecology with Parsons' general theoretical frame of reference. It applies and, at times, redirects Parsonian concepts and theory so as to confront questions facing both policymakers and social scientists.

prerequisites
for synthesis

It is one thing to talk facilely about the expected relations between broad categories of variables. It is certainly more difficult to incorporate the necessary details. To achieve the latter, we must have good linguistic tools.

Today, the Ekistics grid is probably the most systematic exposition of the relationship between aspects of physical environment and other relevant factors. This grid, as reproduced in Fig. 1, gives a feeling for the complexity of relationships involving urban phenomena and acts as a means of classification for any particular research finding.

The horizontal axis of the Ekistics grid refers to the scale of the environment, from the measure of man alone, through dwellings and neighborhoods, up to the ecumenopolis of 30 billion people. It refers to the numbers of people involved at any position on the vertical axis. The latter axis consists of types of elements making up nature, man, society, shells (buildings and transportation units), and networks. These elements, as listed below the grid, are broad categories. They state where to look for significant variables. But they do not state what these variables in fact are. They do not say what, within these social and physical categories, are the critical conditions whose variations are meaningful to human life.

Community Scale	i	ii	iii	I	II	III	IV	V	VI	VII	VIII	IX	X	XI	XII
	1	2	3	4	5	6	7	8	9	10	11	12	13	14	15
Ekistic Units	Man	Room	Dwelling	Dwelling group	Small neighborhood	Neighborhood	Small town	Town	Large city	Metropolis	Conurbation	Megalopolis	Urban region	Urbanized continent	Ecumenopolis
Elements — Nature															
Man															
Society															
Shells															
Networks															
Synthesis															
Population	1	2	4	40	250	1.5T	7T	50T	300T	2M	14M	100M	700M	5,000M	30,000M

Population
T (Thousands)   M (Millions)

Ekistic Logarithmic Scale

EKISTIC ELEMENTS

Nature
1. Water resources and pollution
2. Air circulation, temperature and pollution
3. Mineral resources
4. Land forms and landscape
5. Agriculture and fishing
6. Recreation and preservation of nature

Man
1. Biological needs (space, light, temperature, etc.)
2. Sensation and perception (the five senses)
3. Emotional needs (human relations, beauty, etc.)
4. Moral values

Society
1. Population composition
2. Social relations
3. Cultural patterns

4. Economic development policies
5. Industrial development
6. Education, health and welfare
7. Law and administration

Shells
1. Housing
2. Community services (schools, hospitals, etc.)
3. Commerce and recreation
4. Industrial equipment
5. Transportation facilities

Networks
1. Public utility systems (water, power, sewerage, etc.)
2. Transportation systems (water, road, rail, air)
3. Communication systems (telephone, radio, television, etc.)
4. Physical layout (land use system)

Fig. 1   The Ekistics grid. (Reprinted by permission of *Ekistics* (April, 1968), Athens Technological Institute, Athens, Greece.)

The Ekistics grid serves its purposes nobly. But to fully achieve the potential of the scheme suggested in Chapter 1, we need to break the urban physical environment down into a detailed set of meaningful concepts which represent environmental conditions. Although some highly promising attempts have been made, I do not feel the job has yet been realized, and it is an obstacle which I do not believe can be fully overcome in the present volume.

The need for such conceptualization is equally clear, however. As a prominent architect recently stressed:

The problem of housing any group is not unlike the problem of filing and cataloging books, when we suddenly find that there seems to be an awful lot of material on an apparently new subject and then, faced with the problem of where to put them, for expedience we order another section of shelves or filing cabinets and just dump them in. If we had set up our filing system more carefully initially, there would have been a proper place for them. When we are dealing with human beings, we cannot afford to group them for convenience and expedience and then house them under one classification if we really want to develop a self-adjusting and perpetual solution to the problem.[1]

This chapter represents several types of preparation for the review and synthesis of literature which follows. While acknowledging the difficulties involved, I shall try to move closer to the realization of variables which represent the environment by sketching some criteria which such a conceptualization would have to meet. I shall also outline a point of view which I feel would have to be the foundation for any system of concepts as could be devised. I shall then suggest how common ways of conceiving the environment now might be interpreted from this point of view, so that the current gap between ideal and present concepts won't obscure dissemination and appreciation of findings already on hand.

Following this discussion of concepts representing the physical environment, I shall present a more routine statement of variables from the other systems which give evidence of being relevant, so as to set the stage for the chapters in Section II.

Towards a Conceptualization of the Urban, Man-made Environment

Any review of the concepts which have been utilized to represent the physical environment must emphasize the diversity of emphasis

---

1   K. Izumi, appendix to paper presented at American Psychological Association Conference, September 3, 1966, New York City, p. 1.

in past work. The environment is rich and complex. Even an attempt at full description of every aspect of a particular scene would almost undoubtedly involve some selectivity in what an observer would report. Such is the stuff of fine literature. One writer might come forward with a brilliant description of a waterfall, for example, but it would not prevent the next writer from reporting additional details equally brilliantly. And it would not prevent a "full description" by a physicist from taking on still a different shape. Or that of a geologist, or a civil engineer, and so on.

However, even if we could assume that full description were possible, it is not always desirable. There are times when we want to know only the significant elements of an environment, those elements that are so central to the full picture that a change in them would mean that the whole scene would have different implications. These elements may be individual entities within the scene or they may be abstractions from a whole group of lower level elements. In any case, we deal with only these carefully selected elements of the total picture of reality when we need to generalize beyond the characteristics of a particular case.

Aesthetic appreciation of a single setting may still involve attempts at full description. Flowery description may be a firm requirement of astrological documentation in love stories. But if one wishes a common language with which to discuss a phenomenon such as the environment more generally—to appreciate similarities and differences from place to place—then common concepts which capture the elements whose variations are meaningful are necessary. One cannot systematically compare and contrast, or even outline, environments if the phenomena involved are infinitely variable. Therefore, some degree of conceptualization is in order, just as in any scientific enterprise.

What form do concepts to describe the urban environment normally take? As a prelude to a fuller discussion of criteria for such concepts, let me cite several. They give evidence of one way that current concepts vary—in the scale they describe.

Lynch and his associates have come forward with concepts like "edges" and "focal points."[2] The former refers to land uses that

<hr />

2   See, for example, Kevin Lynch, *The Image of the City*, Cambridge, Mass: M.I.T. Press, 1960, and Donald Appleyard, Kevin Lynch, and John Myer, "The View from the Road," in David Lowenthal (ed.), *Environmental Perception and Behaviour*, Chicago: University of Chicago, Department of Geography, Research Paper No. 109, 1967, pp. 75-88.

tend to serve in people's minds as borders, where one subarea of a city stops and another begins; railroad tracks are a traditional "edge,"[3] although rivers and certain highways serve the same function. Focal points are places which symbolically form the center of a cluster of land uses, holding together a larger area which otherwise might not have any unifying force. Statues, parks, and shopping centers are all focal points for subareas of cities. Indeed, if focal points are dramatic enough they may tie together entire cities or even regional areas.

Others have created concepts based on still broader levels of the environment. They sought patterns in the city as a whole. Blumenfeld, for example, shows that road patterns may impose at least two meaningfully different patterns on the city: circular and gridiron.[4] The former have roads leading from the center like spokes from a wheel. This plan is said to provide security in the absence of naturally protective boundaries, and it was "beloved by chieftains, emperors, priests, and popes,"[5] as whatever was placed in the center would be a natural focus of attention, whether it be temple, palace, or statue. The gridiron system originated from the ownership and subdivision of square fields and has so facilitated subdivision that it became the model for economically-oriented cities. "The open lot and speculation have always gone hand in hand."[6]

To these patterns, Tunnard adds two more: linear and curvilinear. In the former, all development follows a single, straight road, while in the latter, roads curve haphazardly, less for convenience than for amenity. Smith notes, for example, that Portuguese towns in the New World have strictly followed linear patterns, while their Spanish equivalents are gridirons, each for their own peculiar reasons.[7]

Thus it is evident that concepts differ at least by the *level* of the environment at which they are relevant. Some of them, in

---

3   See the use of tracks as edges in, for example, August Hollingshead, *Elmtown's Youth*, New York: Wiley, 1949.

4   Hans Blumenfeld, "A Theory of City Form, Past and Present," *Journal of the Society of Architectural Historians,* Vol. 8, nos. 3-4 (1949): pp. 7-16.

5   Christopher Tunnard, *The City of Man,* New York: Charles Scribner's Sons, 1953, p. 121.

6   *Ibid.,* p. 77.

7   Robert C. Smith, "Colonial Towns of Spanish and Portuguese America," *Journal of the Society of Architectural Historians,* Vol. 14, no. 4 (1955): pp. 3-12.

addition, are meaningful in an aesthetic sense, but not necessarily in a social sense or any other particular way. Others have economic significance. What criteria must an acceptable set of concepts for present purposes meet?

Criteria for Concepts

I propose six criteria for concepts of urban physical environment appropriate for articulation with variables in the cultural, social, and personality systems:

1. They must be relevant to all levels of form.
2. They must systematically integrate lower levels of environment with higher levels.
3. They must be physical, not social.
4. They must be relevant to social phenomena.
5. They must be measurable.
6. They must be man-made.

Let's look at these criteria one by one.

1. **They must be relevant to all levels of form.** There is sufficient evidence from even casual observation that each of the levels at which we might consider the environment plays a part in the daily lives of most people. The home and immediate environment is a very basic one to most people—a point to which I shall soon return. Yet various aspects such as edges and focal points, which are of a higher level than the home and immediate neighborhood, nonetheless fit both consciously and unconsciously into the daily round. Finally, even total patterns which many people may never see or appreciate still potentially make some contribution to the achievement or frustration of some personal, social, or cultural ends. That a person does not appreciate the physical peculiarity of a linear city, for example, does not mean that his access to certain people or to land uses (and hence certain abilities to organize or to realize certain cultural goals) is unaffected by that level of environmental pattern.

2. **They must systematically integrate lower levels of environment with higher levels.** But while all levels should be covered, they are not independent of each other. Indeed, each level becomes a part of the next higher level, so that while the whole may *represent* more than the sum of its parts, it still *consists* of the sum of its parts. It is therefore desirable that the lowest level concepts be system-

atically combined with each other at higher levels, rather than be discarded in favor of new concepts, so that the specific array of elements creating a particular environment at any level may be dissected and analyzed at any time. This is, of course, a systems approach. It makes possible sophisticated accounting of the components of specialized and complicated higher levels of form, as well as the manipulation of component concepts to produce new configurations, if desired.[8]

3. **They must be physical, not social.** Lest the scheme presented in Chapter 1 be tautological, the concepts which represent the physical environment must represent created spatial patterns. They must be more basic than simply the *use* that people make of a place. It is not sufficient to say that people act a certain way in a banquet room because it is a banquet room; "banquet room" is a social term, representing a cultural meaning given to a physical object, left undefined. One would be surprised if (within any culture) behavior were to vary greatly in a banquet room. But it is a valid proposition, though probably not the most fruitful one, to ask if there is any special limitation or encouragement to a specific human behavior or cultural pattern imposed by a 20' X 30' room with particular acoustical, visual, etc. properties. In short, if we are able to measure the relationships among systems, the concepts representing these systems must be independent of each other in definition.

4. **They must be relevant to social phenomena.** I have just stressed that concepts representing the physical environment must be physical, not social in character. But within this requirement, concepts may be many things indeed. A physicist might describe the molecular structure of the environment. An art historian might stress its aesthetic tradition. If, however, on top of such perfectly valid concerns, we must understand physical environment in terms of its articulation with the systems of social science, then the concepts must be such that they stand a chance of having some bearing on social phenomena. Molecules don't appear offhand to be related to the potential that two people will come into contact with each other; therefore, molecular concepts might best be skipped. But a

---

8   On this type of approach, see Christopher Alexander, *Notes on the Syntheses of Form*, Cambridge, Mass.: Harvard University Press, 1964 and Richard Meier, *A Communications Theory of Urban Growth*, Cambridge, Mass.: M.I.T. Press, 1962.

concept incorporating distance may well play a part in this latter type of phenomenon, suggesting its inclusion.

5.   The concepts must be measurable. In order that reliance can be placed on findings based on these concepts, there must be some way of stating the presence or absence of relevant phenomena. There is little agreement right now on aesthetic judgments because the presence or absence of a phenomenon like "dynamic tension"[9] is a very subjective decision. But in scientific propositions of an "if X then Y" character, there must be unequivocal criteria as to whether X is really X. Without this, it is impossible to build knowledge on any systematic basis. I do not argue, though, for the complete quantification of every concept, with absolute zeros, equal intervals, powers of division, and the like. While highly desirable, this goal is at present like asking a novice violinist to try Paganini at the outset. It will be a breakthrough in the environmental sciences when concepts reach even the point of an evenly graded continuum between opposite poles of any phenomenon, such as density. It will be significant to know when a complex phenomenon, such as physical isolation, is in fact present or absent. But scientists can do little until they are certain of the phenomena which they take at the start as given.

6.   They must be man-made. In the preceding chapter, I argued for a definition of the environment considered in this context to be a man-made environment. Therefore, at the least, consistency requires that this be a requirement for concepts. In addition, I would argue that this criterion is one that also puts a spotlight firmly on the city and hence on urban phenomena. While occasional beams may randomly illuminate nonurban phenomena, few aspects of environment are as completely man-made as cities. Indeed, as man comes increasingly to master his environment, the more this will become the case. The urban environment is not the only one man has made, but it is the one that man has made most fully. One cannot dispute that important physical elements of a city—parks, ravines, lakes,

---

9   This was a favorite criterion of project excellence in an architecture school I used to visit. It would be disconcerting to evaluate a project in terms of a criterion which was important to me, such as integration of social classes, only to hear the students' instructors bring the discussion back to "dynamic tension," upon which apparently even they (let alone prospective tenants) did not agree.

etc.—are not originally man-made.[10] Yet their shape, extent, and even future existence are now so much under the control of man that they do not represent exceptions to the rule.

Concepts of the Man-Made Environment

There have been several highly original attempts to break ground in the formation of systems of concepts to represent the urban environment.

Kevin Lynch has been in the forefront in developing concepts to describe cities macroscopically. With Lloyd Rodwin, he proposed a set of concepts based on the following criteria.

. . . the categories of analysis must: . . .

1. Have significance at the city-wide scale, that is, be controllable and describable at that level.
2. Involve either the physical shape or the activity description and not confuse the two.
3. Apply to all urban settings.
4. Be capable of being recorded, communicated, and tested.
5. Have significance for their effect on the achievement of human objectives, and include all physical fixtures that are significant.[11]

The resulting scheme had six concepts. The first, *element types*, amounts roughly to qualitative description of different building types. The second is *quantity*, the total number of units considered. The third is *density*, the number of elements inside a particular space. *Grain*, the fourth concept, refers to the heterogeneity, size, and spacing of elements within a given area; and *focal organization*, the fifth, refers generally to crucial places in the total picture which stand out. The final concept, *generalized spatial distribution*, refers to the entire pattern, grasped for whatever form it may convey to the observer.[12]

10　The continuum "natural to man-influenced" goes along with scale as the two major dimensions of environment sketched by Kenneth H. Craik, "The Comprehension of Everyday Physical Environment," *Journal of the American Institute of Planners,* Vol. 34 (1968): pp. 29-37.

11　Kevin Lynch and Lloyd Rodwin, "A Theory of Urban Form," *Journal of the American Institute of Planners,* Vol. 24, no. 4 (1958): p. 204. Reprinted by permission.

12　*Ibid.,* pp. 205-206.

Lynch and Rodwin's scheme does not adhere to all the criteria sketched in the previous section. Their first criterion is incompatible with my second. Therefore, it is not surprising that these concepts, however valuable, do not satisfy all my criteria. Chiefly, the concepts individually represent different levels of form, ranging from element types at the microscopic end through quantity, density, grain, focal organization, and up to generalized spatial distribution at the macroscopic end. It is not clear how concepts of lower levels fit into higher level patterns. Each, it seems, takes a stab at a relevant spatial arrangement at its own level; some but not all of them make reference to lower level concepts.

On the positive side, Lynch and Rodwin's concepts often summarize, quite brilliantly, socially relevant physical phenomena. The concept, "element types," for example, deals with characteristics of dwellings but is yet more general than particular housing types on the market. Grain is an excellent shorthand for the different and often complicated mixtures of land use.

Lynch, in a later essay, differentiated between the actual physical factors that create macroscopic patterns and the patterns themselves. Under the former he listed:

1. Magnitude and pattern of structural density and condition.
2. Capacity, type, and pattern of circulation facilities.
3. Location of fixed activities that draw on or serve large portions of the population.[13]

The three significant features which could be abstracted from the above factors are: (1) grain, (2) focal organization, and (3) accessibility (in time).

In this scheme, Lynch brings in methods of transportation. It is a matter of debate whether transportation is itself a component of urban form or a mechanism which supports or makes possible given forms, but its importance is certainly valid. The other substantially new element is accessibility, a concept representing ease of human movement within the new environment.

Writing after Lynch, Webber addressed himself to delineating the principal components of metropolitan form.[14] Although his aim

---

13 Kevin Lynch, "The Pattern of the Metropolis," *Daedalus* (Winter 1961): p. 80.

14 Melvin M. Webber, "The Urban Place and the Nonplace Urban Realm," in Melvin Webber *et al, Explorations into Urban Structure*, Philadelphia: University of Pennsylvania Press, 1964, pp. 79-153.

departs from the start from our very first criterion, his results are nonetheless instructive. First, he stresses the need to account for the *communications channels* which form the basis for the particular spatial patterns of a city. Cities where information or money changes hands in face-to-face encounters are likely to have different spatial needs from those dependent on telephone or telex. His second component includes the *spatial properties* of the various places and lines of communication in the metropolis. This accounts for the appearance but not the use of land, which he feels is still a separate component. The third, then, is the *location of the different land uses* as compared with one another. Each of these components of metropolitan form can then be specified in terms of six dimensions, which are consistent with but more detailed than Lynch and Rodwin's concepts.[15]

· Writers from other disciplines have shown complementary concentrations. A.E. Parr, an environmental psychologist, distinguishes between *territory* and *orbit*. Going more deeply into the microscopic end than did Lynch or Webber, Parr makes the following comparison:

Territory is the space which a person, as an individual, or as a member of a close-knit group (e.g., family, gang), in joint tenancy, claims as his or their own, and will "defend."

Orbit is a term I use to define the much wider concept of the space through which an individual habitually or occasionally roams. The orbit may contain two or more territories (e.g., home, office) in addition to all other space traversed or only irregularly occupied by the individual.[16]

The territorial concept goes more deeply into the fact that most people orient themselves around a single location, their home, even though, akin to ecological treatment, it deals with space more as a medium than as a variable. The orbital concept stresses another dimension by putting land uses into the perspective of its users, a noteworthy addition to our previous considerations.

A final emphasis comes from the scheme of a second psychologist, Isidor Chein. His view is one of specific environmental factors that have an impact on the individual. Although put into psychological jargon, these are aspects of the physical environment that have a bearing on behavior. Some are stimuli; they trigger off

15   For details, see the discussion on pp. 102-108 of Webber.

16   A.E. Parr, "In Search of Theory VI," reprint from *Arts and Architecture* (Sept. 1965): pp. 2-3.

behavior that was ready to occur. Others are *directors;* they induce specific directions of behavior. Then there are *goal objects*, which serve to satisfy certain needs. There are also aspects of the environment that are *supports* and *constraints* to behavior, as suggested in the scheme outlined here in Chapter 1.[17] Chein, while virtually ignoring the physical nature of the environment as well as its various levels, nonetheless puts a welcome stress on how the environment has different sorts of impacts on individuals.

The above authors thus differ greatly in their outlook, and they demonstrate how systems of concepts may vary according to this outlook. But they individually add the perspectives that (1) people are affected differently by different aspects of environment, (2) they venture from bases out into the city through often idiosyncratic paths, and (3) buildings and land uses of varying types and sizes contribute through their mixture to certain distinguishable patterns in the city as viewed from on high. Taken generally, all these are important views, and they fit within the criteria sketched in the previous section.

I should now like to outline a point of view which binds them together and which is intended to provide a reference point for the analysis of the social significance of existing buildings, neighborhoods, and cities.

The Ego-Centered Point of View

City planners see cities as entities. Airline pilots are familiar with their shapes. Politicians have to know all areas of cities and how they add up. But most people have no need for such a comprehensive view.

People know parts of cities. They are familiar with the areas in which they live, where they meet people, where they shop, and where they work. As Strauss puts it:

. . . the various kinds of urban perspectives held by the residents of a city are constructed from spatial representations resulting from membership in particular social worlds.[18]

---

17   Isador Chein, "The Environment as a Determinant of Behavior," *The Journal of Social Psychology*, Vol. 38 (1954): pp. 115-127.

18   Anselm Strauss, *Images of the American City*, New York: The Free Press of Glencoe, 1961, p. 67. Reprinted by permission of Macmillan Co.

A recent study by Orleans, for example, demonstrated that residents from different areas of Los Angeles have mutually exclusive images of the city.[19] Only residents of Westwood, where the University of California at Los Angeles campus is located, have a reasonably comprehensive image of the metropolitan area.

Lynch queried a sample of professional people in three cities as to what they noticed and/or remembered about their cities. The images they held of their city were only very partial, as Strauss would have expected, even though they were active people.[20] In this connection, we all know the legendary Bostonian's map of the United States, in which Massachusetts Bay takes up about half of the American East Coast and in which little of the continent lies to the west of Massachusetts (Fig. 2).

There isn't much argument at present against viewing the *immediate* environment in terms relevant to its impact on individuals. The term "human scale" is almost trite by now in architectural circles. What the preceding argument suggests, however, is that even the more macroscopic aspects of environment might fruitfully be conceived in terms of their relevance to individuals.

Our second criterion for concepts of physical environment requires that concepts describing aspects of the immediate environment combine to produce higher levels of environment. And while doing so, these basic concepts must have social meaning. To gather a systematic set of concepts that build a socially relevant picture of the environment, *both* microscopic and macroscopic, we must begin with concepts that apply to each individual who lives in the city—each ego. This would be an ego-centered conception of urban form.

An ego-centered point of view does not ignore the fact that people operate in cities as members of numbers of groups that have well-defined spatial needs of their own. Nor does it suggest that macroscopic environment is any less important. All it suggests is that the environment must be conceptualized in terms that are meaningful to the smallest unit that wanders throughout all levels—the

---

19 Peter Orleans, "Urban Experimentation and Urban Sociology," Annual Meeting of the National Academy of Sciences, Washington, D.C., April 27, 1967.

20 Lynch, *The Image of the City*, Cambridge, Mass.: M.I.T. Press and Harvard University Press, 1960.

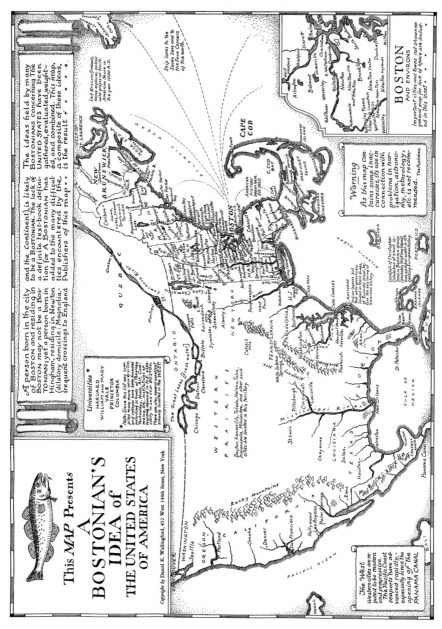

Fig. 2 People's own conception of space is caricatured by "A Bostonian's Idea of the United States of America." (Courtesy of Mrs. Florence V. Thierfieldt.)

Man and his urban environment

individual. I suggest that all concepts of environment must spring from a fundamental truism: *All people are separated in space from other people and from nonresidential activities.*

Men's homes are indeed their castles. To be sure, they meet people elsewhere, and many important activities are elsewhere, but everything starts from the home. Man-made spatial arrangements separate a person from all other people outside his housing unit and from all other types of activities. People and activities are separated at least by sight, by sound, and by touch, and in varying degrees.

Foley argues, when sorting out similar issues, that one must separate the effects of individual buildings from the spatial relations of groups of buildings when assessing the impact of the environment.[21] This point is well taken, but it can be turned around. I would argue that the basic measures of both phenomena are the same—the separation of ego from other people and activities.

People's homes commonly involve more of their time than any other single place in the city.[22] More activities in a man's life and in that of his family begin and end in his home than in any other location. Residences typically cover more of the area of cities than do any other single land use.

Not everyone, of course, has a home, as it is generally conceived. For some, a park bench in the summer and a jail cell in the winter constitute home. Others live in group quarters as part of a job or service. Yet, in the search for a basic element from which to view man in his urban environment, the individual's home unit stands head and shoulders over any other for all but a small segment of the population.

One could easily argue that internal features within homes separate even members of the same family from each other.[23] They do. The following discussion, however, will proceed from the home itself as a unit, since this is in my opinion the most microscopic level contributing to macroscopic urban environment. Internal division of

---

21   Donald L. Foley, "An Approach to Metropolitan Spatial Structure," in Melvin M. Webber *et al., Explorations into Spatial Structure*, Philadelphia: University of Pennsylvania Press, 1964, p. 43.

22   See, for example, the data in F. Stuart Chapin, Jr. and Henry C. Hightower "Household Activity Patterns and Land Use," *Journal of the American Institute of Planners,* Vol. 31 (1965): pp. 222-231, and Chapin and Hightower, *Household Activity Systems—A Pilot Investigation*, Chapel Hill, N.C.: Center for Urban and Regional Studies, Institute for Research in Social Science, University of North Carolina, 1966.

23   See, for example, Dorothy E. Smith, "Household Ecology," unpublished paper, *ca.* 1966.

space within homes and apartment units does not affect higher levels of form, even though it is important in its own right.

Homes offer varying degrees of protection from impingement by people residing outside them. This is the first place for which concepts are needed. Acoustical concerns, concerns regarding visual outlook, and concerns regarding the ability of other people to come in contact with each other are involved at the very least.

"Separation in space of people from other people" is a two-edged sword. It can be viewed, as above, in terms of environmental protection from impingement by others. But the sword can, of course, cut the other way; these concepts can be viewed with respect to their ability to bring people together. Some people value freedom from social contact, while others welcome contact. But the physical concepts should be neutral, referring to *separation* per se as a measurable entity, not as a good or bad goal. Some types of homes separate more fully than do others.

When physical contact, apart from visual or acoustical impingement, comes into the picture, the notion of distance is involved. It is now widely recognized that distance is an omnibus concept that has many aspects which might well be viewed separately. The traditional usage of distance is *physical distance*, the separation between two points according to a standard linear measure.

But contact is dependent on *overcoming* the physical distance between two points. Two identical physical distances may nonetheless represent differing barriers to contact if it takes more time to overcome one than the other. Many factors account for the variability of time, of which an important one (but not *exclusively* so) is transportation. Hence a second relevant type of distance is accessibility, as Lynch pointed out in his concepts cited earlier. Accessibility may be measured continuously in terms of elapsed time.

But the effect of distance can also be created. People can be made to act on the basis of separation from other people and activities by certain manipulations of the environment which create the illusion of distance. Dense plantings, impenetrable railroad tracks, and paths that lead people in divergent directions are all manipulations of physical environment that lead to social phenomena premised on the assumption of separation in space. This kind of distance might be called *manipulated distance.*[24]

---

24 In the past I have called this perceptual distance. See "An Empirical Analysis of Environmental Preferences," *Journal of the American Institute*

Manipulated distance is less quantitatively continuous than is accessibility. One is left with the impression of proximity or distance. Something is near or far as the result of the manipulations. Indeed, one could even argue that the slippery term "neighborhood" can be defined in terms of manipulations which give certain elements of the environment and people the appearance in common of being proximate.

Thus, in considering separations of people from each other, we must bear in mind that distance has several dimensions. These several dimensions of distance also play a part as we turn our focus to the separation in space of people from nonresidential activities.

Macroscopic views of the city often are in terms of major nonresidential uses of land. What is the mixture of land uses? Which land uses serve as focal points in metropolitan areas? The ego-centered point of view carries into this realm because it is people who go to nonresidential land uses, and from one to another. Supermarkets don't visit each other. It is fruitful to regard the placement of nonresidential activities with respect to the various kinds of distance which ego has to overcome in going to one or more of them.

Regarding individual activities this way accumulates information crucial for macroscopic form. If nonresidential land uses are usually separated by at least a nominal distance from most homes, it says something about the mixture of land uses or grain.

According to the number of egos who frequent a certain site, we discover that this site will be either large or small in scale. If egos go to land uses that are grouped together, we learn of clusters that form a part of the macroscopic pattern. Where large scale and clustering occur simultaneously, we learn of some possible focal points in the urban fabric.

This argument might appear to ignore considerations such as agglomeration with respect to land uses. Stores or factories may be near others of a similar nature because, for the former, groupings bring forth more customers and, for the latter, management may need to know what their counterparts in other similar enterprises are

---

of Planners, Vol. 32 (1966): pp. 355-360. It has also been called "functional distance" by Leon Festinger, Stanley Schachter, and Kurt Back, in *Social Pressures in Informal Groups*, New York: Harper and Brothers, 1950. However, I now use the term "manipulated distance" because of its happier fit with the criteria for concepts sketched earlier. The social connotations of the other terms are misleading inasmuch as the manipulations are physical in nature.

doing. Yet, these factors are not divorced from the daily path of the individual person. Better retailing is done in clusters of like stores because of the preferences (not to speak of the ability) people have to avoid several long trips for the purpose of purchasing consumer items. That people go to the stores helps dictate their location regardless of any secondary relations stores have with one another. The same is true for industries like the garment industry, whose executives could not trade gossip over lunch, keeping themselves informed about a volatile field, without agglomeration.

Thus, focusing on the concepts of the city from the individual's viewpoint does not rob us of the ingredients for macroscopic levels of environment and, on the positive side, it gives us a basic unit from which to start. Total environment is, after all, built of sub-units that relate in different ways to different people.

To this point I have argued that in search of concepts of the urban physical environment, it is advisable to select units taken from the premise that people are separated in space from other people and from nonresidential land uses. I have outlined how the ego-centered point of view contributes above the most microscopic level to the creation of concepts which make up the higher levels of form, through the collation and addition of lower-level concepts.

We do not now have these concepts. How, then, in the absence of them, do the implications of the point of view enable us to use observations which rely on current, commonly recognized housing, neighborhood, and city forms?

A Fresh Look at Current Nomenclature

Any suggestion that we need new concepts to represent the environment implies that our present terms are inadequate. This is certainly the case. Yet there is something to be salvaged from them with an adequate point of view.

Take housing type, for example. There can be no doubt that the thickness of walls and the location of apartments in relation to one another can make a big difference between apartment houses that look similar from the outside. Yet, even though our concepts now ignore these differences, building types still say something about the separation of people from other people.

In the single family house (Fig. 3a) a family shares no walls with other people. In the typical row house, town house, or garden apartment (Fig. 3b), at least one and usually two walls are shared with other families, adding a medium through which each could

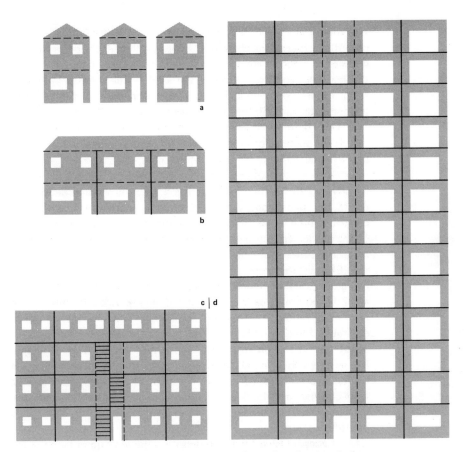

Fig. 3 The solid lines in these two-dimensional, front-view drawings indicate the walls, floors, or ceilings that are shared by neighbors in (a) single family homes, (b) garden apartments, (c) walkup apartments, and (d) high rise apartments. Although architectural variations within a single housing type make huge differences in impingement, it is also obvious that housing types make a difference per se.

impinge on the other. But each family still has its own front door.[25] In a typical walkup apartment (Fig. 3c), floors and ceilings start to be shared and people start to come in contact with other people in shared entrances, stairways, and hallways. In the high rise apartment (Fig. 3d), the sharing of walls, floors and ceilings is more

25 At least one architect, Mr. Irving Grossman of Toronto, claims that this is essential for a feeling of responsibility among families in multiple dwellings. It also facilitates living in a multiple dwelling with children.

the rule than the exception, and contact in elevators is with a potentially more diverse group of people, although the percentage of chances of meeting any particular person is greatly decreased. Thus the housing type itself suggests the kind of distances people have from others, even though we miss a complete picture of this phenomenon through the lack of adequately refined concepts.

The common concept of density has a number of referents.[26] One is the number of persons per room within a dwelling unit (e.g., inside an apartment or flat). Where high, this type of density is referred to by the common term "over-crowding." A second type of density is a direct function of housing type: how many people live under the same roof (i.e., in the same apartment house). This particular type of density may be refined so as to view the potential of the particular housing arrangement to bring people into desired or undesired contact with each other.

Still another type of density refers to the number of people living on a certain amount of residential land: how many people per acre? Often lot sizes are a rough but handy index of this, as are floor-area ratios in apartment buildings. The amount of space separating housing units from each other provides more information about the separation of people from other people. Even if people live in a detached house, their potentiality of contact with others is by no means constant. Living on a fifth of an acre differs greatly from having a full acre or more, and any child hater in the mass-produced suburbs will gladly testify about the density of youthful activity.

Besides housing types and densities, the mixture of land use (or segregation of land uses on the other hand) plays an important part in current terminology. This term makes additional suggestions concerning the concepts we really would like to have regarding the separation of people from various land uses. Consistent mixtures of land uses, or fine grain, imply consistently low separations between people and these activities. This could be (and has been) documented as it affects individual people and contrasts with great amounts of separation of land uses. This is a set of physical conditions which, like the others listed above, could be analyzed for its relationships to phenomena in the personality, social, and cultural systems.

---

26 For a good discussion of this, see Robert Schmitt, "Density, Health, and Social Organization," *Journal of the American Institute of Planners*, Vol. 32 (1966): pp. 38-40.

Neighborhood, as I have suggested, is a slippery term. Keller and Lee, for example, have documented ably the lack of physical parallel between the entities that different people call neighborhoods.[27] Yet, for cohesive neighborhoods, one might easily study what more basic aspects of any particular neighborhood may have led people to consider it *their* neighborhood—something whose contents are viewed in common as proximate. The spatial patterns which influence the shared perception of an area as a neighborhood may be valuable physical variables for analysis regarding social phenomena.[28]

Even the most major focal points defining the overall, macroscopic urban environment have social implications under the ego-centered point of view. Individuals are for the most part quite removed from these land uses when they in fact exist. But the presence of one or two commercial focal points shows that these lands uses are sufficiently accessible and important to people. They contribute to a sense of unity with respect to the total metropolis. The *absence* of a well defined overall pattern on the other hand implies lower distances of people to all kinds of land uses and probably greater fragmentation among land uses. The contrasting macroscopic forms of Chicago and Los Angeles, for example, are socially significant as viewed from the level of the individual resident of these cities (Fig. 4).

Thus, while current usages leave a lot to be desired, they nonetheless are meaningful when dissected on the basis of the ego-centered point of view.

SUMMARY

In this section, I have (1) outlined some requirements for concepts of representing the urban environment, (2) discussed some illustrative schemes that have been offered, (3) presented a point of view which I feel to be fundamental to any workable set of concepts for this context, and (4) sketched how the point of view allows use of current terms to some extent in the absence of ideal concepts.

---

27 Suzanne Keller, *The Urban Neighborhood*, New York: Random House, 1968, and T. Lee, "Urban Neighborhood as a Socio-Spatial Schema," *Human Relations,* Vol. 21 (1968): pp. 241-267.

28 Recent evidence shows, however, that such shared perceptions are not at all common. Different sub-groups living in what outsiders consider a single area often do not view it similarly. See Lisa Peattie, "Reflections on Advocacy Planning," *Journal of the American Institute of Planners*, Vol. 34 (1968): pp. 80-88.

a

Fig. 4 Although traditionally the "center" of Los Angeles, the Civic Center (a) has far less impact as a node in that sprawling, multicentered city than does the Loop (b) in Chicago. These two cities have strikingly different macroscopic environments. (Photos courtesy of the Los Angeles Area Chamber of Commerce and the Chicago Association of Commerce and Industry.)

Realistically, we do not have ideal concepts today. Certainly they were not part of past research efforts. Therefore it is necessary to search for the effects of more basic concepts while looking at terms that are commonly bandied about and which form the basis of past research. The six criteria are to guide the eventual emergence of a set of concepts which are now present only by implication, and the ego-centered point of view is to give direction to the search for these concepts. Therefore, reviewing and synthesizing past literature in this subject area at times require reading between the lines. It is, however, explicitly with the ego-centered frame of reference that any such interpretation will occur.

I have to this point spoken of concepts concerned with the physical environment. I should now like to turn to those representing the behavioral systems, although this treatment will be more brief.

Man and his urban environment

b

Concepts from the Behavioral Systems

In the absence of a clear cut set of concepts giving photographic clarity to differences in the physical environment, concepts from the other three systems—personality, social, and cultural—will form the organizing basis for the analysis of past literature.

As I stressed in the first chapter, a list of all possible variables in these systems would be encyclopedic. It is also unnecessary. The studies which make up the literature in this area have shown the specific relevance in this context of only a small number of concepts, certainly less than is contained in the arsenal of social science. The *number* of relevant variables is small, but their potential importance is not.

The relationships of each concept from the behavioral systems to relevant aspects of the physical environment will be the subject of a separate chapter.

Concepts falling within the social system will contribute to Chapters 3-5. Chapter 3 is devoted to the relationship of *life style* to the urban environment. Chapter 4 deals with *stage in the life cycle:* age and family considerations. Chapter 5 has to do with considerations of *social status*. Social status is probably the most central concept in sociology. Life style and stage in the life cycle are less often cited per se, but represent inclusive concepts which have been frequently used in urban sociology and which take into account many detailed elements on which sociologists concentrate, such as social structure and roles. A rationale for the choice of each topic, together with an explicit definition, will be found at the beginning of each of these chapters.

The cultural system is represented in Chapter 6, in which *value orientations* are related to the urban environment. The cultural system is without question richer in content than just the concept of value orientations, even after disregarding "material culture." Various kinds of normative prescriptions shade off into each other in this system. But value orientations, depending on their exact definition, are central to this range of phenomena, and their inclusion under eclectic terms of definition serves to represent a large part of whatever aspects of this system are relevant to the present context.

Much less work has come into this context on the personality system. A few classical studies attempted to tie personality into the physical structure of cities,[29] but this line of reasoning has not been systematically pursued, let alone refined to refer to specific aspects of the urban environment. There has been much work on perception of the environment, but as I indicated in Chapter 1, the work on perception is but complementary to that explored in this volume.

Much more ambiguous than the other psychological concepts is the idea of pathology. Yet it appears repeatedly in the psychological literature. In some cases it is personal breakdown, a *disruption* to personality development. In other cases, authors refer to what has been traditionally called social disorganization; this may more aptly be seen as a type of social organization which the standard bearers of society view as pathological. In other cases, it may refer to the weakness of cultural rules or their replacement by sets of rules which deviate from those which are commonly accepted. Thus these different kinds of pathology stem from different systems, only one of which is personality. But given its

---

29 See, for example, George Simmel, "Metropolis and Mental Life," in Paul K. Hatt and Albert J. Reiss, Jr. (eds.) *Cities and Society*, New York: The Free Press of Glencoe, rev. ed., 1957, pp. 635-646, and James Plant, "The Personality and an Urban Area," in Hatt and Reiss, *op. cit.*, pp. 647-665.

common theme, *pathology* stands as the concept explored in Chapter 7.

Chapter 8 deals with the direction of interaction. While the previous five chapters ask whether there is any systematic relationship between particular behavioral states and particular arrangements of physical environment, Chapter 8 takes a different tack. It asks, *given* all situations of congruence or incongruence between conditions of a social and a physical variable, does the physical environment nonetheless *determine* to any extent the direction that a person's contact with others will take? If a person is inclined to socialize and his setting permits some amount of it, can environment specify *with whom* he will likely be friendly?

As can be seen by the rapid de-escalation of terminology in the last few pages of this chapter, it is evident that Section II is a bit of a "come-down." Sophisticated points of view with respect to the environment are largely implicit, and the concepts of social science justified by past research in this area are few in number and gross in content. Yet, many of the individual findings and several of the points on which there is some degree of accumulated knowledge are highly valuable to social scientists and designers alike. They represent a great amount of research activity, and they represent the basis for correcting errors made in the past by designers and urban decision makers. The inventory of findings to follow thus serves a dual purpose: (1) as a record of findings and comments for readers searching for existing knowledge, and (2) as a benchmark for other readers wishing to advance the state of knowledge in this field.

Then, in Section III (Chapter 9), I shall evaluate the state of this body of knowledge and look to the future with such considerations as the relevance of *past* and *present* studies for *future* urban needs, how research can utilize and make gains from current projects whose construction couldn't wait till all the answers were in, and some suggested research strategies for maximizing research efforts in this area.

section II
the urban environment

life style and urban environment 3

In this and the chapters that follow, I shall present material on a
series of relationships which link social phenomena to the physical
environment, together with evidence from the far flung literature of
this field which bears upon them.

What is life style? Most people have images of different
life styles. One is of the hard-boiled businessman who spends
all the time he can on business, and even whose pleasures, or
what would be pleasures to other people, are derived from activities
related to his occupational world. He lives near his work. His
holidays are "busman's" holidays. His children, if any, are planned
to fit his career pattern, and they are left to other socializing agents
whenever his workload gets too high, which is normally. He seeks
success, and every accomplishment is belittled when compared with
his ultimate aspirations.

People have other images of life styles as well. One is of the
ideal father, a man who, without visible effort or concern, is a
success at his vocation, but whose active interests and thoughts are
lavished on his children, usually through leisure time activities. He is
not afraid to live some distance from his job if it provides green
pastures for his children. His vacations are spent with the whole

family, and their intent is usually educational or at the least in pursuit of wider personal experiences for the children. He is a handyman who wants to set a good example, and he works in his community to make it a better place in which his children will grow up.

Still another image is that of the person who lives for the joy of it. He spends money on the up-to-date, the enjoyable. He patronizes restaurants, nightclubs, entertainments of all kinds. He knows many people and participates in many crowds. While not necessarily selfish in any moralistic way, his life and its pleasures primarily benefit himself. He likes to live in the middle of things. Suburbia is Endsville.

We all have such images. The ones presented above happen to be three which Bell has codified into life styles which he called careerism, familism, and consumership.[1] These life styles are commonly recognized, if highly general phenomena. While there are pure, ideal patterns, most people represent some type of combination of these phenomena. But what, theoretically, are life styles as social variables?

Life style is based on *role emphasis*. City dwellers potentially play an appreciable variety of roles as they participate in a number of intersecting groups throughout the day. They might be father, subway rider, store clerk, friend, good samaritan, and many, many more in the course of a single day. Each one of these positions normally contains expectations of a pattern of behavior: the role. But all roles are not equally meaningful to each person. Some stand out; they are central to a person's image of himself, and they at times present special needs which extrude into the physical environment.

Two elements at the minimum are included in life style. One is a set of behaviors which must be performed to satisfy a role. This element will usually include interaction with other people. Depending on the role, these people must be appropriately present or absent for proper performance of the role.

The second element is the *sphere of life* which is emphasized. Social scientists generally cite at least five spheres as central elements

---

1   Wendell Bell, "The City, the Suburb, and a Theory of Social Choice," in Scott Greer, Dennis L. McElrath, David W. Minar, and Peter Orleans (eds.), *The New Urbanization*, New York: St. Martin's Press, 1968, pp. 132-168.

of any society: political control, economic supply, propagation, socialization of the young, and explanation of the supernatural.

For example, with our hard-boiled businessmen, certain achievement oriented behaviors with business colleagues and/or customers would be emphasized, together with the economic supply sphere of life. He would typically deemphasize socialization of the young.

Together these elements help define the content of roles. Life style, then, is a composite of those aspects of the roles a person strongly emphasizes. It refers *not* to styles of dress or furnishing, but *rather* to styles of *living*.

INTENSE FAMILY INTERACTION AND HIGH "DENSITIES"

On the Lessons of Ghettos

There is currently a spate of literature on life style and housing in so-called ethnic ghettos in cities.[2] This has become an issue because researchers have recently recognized, with a measure of surprise, that ethnic identity seems every bit as strong today as it was in the days when mass immigration was a regular phenomenon in the United States.[3] In some cases, where groups are disadvantaged by a lack of skills or by skin color, they are forced in upon themselves. In other cases, people choose to remain together for various benefits which their propinquity can provide. In any case, different subcultures frequently maintain different life styles among their other differences.

In *Beyond the Melting Pot,* Glazer and Moynihan, for example, discuss the thriving and separate existence in New York City of Jews, Negroes, Puerto Ricans, Irish, and Italians. True to their title, these authors suggest strongly that any notion of a "melting pot," in which all immigrants would in time be refined to a single specimen of red-blooded American, is fallacious. It did not happen. Instead, the day-to-day basis of ethnicity has been changed among the older groups, while the binding and at times divisive force of ethnicity has

---

2   Its importance to design has been subject to sharp debate. Among at least one group of architects, this is known as "ethnic crap."

3   This is still a current phenomenon in Canada.

not changed.[4] Kantrowitz put it succinctly, "We think voluntary ethnic segregation is still a viable force."[5]

The groups involved in any city tend to differ. In Boston, there are still significant clusters of people of Italian extraction. In Census Tract 43, for example, a tract roughly synonymous with an area called the North End, over two-thirds of the residents were classified as of Italian stock in 1960. In nearby Beacon Hill, that figure is less than 10%.[6] Some of the largest "Italian cities" in the world have been on New World soil, and there is no evidence that this was purely a temporary phenomenon.

In Detroit, there is a Polish enclave named Hamtramck. One writer, after studying this area, was moved to state:

Though the proportion of the Polish-born in the population will decline further in the coming years, at present there seems to be no diminution in the essential Polishness of the Community . . .[7]

In 1927, for example, 47.7% of the residents of Hamtramck spoke only Polish in their homes, and by 1945 this had increased to 49.3%,[8] although the melting pot theory would have led to the expectation of a reduction.

Elsewhere in America, one can point to Spanish-Americans, to orientals, and even to old-line American hillbillies maintaining separate images and residences.

Many sociologists keep active trying to account for the existence of ethnic ghettos and the manner in which they change. They also ask what influences *individual* mobility into and out of ghettos even at the same time that ghettos remain stable. The classic

4   Nathan Glazer and Daniel Patrick Moynihan, *Beyond the Melting Pot,* Cambridge, Mass.: M.I.T. Press and Harvard University Press, 1963.

5   Nathan Kantrowitz, "Ethnic and Racial Segregation in the New York Metropolis, 1960," *American Journal of Sociology,* Vol. 74 (1969): 685.

6   U.S. Bureau of the Census, *U.S. Census of Population and Housing: 1960,* Final Report PHC (1)-18 (Boston, Mass.), Washington, D.C.: Government Printing Office, 1962, pp. 19-20.

7   Arthur Evans Wood, *Hamtramck: Then and Now,* New Haven: College and Universities Press, 1955, p. 10.

8   *Ibid.,* p. 36.

line,[9] although one that has been recently questioned on a variety of grounds,[10] is that strict residential segregation is connected to the economic position of a group. As the people are able to successfully cope with the larger world financially, they also gain whatever additional leverage is needed to locate in a desirable location which is not necessarily the primary turf of their ethnic group.

Yet one can inevitably point to the exceptions to this rule: colonies of wealthy members of particular ethnic groups in select locations (the so-called "gilded ghetto"[11]), and wealthy members of ethnic groups who choose to remain with their brethren because of a common style of life.[12] The complex of factors that governs the erection and maintenance of ghettos is, however, less important to this chapter than the fact of their existence today. It is indeed important that clusters of people persist who share similar life styles in local areas.

After an inspection tour of American cities, the British town planner, Marris, wrote:

It is, I think, a mistake to conceive the assimilation of immigrants in terms of two cultures: the dominant culture of America, represented by city life, and the culture of the rural society from which they came. The city contains subcultures as stable and viable as the conventional norms, and it is to one of these subcultures that the newcomer is first introduced. The more successfully he becomes integrated in it, the more difficult it becomes to interest him in the values of the dominant culture . . .[13]

And the same phenomenon has been documented, with particular reference to housing, very recently in England, as well, by Burney.[14]

---

9   See, for example, Otis Dudley Duncan and Stanley Lieberson, "Ethnic Segregation and Assimilation," *American Journal of Sociology*, Vol. 64 (1959): pp. 364-374.

10   See, for example, Edward O. Laumann, James Beshers, and Benjamin Bradshaw, "Ethnic Congregation-Segregation, Assimilation, and Stratification," *Social Forces*, Vol. 43 (1964): pp. 482-489.

11   Judith Kramer and Seymour Leventman, *Children of the Gilded Ghetto*, New Haven: Yale University Press, 1961.

12   I am informed that this is common in Boston, for example.

13   Peter Marris, "A Report on Urban Renewal in the U.S.," in Leonard Duhl (ed.), *The Urban Condition*, New York: Basic Books, 1963, pp. 121 and 125.

14   Elizabeth Burney, *Housing on Trial*, London: Oxford University Press, 1967.

What we must investigate is whether some of the styles of life found among residentially propinquitous ethnic groups thrive in the spatial arrangements presented by their current setting. Researchers will debate whether these styles of life are really bound to the cultural group or whether they are in fact functions of social class;[15] but the whole point, for present purposes, is that among many such groups an emphasis on a life style which includes very strong, frequent, and intense interaction with a large number of relatives seems to require that they live in some arrangement of buildings, streets, and open spaces (or the lack of them) that promotes the easy availability of person to person.

Hence, the first relationship which studies would seem to support is: *Intense family interaction is congruent with low separations of people from other people.*

What general style of life is involved here? It is highly organized. Gone are the days when well-meaning social scientists would examine an area, discover that the behavioral blueprint for middle-class America was not being followed, and as a consequence declare that the area was "disorganized," a term with strong negative implications. Whyte, for example, studied an Italian ghetto which people called disorganized and concluded that it had a highly structured internal organization. Its structure simply differed from that which most middle-class people were accustomed to recognize. Even the bowling scores of the streetcorner gang with whom Whyte associated came out completely consistent with the complexities of internal organization within that group, although the *objective* skill of the bowlers had no relation to these scores.[16]

The differential organization in certain groups of society was also brought out in studies of voluntary organization. Studies had traditionally shown that the higher in the status hierarchy people happened to be, the more they participated in voluntary associations. Hence, many people concluded that life among people at the bottom of the status hierarchy was disorganized. It took Dotson's study of interpersonal relations to show that, at least in New Haven,

15   See the arguments for the latter by Herbert Gans, *The Urban Villagers*, New York: The Free Press of Glencoe, 1962.

16   William F. Whyte, *Streetcorner Society*, Chicago: University of Chicago Press, 1943. For a highly consistent pattern, see Gerald Suttles, *The Social Order of the Slum,* Chicago: University of Chicago Press, 1968.

lower class people hadn't abdicated from the human race; when they saw people, they saw *relatives*, and they met these relatives more frequently than did other people.[17]

Disorganization is a loaded concept. Yet there are areas which are characterized by a "reorganization" with consequences that many will argue are harmful to those involved in them. Gans has called this the "urban jungle."[18] There is no question that not all rundown areas are well organized socially. But some of them are, and the basis of this organization frequently appears to be kinship.

Boston's West End

The devotion of energy and attention to frequent meetings with like-age relatives was a consistent and important finding throughout the variety of reports issuing from the West End Study in Boston in the late 1950's and through the '60's. The West End was an older section of Boston, with five-story walk-up apartments, tiny back yards, and no setback from the narrow, winding streets. Its homes were not kept in good repair, and the city declared it fit for renewal. The West End Study utilized the tools of psychiatry, psychology, anthropology, and sociology to study in longitudinal dimensions the impact of the redevelopment on the residents of the area.

In studies conducted before the move, a clear picture was gained of the place that kinship activities played in the lives of these people. A good person was one who was loyal to relatives of his own generation. He had no sources of counter-loyalty. He was always on call for spontaneous get-togethers. He responded enthusiastically to other people. Hardly the hard-boiled businessman, he was, as Gans put it, person oriented—interested primarily in the people in his group, *not* in anything abstract or objective such as is often involved in the occupational world.[19] The values underlying this life style are said to be expressiveness and group integration, *not* achievement.[20]

If one is person oriented in this "peer group society," then it is important to ensure that those with whom the society is shared are

---

17 Floyd Dotson, "Patterns of Voluntary Association Among Urban Working-Class Families," *American Sociological Review*, Vol. 16 (1951), pp. 687-693.

18 Gans, *op. cit.*, p. 4.

19 *Ibid.*, Part Two.

20 Edward Ryan, "Personal Identity in an Urban Slum," in Leonard J. Duhl (ed.), *The Urban Condition*, New York: Basic Books, 1963, pp. 135-150.

also adhering strictly to this life style. Therefore, "behavior control" plays an important part in the maintenance of this life style. It was common in the West End for people to constantly check and reinforce with others' behavior, lest some alternative pattern develop and disrupt the social networks binding the community. For this, surveillance of everyone by everyone else was of prime importance.

There is every evidence that the physical environment of the area strongly supported this life style.[21] The people were living in high enough densities so that many related families could live near each other. While not a purely physical factor, procedures governing occupancy were anything but rigid, so that they did not block what the densities allowed. People, via their residences, were close to many other people.

But the pattern of streets also helped maintain this life style (Fig. 1). From their windows, people could easily view passers-by, and they were close enough to hail them if desired. Windows in one home were usually pretty close to those in others, so that conversations among the many residents of adjacent buildings did not require arrangement in advance. Stores which the local residents patronized were scattered throughout the neighborhood, so that even the pursuit of routine daily errands would bring people within range of the doors and windows of a wide number of potential contacts.

The people never idealized their housing itself. What they did value, however, was the combination of type of building and siting of buildings relative to each other, the streets, and the commercial land uses. This combination brought people into frequent, spontaneous, and intense contact with their relatives. It strongly supported their style of life. As one of the researchers put it:

In the West End, and in most working class communities which have been reported in the literature, there was considerable interaction with the surrounding physical and social environment, an interaction which formed an integral part of the lives of the people . . . Among a population for whom sitting on stoops, congregating on street corners, hanging out of windows, talking with shopkeepers, and strolling in the local area formed a critical part of the **modus vivendi**, the concept of personal living space must certainly be expanded to include outdoor as well as indoor space.

. . .In other words, if the prevalent life-style is such that the street scene, hallways, and the apartments of others are the locus for a

---

21   Gans, *loc. cit.*

Fig. 1 A typical street in the old West End of Boston. (Photo by Herbert Gans.)

considerable part of the day's activities, measures and standards of residential density must be revised to include a realistic assessment of available living space as well as consideration of the preferred pattern and intensity of interpersonal contact.[22]

Residents of the West End pictured suburbs as cold, dreary places, which could not support their way of life.[23] How could people meet their confreres frequently and spontaneously when they might have to *drive* to get to each other's homes? This number of families simply can't locate as closely to each other in the low densities that characterize so many suburbs. How do you run into people without prearrangement when homes are set back well beyond the sidewalks (if there are any) and when strict separations

22   Chester W. Hartman, "Social Values and Housing Orientations," *The Journal of Social Issues,* Vol. XIX, No. 2 (1963): pp. 128-129.
23   Gans, *op. cit.,* pp. 22-23.

of land use remove convenience centers from the midst of where people live?

Gans also tells the story of a group of boys who were given the opportunity to spend a summer holiday at Cape Cod. They couldn't imagine, after having been there, why anyone would consider it worth visiting, let alone having as home. It was desolate. There was no "action." These boys much preferred the person-centered life style that was part and parcel of the particular arrangement of their "hot city streets."

In short, for people with this life style, regardless of whether it is a function of their ethnicity or social class background, the immediate neighborhood (i.e., a pattern of several streets) is far more important to them than the condition of their housing. And the particular arrangement of the neighborhood appears to support this life style, while the latter might be considerably more difficult to maintain elsewhere, or indeed impossible.

One must note that this relationship includes not just the nature and arrangement of the housing, but just as vitally the integration of commercial land uses with others in the general area.

This does not require, however, that cities be forced to absorb whatever inefficiencies or costs accompany neighborhoods which represent menaces to health, safety, or welfare, or which stand in the way of more efficient use of land which could prove of overwhelming benefit to the entire city. What it does require is attention to the spatial components—the basic concepts of environment—that make a particular old neighborhood so viable socially to some people. These components could, with hard work and ingenuity, be intrinsic to replacement housing provided to play fair with the dispossessed ghetto-dwellers. If voluntary ghettos play such a part in people's lives, then safe and clean ghettos can be designed to replace those that must disappear. There is potentially far more choice for those forced to relocate than that between stereotypic public housing, on the one hand (built according to criteria of economy of construction and maintenance, noncompetitiveness with the private market, and standardization of form), and the vagaries of the private market, on the other, even if mediated by a public agency.

What is fascinating to observe among the West Enders is the similarities among the areas to which they moved after redevelopment in the West End. While they dispersed quite widely, the concentrations which occurred were in parts of greater Boston known for their high densities and mixtures of land uses: the North

End, Charlestown, Somerville, and East Boston.[24] While by and large the people ended up gaining more private open space, this was almost inevitable given the difficulties in finding exact duplicates of the West End. A final aspect of the choice of new housing which gives a clue as to the purposive nature of this search is the fact that so few people (only about 15%) found replacement housing through the aid of relocation officials, although this figure also includes those who accepted public housing.[25]

The West End Study was thorough, and its findings have been disseminated to scientists and policy makers alike. But its findings regarding the congruence of frequent and intense family interaction with low separations of people from other people are not isolated. Similar findings have come from studies conducted elsewhere in the world.

London's East End

Another thorough study was conducted in and around London, England.[26] London's East End was old and densely settled. Like Boston's West End, there was a mixture of small stores among the residences, which were apartments in old buildings, with little, if any, open space other than the streets. Like the West Enders, the people whom the researchers studied were working class. But they were not of Italian extraction, and their lives did not center on relatives of the same generation.

Nonetheless, interaction with relatives was highly valued. But in Bethnal Green, the area studied, this interaction focused around the family matriarch. "Mum," the oldest female in a chain of descendence, was the consistent element in this world. It was at her house that families would convene regularly. She would look after grandchildren when their mothers worked. She would hold the fort

---

24 Chester Hartman, "The Housing of Relocated Families," in James Q. Wilson, *Urban Reversal: The Record and the Controversy*, Cambridge, Mass.: M.I.T. Press, 1966, p. 296.

25 Every West Ender was guaranteed space in the luxury apartments which will be built on the site, but this was not a realistic alternative financially. Subsequent government action has put an end to the approval of renewal projects that primarily benefit others than the residents of the area, at least in principle.

26 Michael Young and Peter Willmott, *Family and Kinship in East London*, Baltimore: Penguin Books, revised 1962.

during times of illness or childbirth. She would lend money to those who needed it.[27]

Newly formed families would often live with Mum after marriage, since flats were scarce. And it was Mum whose influence with the rent collectors procured apartments within a short distance for the families that outgrew Mum's flat.

The daily round of life thus revolved around family, just as did the West Enders'. Only in this case, the particular conception of family is vertical through generations rather than horizontal through more distant relatives of the same generation. But this life style, despite the change in the exact structure of the intense family interaction, nonetheless requires that everyone be living within easy access of a number of significant others. And like the West End case, the mixture of stores around the area facilitated the frequent contact among members of a family.

The congruence of the environmental setting to the style of life is brought home dramatically in this study by some data that the researchers gathered before and after a number of families were forced to move to a relatively low density estate of semi-detached houses in a suburb of London given the name of Greenleigh. When living in a suburb with other families, people just couldn't get to see their Mums, who were left behind in Bethnal Green and who were now seen only occasionally, when people made other trips back to that area (e.g., to work or to shop). While husbands had seen their mothers an average of 15.0 times per month before their move, after the move to Greenleigh this had declined to 3.8 and then to 3.3 after two years. The comparable figures for wives, who formerly had been closer to their mothers than the men but who later hadn't even the excuse of working in the East End for visits back, were 17.2, 3.0, and 2.4.[28]

Similar figures were given by Mogey for people moving from central Oxford to a suburban tract, as compared to the old neighborhood. In Oxford, 60% of those with relatives saw them regularly, while on the periphery, only 30% had regular meetings.[29]

---

27 An additional description of Mum can be found in Madeline Kerr, *The People of Ship Street*, New York: Humanities Press, 1958.

28 Young and Willmott, *op. cit.,* p. 131.

29 John M. Mogey, *Family and Neighbourhood*, London: Oxford University Press, 1956, p. 81.

Table 1 Care of Children at Last Confinement*

	Bethnal Green Sample	Greenleigh Sample
Relatives	29	4
Husbands, children, or neighbors	15	15

*   Taken from Michael Young and Peter Willmott, *Family and Kinship in East London,* Baltimore, Md.: Penguin Books, revised 1962, p. 141.

The nature of mutual aid also changed after the move from Bethnal Green to Greenleigh, since Mum was much less available for her regular services. As Table 1 points out, when a new child was born into a family, relatives had been relied on in Bethnal Green by a margin of 2:1 over other people to take care of the other children. After the move, this ratio reversed itself to practically 4:1 in favor of people other than members of the extended kinship network, in the absence of relatives within easy reach.

Indeed, not only was there a change *away from* the life style emphasizing intense family interaction in the new setting, but the people in Greenleigh adopted an altogether new life style. What is significant is that the people were not left in a disorganized state after having been stripped of environmental support for their old life style. Although they did not consciously seek its replacement, there is every indication that the new life style was the path of least resistance given their new surroundings.

The question remains, however, as to whether the drastic change in life style was not just a function of upheaval in the lives of the Bethnal Greeners. They were, after all, arbitrarily uprooted and separated from familiar places and people. Wouldn't time heal these wounds and enable people to make the arrangements necessary to reinstitute the style of life centering around Mum?

One of the researchers from the Bethnal Green study sought to investigate this question by studying life in a working class estate much like Greenleigh, except that it had been settled by refugees from urban ghettos much earlier in time.[30] He discovered that it was indeed possible for people to reinstate a Mum-centered way of life in

30   Peter Willmott, *The Evolution of a Community*, London: Routledge and Kegan Paul, 1962.

a

Fig. 2 Nigerians used to housing such as the compound shown in (a) did not
believe that their life styles would be accommodated in the new housing shown
in (b). (Photos by Black Star and by Michael Wheeler.)

the lower density suburbs with segregated land uses. But it was
difficult to arrange in a setting in which few homes were really close
to each other. The number of homes which were potentially open to
members of a family who wished frequent contact with each other
were small, and the turnover among the potential homes could
neither be anticipated nor channeled to benefit particular families as
it could in the ghetto. An additional obstacle lay in the fact that
most surburban homes were built for families, so that the number of
potential units for older people either without children at home or
living alone was negligible.

Thus, while the life style centering around Mum did reappear
with time—it usually took a generation (i.e., when girls who moved to
suburbia as children had their own children)—it was anything but the
path of least resistance in that setting, and it did not become a
modal life style as before.

Downtown Lagos

Evidence on this relationship comes also from Nigeria.[31] There, in Lagos, family interaction (above and beyond just parents and children) took still another form. Families here congregated around the surviving patriarch, and spontaneous contact was maintained and valued among large numbers of families descended from the same older man. These groups lived in large square-shaped compounds, with open space in the center for congregation, cooking, and like activities. Each family would have one section of the compound as its own domain (Fig. 2a).

As in other studies, the relation of a life style to arrangements of space came into focus with the threat of urban renewal. The public officials of the area decided that downtown Lagos, which contained numerous extended family compounds, was not impressive as a capital, in the growing international style characterized by tall office buildings and wide boulevards. To replace the compounds, which would be bulldozed from existence, the planners proposed a

---

31 Peter Marris, *Family and Social Class in an African City,* Evanston, Ill.: Northwestern University Press, 1962.

series of row houses, with yards separating them from each other. Located some distance from the central area of Lagos, these new homes incorporated strongly ingrained Western notions of sanitation and privacy (Fig. 2b).

The residents of the compounds complained. The researcher captures the gist of complaints which touch on interaction patterns in the words of one of his respondents:

And then, the condition of the houses at Suru Lere doesn't suit me. It's European style of building, there's no yard. They're just self-contained houses, and I'm used to communal living. When you come into the yard now, you see people coming and going, but out there it's just empty land. Unless it's compulsory, it's not the kind of place for people used to communal life . . .[32]

But others did like it. Most favorably disposed to the new housing were Nigerians returning from work or study abroad. They had in many ways shed more traditional life styles, and they had adopted those more congruent with the environment created by the replacement housing. As the researcher put it:

It was this peace and isolation, the self-sufficiency of a well appointed house, which most appealed to those who liked it there: and underlay the frustrations of those who hated it.[33]

Thus data from a variety of sources point to a relationship between intense family interaction and low separations of people from other people. They suggest that people have access to a number of other people to support this life style fully, and that not just housing shells, but also open space and the mixtures of land use are important aspects of this type of environment.

Some recent evidence in the southern United States supports these contentions. In a study of Greensboro, North Carolina, Adams discovered that contact with kin of all kinds, *including telephone and letters,* decreased with increasing degrees of separation. This occurred despite the fact that people considered their kinfolk no less important to them if they were distant.[34]

---

32 *Ibid.*, p. 94.

33 *Ibid.*, p. 97.

34 Bert N. Adams, *Kinship in an Urban Setting*, Chicago: Markham Publishing Company, 1968.

THE NUCLEAR FAMILY IN SUBURBIA

The preceding observations have another side to them. Extended families differ from nuclear families, those in which intense contact is maintained primarily between spouses and their resident children. Urban ghettos are counterbalanced by popular conceptions of suburbia; even though suburbs differ greatly from each other, the principal elements intrinsic to this discussion are lower densities, created by a combination of housing type and open space, and a more strict segregation of land uses, particularly the placement at a distance of large-scale sources of employment. Evidence seems to suggest that a style of life which emphasizes activity with this type of family is the path of least resistance in areas so characterized.

One set of authors, for example, states directly that Australians live for the most part in single family dwellings (83% of all dwellings in Melbourne are of this type) and that this is connected with tremendous emphasis in Australia on the nuclear family.[35]

Some of the studies cited in the previous section illustrate this relationship.

When the Bethnal Greeners arrived at Greenleigh, they took on a new life style—one that centered around their nuclear family as a unit.[36] They began to "keep up with the Joneses" for the first time. Possessions began to matter. This required money, and money in turn required a new dedication to work routines. The environment set out families as isolated units, and hence its members worked to enhance and put the best light possible on this unit.

The same researchers took a look at a more settled suburb called Woodford.[37] There they described what they termed house centered couples, families living largely independent of their kin with activities shared by the couple and focussed on their family unit as an entity. Handyman activities, which portray a positive role of a father to his children and which serve to improve property held by the family, were stressed. Only 16% of these adults had parents within a five minute walk, compared with 41% in Bethnal Green.[38]

---

35   O. H. Oeser and S. B. Hammond, *Social Structure and Personality in a City*, New York: Macmillan, 1954, p. 14.

36   Young and Willmott, *op. cit.*

37   Peter Willmott and Michael Young, *Family and Class in a London Suburb*, London: Routledge and Kegan Paul, 1960.

38   *Ibid.*, p. 29.

Interaction was not something pursued by members of the family individually according to kinship lines, but was rather centered on nonrelated "friends."

The common pattern, it seems, is to belong to a small, intimate network of 'friends,' mostly coming from the surrounding 20 or 30 houses. Though some people, particularly in professional or managerial jobs, also have friends living farther afield.[39]

This follows the lines of Bott's distinction between family interaction styles. In some, husbands and wives maintain separate networks of friends and activities. In others, people are known and seen jointly. More generally, in the former case, the roles of the husband and the wife are quite divergent, while in the latter there is much overlap. The two put different requirements on physical environment and hence flourish in different environments.[40] In the suburbs, husbands and wives are more likely to do the same things—and together.

Mogey, for example, found a strong division of labor among only 20% in his surburban Oxford sample as compared with 65% among his center city group.[41]

This general trend away from husbands and wives parting ways is also no doubt aided by the provision of only occasional, large scale pubs in the suburban locations, literally separating men from something which was formerly close to them, both literally and figuratively.[42]

Gans studied people moving to a newly constructed suburb emphasizing low densities and segregated land uses: Levittown, New Jersey.[43] After a lengthy look at the adjustment of these people, he

---

39   *Ibid.*, p. 102.

40   Elizabeth Bott, *Family and Social Network*, London: Tavistock Publications, 1957.

41   Mogey, *op. cit.*, p. 58.

42   Young and Willmott, *op. cit.*

43   Herbert Gans, *The Levittowners*, New York: Pantheon Books, 1967. See also his "Planning and Social Life: Friendship and Neighbor Relations in Suburban Communities," *Journal of the American Institute of Planners*, Vol. 27 (1966): pp. 134-140; "Urbanism and Suburbanism as Ways of Life: A Re-Evaluation of Definitions," in Arnold M. Rose (ed.), *Human Behavior and Social Process*, Boston: Houghton Mifflin, 1962, pp. 625-648; and "Effects of the Move from City to Suburb," in Leonard Duhl (ed.), *The Urban Condition*, New York: Basic Books, 1963, pp. 184-198. Levittown has since changed its name back to the original name of the area: Willingboro.

found that most of them were extremely happy and well adjusted after their move. Indeed many of them had chosen Levittown because they desired to break out of life styles which bound them to their extended families. And they found that it worked. Most of the changes resulting from suburban living were anticipated. They could act out new life styles based on nuclear family activities successfully in the changed environment. They could "be left alone" to themselves.

Life styles emphasizing the nuclear family thus appear happily congruent with suburban spatial patterns. What then appears incongruent with it? Few new residents were unhappy in Levittown. But one of the most pronounced groups of these consisted of women leaving their mothers and sisters in Philadelphia who did *not* realize that the new setting would place limits on their extended family participation. They did not desire that the apron-strings be cut, and they were unable to cope with a situation in which they did not have easy contact with their kin. Telephones allow instant contact, but the intensity of contact to which these ladies were accustomed was too time consuming and hence expensive to maintain via telephone.

Berger studied a group of automobile workers whose plant and hence homes were transferred from an urban location in California to a typically suburban locale.[44] Berger argues that some typical forms of reaction to suburbia which popular magazines had established as universal did not occur among his blue collar workers: They didn't attend church more; they didn't join great numbers of voluntary organizations; they didn't vote more conservatively; they didn't take on aspirations of upward mobility; and they didn't decorate their homes more stylishly.

But one datum which Berger reports is quite relevant to our present relationship. He mentions that two families broke up—on the wife's initiative in each case. The wives had held jobs in their previous urban location. When faced with the lower densities and great distance to potential jobs in the new setting, they could not adopt the role of the housewife, rooted in her own home, receiving human companionship from immediate neighbors through *kaffee klatching*, as did many women. They could not subordinate the occupational aspects of their roles to those centering on the household. Since

---

44   Bennett Berger, *Working Class Suburb: A Study of Auto Workers in Suburbia*, Berkeley, California: University of California Press, 1960.

there was then *incongruence* between the continuing life style and their environment, these two women changed the latter so as to restore congruence.[45] Gans discovered this phenomenon in Levittown as well.[46]

Fava has stressed this aspect of neighboring as part of a suburban "way of life."[47] She studied the association of women with the people living near them among matched samples in a central city in an outer city area, and in a typical suburban area, finding the amount of neighboring much higher in the last area. Doubtless this is because other roles could not be fulfilled in the suburban area so easily, while this one, highly desirable to many people, could be. Local participation, then, may represent a functional reaction to conditions of isolation from large scale enterprises.

A Detroit Area Study produced similar data. Tomeh demonstrated that social participation increases, *all else equal*, with distance from the center of the city.[48]

Much the same problem presented itself in Lagos. Objection to the renewal there was based on more than "just" what it would do to the interaction of extended families. Women objected for reasons having to do with the nature of their role as women. A good woman was not a hausfrau who sat at home and kept things in order; *that* could have been accommodated in the suburban setting. Rather, she was a trader, one who sold goods to government employees who commuted into the city daily. She had to be near her customers, who would seek her out for goods. The women living in compounds in Lagos could not conceive of changing their role emphases and hence their life styles, yet a life style congruent with one setting was quite incongruent with another.

Having observed congruence and incongruence between aspects of the life styles of women and their environment, let's turn for a

---

45   This is, of course, Berger's fact as reported through the lenses developed in the first two chapters of this volume. See footnote 31 on page 70 of the second edition, 1968.

46   Personal communication.

47   Sylvia Fleis Fava, "Suburbanism as a Way of Life," *American Sociological Review*, Vol. 21 (1956): pp. 34-37, and "Contrasts in Neighboring: New York City and a Suburban County," in W. M. Dobriner (ed.), *The Suburban Community*, New York: G. P. Putnam's Sons, 1958, pp. 122-131.

48   Aida K. Tomeh, "Informal Group Participation and Residential Patterns," *American Journal of Sociology*, Vol. 70 (1964): pp. 28-35.

second to men's roles. Wallace treats the conception of the male as a pioneer—a leader and doer of great deeds before the eyes of his children, as well as one who reinforced his own ideas of what a man should be.[49] This conception may be mythical—it's possible that few men ever did it. But it is nonetheless widespread. Many men think it is worth doing.

Wallace points to several limits to the accomplishment of this role imposed by physical environment. When a man lives in a multiple dwelling, particularly when he is surrounded on all sides by other tenants, he can't perform any activity which is violent inside his own dwelling unit without provoking his neighbors—not unless there is adequate soundproofing, an expensive proposition. He can by no means alter the interior of his dwelling to any major extent without typically invoking the wrath of his landlord and probably a lawsuit.

But where else can he perform this role? Private outdoor space provides a suitable outlet. The man who has just completed an active job and stands talking with his neighbor, foot on split-rail fence, is out of the American dream. Yet most multiple dwellings, particularly high rise apartments, have no provision for private open space for such purposes. In some cases, large amounts of *shared* open space are provided with the expectation that they allow amply for all man's spatial needs, even better than tiny private parcels.[50] But they don't provide for these aspects of life style. In other cases, hobby rooms are provided in apartment complexes in their basements. While setting aside space in this manner may eventually change what is now a matter of incongruence, this is still rare in luxury housing, not to speak of public housing, although it exists in both.

What Wallace argues, then, is that in some modern combinations of housing and arrangements of outdoor space, fathers are forced into a role of star boarder.[51] Their traditional role is incongruent with their residential surroundings, yet they are still

---

49   Anthony F. C. Wallace, "Housing and Social Structure: A Preliminary Survey with Particular Reference to Multi-Storey, Low Rent Public Housing Projects," Philadelphia: Philadelphia Housing Authority, 1952 (mimeo).

50   See William H. Whyte, Jr., "The Cluster Concept, Cluster Development," in H. Wentworth Eldredge (ed.), *Taming Megalopolis*, Garden City, N.Y.: Doubleday Anchor Books, 1967, Vol. 1, pp. 462-477.

51   Wallace, *op. cit.*, p. 41.

treated as top banana. About all they can do[52] within their dwelling area is sit in a chair, watch television, and drink beer.

Kumove, in a pilot study patterned after Wallace's, noticed in informal visits to a number of multiple dwellings of different sizes that in high rise apartments men were not to be seen.[53] They undoubtedly lived there, but they were not in evidence to the visitor to the building. In town-house arrangements, on the other hand, where dwelling units had contact with the ground, even though that ground wasn't necessarily staked off under private ownership, men could be seen *doing* things. They were usually playing ball with other men or with their children. But they were there!

David Riesman is a critic of just these aspects of life style in suburbia.[54] That people find in suburbia a vehicle for the devotion of large parts of their efforts, whether through gardening or the Little League, is detrimental to society, according to Riesman. It connotes a general aura of low keyed pleasure and aimlessness. Nothing great is being achieved when family men, in splendid isolation, devote their time to their family roles. By opting for this life style, they reject participation in public affairs in the central city. Those still residing in the city are less likely to have the educational and social skills to provide sound leadership where it's most needed. In effect, they have put emphasis on one role over another, with what Riesman believes are deleterious results for the inner city.

Men in this situation are also slackening their support for the high culture that traditionally has flourished almost exclusively in city centers. While living away from large scale land uses and in low densities *enables* some roles to be played in families, such as those reported by Wallace, it also provides the kind of isolation that encourages a man to focus on his family. As he does this, he loses the will to overcome the frictions of space to participate in the specialized cultural activities of the city center, which will then wither for lack of support. Riesman claims that the numbers of

---

52 Wallace apparently did not consider creative activities among his samples of public housing tenants.

53 Leon Kumove, "A Preliminary Study of the Social Implications of High Density Living Conditions," Toronto: Social Planning Council of Metropolitan Toronto, 1966 (mimeo).

54 David Riesman, "The Suburban Sadness," in William M. Dobriner (ed.), *The Suburban Community*, New York: G. P. Putnam's Sons, 1958, pp. 375-408.

Man and his urban environment

people in suburbs, within easy reach of each other, are barely enough to support classical music, let alone groups specializing in Wagner or Verdi, as exist quite independently in the center city. Again, emphasis on one role and its physical component has taken precedence over another.

While Riesman poses our proposition well, the pejorative tone of his remarks has not gone unchallenged. Vernon, for example, claims that the life style choices made in suburbanization are gladly endured by most people.[55] Certainly there is a congruence between life style and the spatial arrangements found in many suburban areas. But in arriving at this happy congruence, most of the people are not enduring the cultural sacrifice suggested by Riesman. They never liked either Wagner or Verdi. Those who do, according to Vernon, form two distinct groups: wealthy patrons of the arts and upper-middle-class intellectuals with elite tastes but not elite pocketbooks. The former are not bothered by the trends of suburbanization and subsequent removal of middle class residents from the central city because they are affluent enough to live in large apartments in the luxury high rise accommodations that cling to the centers of cities, close to cultural facilities. It is only the latter groups, people with elite tastes but not purses, who suffer from the current trends. They cannot any longer afford to live near the center. They feel that it is unwise to remain living in areas of the city which are decaying, but they find that their life style is incongruent with that which is the path of least resistance in the suburbs.

Indeed, in Gans' study of Levittown, a second group of dissident women consisted of well-educated Jewish women with specialized tastes. They were unable to find bases for friendship among the limited number of women near them, and the nonresidential activities at hand were not of the scale to permit specialization. They were either unwilling or unable to adopt the life style of the others in Levittown.[56]

Some indirect evidence on the relation of life style to physical environment[57] stems from a series of interviews conducted by Survey Research Center of the University of Michigan with a sample

---

55   Raymond Vernon, *The Myth and Reality of Our Urban Problems*, Cambridge, Mass.: Joint Center for Urban Studies of M.I.T. and Harvard, 1962.

56   Gans, *The Levittowners*.

57   William Michelson, "Potential Candidates for the Designers' Paradise," *Social Forces*, Vol. 46 (1967): pp. 190-196.

representation of families in all the metropolitan areas of the United States except New York, which was considered atypical.[58] Some idea of style of life could be gleaned from questions asking whether respondents enjoyed each of the following spare time activities:

a) going for a drive in the car
b) gardening or working in the yard
c) cooking out in the yard at home
d) going on picnics away from home
e) fishing
f) hunting
g) golf
h) going to plays and concerts
i) workshop activities
j) watching television.

Respondents who had moved from a multiple dwelling to a single family home but who in retrospect thought it a *bad* idea were much less likely than people who had done the same without regret to enjoy gardening and cooking out at home. Turning this around a bit, it would appear that the life style which incorporates these *family and home-centered activities* is congruent with the access to private open spaces provided by single family homes—one component of the basic spatial conditions involved in suburbanism. This finding is tempered, however, by the small number of cases reporting dissatisfaction (Table 2).

Another factor on which this analysis sheds light is the cultural taste of suburban people living removed from large scale or specialized land uses. When interviewed, Americans who lived in uncrowded areas but who nonetheless preferred living closer to the center of their city were significantly more likely to enjoy plays and concerts than were the other people interviewed. Among the former, 48% claimed to enjoy these pastimes, compared to only 31% of the latter, a difference not likely to have occurred by chance.[59] This, of course, supports Riesman's argument.

---

58   Details about this study and its principal findings are available in John A. Lansing, *Residential Location and Urban Mobility: The Second Wave of Interviews*, prepared for U.S. Department of Commerce, Bureau of Public Roads, Ann Arbor: University of Michigan, Institute for Social Research, 1966.

59   Michelson, *op. cit.*, p. 194, Table 5.

Table 2 Satisfaction with Move from Multiple Dwelling to Single Family Home by Whether Enjoy Selected Pastimes (in %) *

	Satisfaction Poor N = 9	Satisfaction Good N = 156
Mention enjoy gardening or yard activities	33.3	59.6
Mention enjoy cooking out in yard at home	44.4	59

* Adapted from William Michelson, "Potential Candidates for the Designers' Paradise: A Social Analysis from a Nationwide Sample," *Social Forces,* December, 1967, p. 194.

Indeed, Zelan discovered from a secondary analysis of national data that graduate students stating a preference for the suburbs as a place to live were significantly lower on a "culture index" than were those with other preferences.[60]

Similarly, respondents in a socially homogeneous sample in Toronto who lived close to public facilities and conveniences were significantly more active in their social participation than were respondents living distant from them. This was true, moreover, even with respect to activities not found in the centers near these people's homes; their life styles were simply of a different nature. In a like vein, those respondents lacking private open space were much more likely to express frustration over an environmentally induced restraint over their activities.[61]

These various pieces of evidence tie in with some of the major treatments of suburbanization in orthodox sociology. Martin,[62] for example, suggests two definitive physical characteristics of the

---

60 Joseph Zelan, "Does Suburbia Make a Difference: An Exercise in Secondary Analysis," in Sylvia Fleis Fava (ed.), *Urbanism in World Perspective*, New York: Thomas Y. Crowell Company, 1968, pp. 401-408.

61 William Michelson, "Analytic Sampling for Design Information: A Survey of Housing Experience," presented to the first annual meeting of the Environmental Design Research Association, Chapel Hill, North Carolina, June 8-11, 1969.

62 Walter T. Martin, "The Structuring of Social Relationships Engendered by Suburban Residence," *American Sociological Review*, Vol. 21 (1956): pp. 446-453.

suburban location which affect social characteristics of the people living there: distance from the city center and commuting. Bell, in a separate but complementary statement,[63] posits that people living in such a setting have chosen a life style emphasizing *familism* over such alternatives as *careerism* and *consumership;* the latter flourish much more successfully in urban cliffs.

What the current evidence would indicate is that these ideas are generally correct but must be made more specific than what Martin suggests. Current urban trends involve great amounts of decentralization of job locations;[64] Gans, for example, points to no significant increase in the commuting time of his Levittowners as a result of their move.[65] What does appear physically definitive of suburbs so as to convey some social meaning is the low access of people to many other people and the removal of the area from well defined centers.

Supporting data stemmed from a study of my own which I shall describe more fully in the following section. In this study, people decided, among other things, whether or not certain land uses should be present in their ideal neighborhood. There turned out to be a strong relation between current residence in one of Boston's suburban areas (as opposed to the City of Boston and inner ring cities) and a preference for completely residential neighborhoods. This was, moreover, the only aspect of ideal environment for which suburbanites had common preferences. Therefore, the relevance of the physical component of suburban residence that stresses removal from large scale centers appears strongly underlined.[66]

But the evidence of this section would also clarify what Bell means by "familism." What is stressed under these circumstances is not just the family, but the nuclear family. People in some high density areas also stress their families, but their style of life is far different, as is the way in which their environment serves to support it.

---

63 Bell, *op. cit.*. See also his "Social Choice, Life Styles, and Suburban Residence," in Wm. M. Dobriner (ed.), *The Suburban Community*, New York: G. P. Putnam's Sons, 1958, pp. 225-247.

64 See, for example, Raymond Vernon, "The Economics and Finances of the Large Metropolis," in *Daedalus* (Winter 1961): pp. 31-47.

65 Gans, *The Levittowners*, p. 222.

66 William Michelson, *Value Orientations and Urban Form*, unpublished doctoral dissertation in Sociology, Harvard University, 1965, p. 215.

Thus it would appear that low densities and segregation of land uses support a life style involving an emphasis on the activities of the nuclear family, including the visiting of nonrelated neighbors and pioneer types of activities on the part of fathers. Again, stress has been put primarily on the environment external to the housing type, although the latter is certainly a factor in density as well. But neighborhood considerations are just as vital as with those who emphasize extended family relations.

LOCALS VERSUS COSMOPOLITANS

A final distinction in life style worthy of mention in this context is the local-cosmopolitan distinction. Some people are citizens of their local area, with limited horizons. Rich or poor, their interests lie within a limited range of territory. Their standards are local standards, and they evaluate others on a basis of idiosyncratic knowledge. Other people are very different. They are not bound to one place. They tune in to national or local media. They evaluate people and situations according to universal, objective criteria. The former people are locals; the latter, cosmopolitans.[67]

This distinction can be applied to environmental phenomena.[68] It is particularly relevant in light of recent attacks by several writers on physical plans like the "neighborhood unit plan,"[69] that assume that local neighborhoods can be created which through their design alone can re-create the relations among neighbors glorified in rural America.[70] Webber, for example, has pointed to a trend of

---

67 Some classic statements of this distinction are: Robert K. Merton, "Patterns of Influence," in Paul F. Lazarsfeld and F. N. Stanton (eds.), *Communications Research, 1948-49*, New York: Harper Brothers, 1949, pp. 180-219, and G. M. Sykes, "The Differential Distribution of Community Kinship," *Social Forces*, Vol. 29 (1951): pp. 376-382.

68 See, for example, Desmond M. Connor, "Selective Migration and Residence," *International Migration Review*, Vol. 2 (1964): pp. 97-106.

69 Clarence Perry, "The Neighbourhood Unit Format," in William Wheaton *et al.* (eds.), *Urban Housing*, New York: The Free Press of Glencoe, 1966, pp. 94-109.

70 See, for example, Reginald Isaacs, "The Neighbourhood Theory, An Analysis of its Adequacy," *Journal of the American Institute of Planners*, Vol. 14 (1945): pp. 15-23, and Richard Dewey, "The Neighbourhood, Urban Ecology and City Planners," in Paul K. Hatt and Albert J. Reiss, Jr., *Cities and Society*, New York: The Free Press, rev. ed., 1957, pp. 783-790.

a

b

Fig. 3 Photographs used as stimuli for projective questions on housing type. [(a) Courtesy of Levitt and Sons; (b) and (c) taken by the author; (d) courtesy of Real Estate Forum.]

c

d

"community without propinquity."[71] People, he claims, no longer live within shouting distance of their closest friends. They can live half a city apart, but with modern means of communication and transportation, they can get in touch with them easily whenever desired.

There is no question of the validity of Webber's argument. Yet it must be put into context. There are people, and then there are other people. Many claim the whole city as their empire, if not more. Still others are yet bound to local areas. The former may well bear the mantle of cosmopolitan (at least relative to the others), and they are the ones of whom Webber and others speak. Furthermore, this aspect of life style may be independent of considerations of family type and emphasis.

Evidence on this with respect to physical environment stems from the study to which I briefly alluded in the previous section. To obtain data on the systematic association of people's preferences in urban environment to their social characteristics in a manner affected as little as possible by extraneous factors, I conducted lengthy interviews with a sample of 75 respondents whose general level dominant value orientations had been previously determined by means of the Kluckhohn Value-Orientation Schedule, but who otherwise differed greatly from each other. Their distribution among diverse categories of education, occupation, age, and the like were independent of the value orientation categories, which had been used so as to have some a priori control over a factor of some interest. All the respondents were either Italian- or Irish-Americans, so as to assess ethnic differences as well; this type of difference was also independent of individuals' value orientations.

The people interviewed were given photographs of buildings and neighborhoods unambiguously representing variations in environment as stimuli for open-ended and undirected responses, much as in psychological projective testing. These photographs, reproduced in Fig. 3, were also compared and ranked with respect to one another, with valuative rationales demanded after every choice. A content analysis was made of transcripts of tape recordings of these free-flowing answers, which provided data on the value orientations expressed with respect to each variation of environment for each person; these value orientations were of a lower level of generality

71 Melvin Webber, "Community Without Propinquity," in Lowden Wingo (ed.), *Cities and Space*, Baltimore: The Johns Hopkins Press, 1963, pp. 23-54.

than those gathered by the Kluckhohn schedule, applying primarily to the realm of urban habitation.

Each respondent also planned his ideal urban environment piece by piece, mapping his choices simultaneously, again explaining his reasons for each step. When dealing with standard conceptions of form, starting with the dwelling unit and progressing outward through lot sizes and the placement of different kinds of land use, people were easily able to diagram the communities they preferred. While out of scale, the physical plans they drew located all land uses in relation to each other with distances labeled. Two prototype plans are reproduced in Fig. 4.

Finally, each person provided data on his interpersonal activities and on the nature and his own use of his present and past neighborhoods.

One part of the data relevant to the foregoing stemmed from how far apart people ideally desired their own residence from those of neighbors. The social characteristic which was most congruent with this element of environment in a statistical sense was the distance that people currently lived from their friends. The greater this distance, implying a more cosmopolitan friendship pattern, the larger the separation people wanted from immediate neighbors. On the other hand, the more that friends were local, the less desire they had for space to separate them from other people. Large lots under those circumstances were a hindrance rather than a help to a local friendship pattern.

This distinction was also relevant to segregation of land uses. The more that people were cosmopolitan in their current shopping habits, the more likely they were to propose all residential neighborhoods as their ideal places of habitation. Those who did not just utilize the various kinds of stores and facilities that were nearest to their homes, but who went beyond these to patronize establishments that met their particular desires, were significantly more inclined than those with local habits to place all commercial facilities *outside* their ideal neighborhoods.

SUMMARY

There is thus support from the literature with respect to several types of congruence between life styles and physical environment.

a

Fig. 4 Sample sketch maps detailing aspects of ideal environment.

Conclusions from such far-flung and diverse sources are risky. The following, however, are suggested in the present chapter:

1.   Intense, frequent association with a wide range of relatives thrives in areas in which many people have easy physical access to each other, while the same people find this style of life diminishes involuntarily in areas of low "density."

2.   An emphasis on the nuclear family and its joint activities is most congruent with the access of people to each other and to various activities which are now provided by the typical housing, open space, and land use patterns of the suburbs.

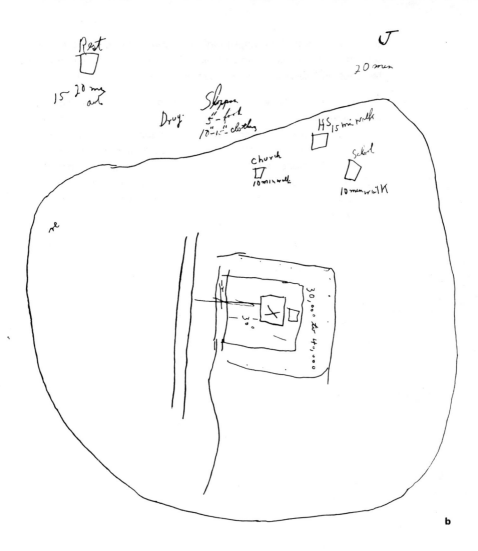

Rest

15-20 min. art.

Drug.

Shopping
5" - food
10"-15" clothes

church
10 min walk

J

20 min

HS 15 min walk

School
10 min walk

re

30,000 to 40,000

b

3. Active, traditionally "masculine" pastimes are part of home life only when the environment is structured so as to minimize the impingement of neighbors on each other.

4. Specialized interests which require co-enthusiasts are difficult to satisfy in low density areas. Adaptive behavior, often expressed in terms of *kaffee klatching* or organizational participation, is essential for those whose lives have previously included other people and activity but who are suddenly relatively isolated.

5.   People with "cosmopolitan" life styles desire more physical separation from neighbors and place less emphasis on proximity to facilities and services than do people whose interests are "local."

All these tentative conclusions would point in the direction of the "obvious" point (indeed the very heart of the discussion in Chapter 2) that relevant environment of people and their life styles consists of much more than just their four walls; it includes such vital considerations as the type, size, and arrangement of open space and the land use mixture of the community generally. These factors are not matters of indifference to people with particular life styles.

stage in the life cycle
and urban environment

4

Social scientists find age a useful variable. As a person ages, he progresses through meaningful stages of physical development, schooling, and productive capacities. Similarly, social scientists benefit from knowledge of a person's position in or out of a family. But far more meaningful than either of these two notions alone has been a third concept—stage in the life cycle—which binds together the insights of the previous two. It is much more meaningful, for example, to realize that a man is 25 and has a wife and two children, than to know either that he is 25 or that he has a wife and two children.[1]

People pass through many stages in the life cycle, although obviously not all people follow the same path. A person passes typically through infancy and childhood as a member of a family, and he usually spends his teenage years (a relatively new stage) there as well. Then follows young single adulthood, sometimes alone or with roommates and sometimes still with the family. Our prototype

---

1   For evidence on this, see John Lansing and Leslie D. Kish, "Family Life Cycle as an Independent Variable," *American Sociological Review*, Vol. 22 (1957): pp. 512-519.

then gets married and most likely sets up housekeeping independent of any other family unit. Some time later, young children are part of this menage. At first they are immobile; then they turn most mobile. Later they start school. Soon they are teenagers and young adults themselves. Then they leave the family nests. At that point their parents are left to themselves again. In many cases, one spouse will predecease the other, leaving a single person once again, but one who nonetheless is bound by the limitations of his age.

Clearly there are many stages in the life cycle. One does not remain in any single one for a very great percentage of a normal lifetime. Indeed at a time when the average American wife gives birth to her last child at age 25,[2] no less than 30 years of a normal life span is spent outside the nuclear family situation (being raised as a child and raising one's own children).

In this chapter, I shall examine several stages in the life cycle which researchers have shown as relevant to the physical environment.

RAISING CHILDREN

There seems to be little argument about the desirability of raising children in the most self-contained units possible.

Wallace points to the problems of raising a family in high rise units in terms of the amount of control that parents potentially have over their children once the latter leave the apartment unit.[3] When a child leaves his home to play many stories below, his actions cannot be followed from the apartment (see Fig. 1). He could go to China just as easily as to the corner store, as far as his parents are concerned. One informant described the situation in a high rise apartment in Chicago as follows.

It's no place to raise a family. A mother can't look out for her kids if they are fifteen floors down in the playground.[4]

---

2   Statistic cited in Murray Gendell and Hans L. Zetterberg (eds.), *A Sociological Almanac for the United States*, New York: Charles Scribner's Sons, 2nd ed., 1964, p. 45.

3   Anthony F. C. Wallace, "Housing & Social Structure: A Preliminary Survey with Particular Reference to Multi-Story, Low Rent Public Housing Projects," Philadelphia Housing Authority, 1952 (mimeo).

4   Edward T. Hall, *The Hidden Dimension,* Garden City, N.Y.: Doubleday and Company, 1966, p. 159.

Fig. 1 What children look like from the upper reaches of a high rise apartment. (Photo by Richard Brause.)

The greater number of corridors, elevators, and stairways of high rise buildings provide additional unsupervised areas where trouble might arise. Loss of control is by no means inevitable when children are let out of apartments in high rise buildings. Among many middle class apartment dwellers, mothers regularly accompany their children out to play. In more affluent cases, this becomes the duty of the nanny. However, more typical are the cases where the nanny does not exist and where the mother has younger children at home whom she either can't or won't move around in the interests of supervising the older children. In many other cases, the mother works and is absent entirely, leaving no one who could supervise any more than she could have from her apartment window.

This differs, says Wallace, from the low-rise situation where children's play areas can be seen from kitchen windows.[5] When necessary, mothers can call their children and children can be heard, and the mothers are at most a few flights of steps from the ground.

5   Wallace, *op. cit.*

In addition, there are fewer nooks and crannies in buildings in which children may lose themselves.

Kumove, after a series of unstructured interviews with mothers in a variety of buildings, formed the impression that children up to about age seven living in high rise buildings cling much more closely to their parents than their counterparts in single family homes, who are independent at a much earlier age. But once past that point, the patterns reverse themselves. Once children reach a fully mobile stage, when parents can't greatly restrict their movements lest they prohibit normally expected behavior patterns, the children in high rise buildings spend much more of their time outside their family's housing unit than do children living in single family houses.[6]

A study of matched groups of junior high school students living in apartments and in detached homes in the Toronto area brought out the same phenomenon. The apartment dwellers were more likely to meet their friends, even casually on school nights, outside the confines of their homes than were the others. Such meetings take additional time in transit (for at least one child), and they again lie outside parental supervision.[7]

This last finding is by no means a blanket indictment of multiple dwellings as a home for families. There is nothing in the nature of the high rise apartments per se that restricts the number of rooms available to families. Wealthy Manhattanites, for example, have been known to maintain upwards of 20 rooms in high rise buildings. Furthermore, nothing prevents the provision of meeting or game rooms where teenagers can pursue their activities within sight of their own apartment doors. But apartment living has *not* generally provided such amenities. The baseline pattern is of small, costly dwelling units, for eating, sleeping and generally quiet activities, with little if any other use of inside space to detract from the rent producing capacities of a building. Where additional facilities are provided, such as swimming pools, they are as often a fad as the result of an assumed demand of the tenants. For example, in some cities, landlords can't rent apartments unless they provide a swimming pool, although few tenants ever subsequently use the pool.

---

6   Leon Kumove, "A Preliminary Study of the Social Implications of High Density Living Conditions," Toronto: Social Planning Council of Metropolitan Toronto, 1966 (mimeo).

7   Term paper by Mr. R. E. Matheson, Willowdale, Ontario.

Willis, however, suggests a reason why children might best be raised in detached homes.[8] Many people believe, she says, that it is harmful to continually frustrate children in what they want to do. What do children want to do? They like to make noise—vocally or through strenuous activities. Where a family shares walls with less than perfect soundproofing with other families, though, this noise must continually be nipped in the bud lest one antagonize the neighbors or invite retaliation. But in being a good neighbor, often a prerequisite for continued residence in a given building, a parent runs the risk of stunting the mental health of his child.

This argument by Willis is directed at all multiple dwellings regardless of how large each family's apartment might be, because walls are shared and soundproofing is expensive. Nonetheless, it is obvious that it is a more serious question the more frequently walls and ceilings are shared and the more sound conductive these walls are. Here we approach the need for our most basic concepts of physical environment, as findings based merely on the conventional terms, multiple dwelling or high rise apartment, are too unspecific.

This is indeed salient in light of a recent report on housing:

While it is true that people who live in flats suffer more from noise disturbance than people who live in houses, this is not the main complaint. More important is the **restriction people feel on making noise themselves**. This affects their whole pattern of leisure and makes for more sedentary hobbies such as television viewing.[9]

The original desire to move to suburban locations which, among other things, feature single family housing, is almost always put in terms of their being good places to raise children. In a study of Levittown, New York, for example, this was by far the greatest reason for moving to Levittown given by its new residents, 66% of whom had come from New York City and 65% of whom had previously lived in apartments (although not necessarily the same people).[10] Whyte stresses the same factor, together with easy

---

8   Margaret Willis, "Living in High Flats," London: London County Council, Architects Department, 1955 (mimeo).

9   John Raven, "Sociological Evidence on Housing; (2: The Home Environment)," *The Architectural Review*, Vol. 142 (1967): p. 236.

10   Harold Wattel, "Levittown: A Suburban Community," in William M. Dobriner (ed.) *The Suburban Community*, New York: G.P. Putnam's Sons, 1958, p. 290.

financing, as the chief motivation for moving to Chicago's Park Forest,[11] as does Gans in Levittown, New Jersey.[12]

In the Toronto study to which I alluded in the preceding chapter, respondents were shown pictures of several different housing types: single family homes, town houses, walkup apartments, and what we called a "futuristic" complex (something quite unfamiliar to the respondents). Each respondent was asked to select the best and worst housing types shown with respect to specific criteria: (a) privacy, (b) raising children, (c) most easily do the things you want to, (d) outside design, (e) contact with neighbors. Although, as is the norm in North America, the single family home was most frequently chosen as best, regardless of the criterion in question, the percentage of people choosing it varied greatly according to criterion. With respect to the first three criteria, about 90% chose the single home; with respect to the last two, only 50% and 40%, respectively.

With respect to all such reports, we must ask what aspect of the environment is really operating in the relationships. After all, in Chapter 3, I stressed the importance of typical suburban densities and land use mixtures to certain styles of life. The evidence of this chapter, however, suggests that the specific process of child raising is much more salient to two much more microscopic aspects of environment: (1) ease of access to outdoor space, and (2) the amount of separation from adjacent neighbors.

The first aspect would suggest that the interests of child raising are best served when children can step directly outside into an easily observed area, to which the parent is handy inside. In some large new buildings, outdoor walkways (Fig. 2) make possible an outside door for every tenant.[13] When they are high above the ground and by definition narrow, however, this concentrates children's activities and noise near other people's units, which is not always appreciated.

---

11   William H. Whyte, Jr., *The Organization Man*, Garden City, N.Y.: Doubleday Anchor Books, 1956.

12   Personal communication. See also Herbert J. Gans, *The Levittowners,* New York: Pantheon Books, 1967.

*   William Michelson, "Analytic Sampling for Design Information: A Survey of Housing Experience," a paper to be published in the proceedings of the first annual meeting of the Environmental Design Research Association, Chapel Hill, North Carolina, June 8-11, 1969.

13   Architect Irving Grossman of Toronto feels that a door leading directly outside also gives each family more of a feeling of possession of their unit and pride in it, which helps later maintenance.

Fig. 2 Balconies are frequently used as access to units in "family" high rise apartments, with mixed results. (Photo by City Architect, Sheffield, England.)

The second aspect above would suggest the ultimate desirability of single family housing in today's technology. Where this is beyond question, it would suggest altering the design of multiple dwellings. There are some activities among children that are incongruent with allocations of space as buildings are now designed. The challenge is how to provide for desired, active human functions (however "childish") within multiple dwellings in such a way that: (1) neighbors do not bother each other, and (2) these functions remain within the jurisdiction of the family.

For example, in the nationwide survey cited in Chapter 3, the desire for a detached home, while strong in all subsectors of the population, was significantly stronger among respondents who were married and had children. Whereas 51% of the persons interviewed were married and had children, only 26% of the people who were desirous of exchanging detached homes for apartments were in this stage of the life cycle. In addition, it was the married couples *without children* who were significantly over-represented among people who desired private lots smaller than their present ones; there was certainly no such over-representation among couples with children.[14]

---

14 Michelson, "Potential Candidates for the Designers' Paradise," *Social Forces,* Vol. 46 (1967): pp. 190-196.

Thus different physical aspects of the typical suburban pattern serve different social purposes. Macroscopic density and separation of land uses are related to a life style emphasizing the nuclear family. Separation from adjacent neighbors and access to the outside are related to child raising. They are separate factors, but there is no reason that they should not go hand in hand. For example, in Rossi's study of "Why People Move," people's complaints about dwelling unit space *and* the physical environment around the home were found to have extremely strong predictive power on future residential mobility.[15]

This combination of a style of life which people increasingly desire, together with considerations of child raising, has undoubtedly accounted for the overwhelming attraction of suburbs to hordes of people. And this has been aided by government financing policies which did not apply to homes in the center city. Critics may bemoan the aesthetics of suburbia, but aesthetics are largely irrelevant to the reason for its popularity.

This does not mean, however, that today's suburbs need to be the yardstick for tomorrow's general habitat, if the social factors underlying them persist. Just as with multiple dwellings, there is no reason why the various social needs cannot be incorporated into the newly designed buildings, neighborhoods, and cities of the future, based on technologies not known or used today.

One reservation should be entered, however, before leaving this stage in the life cycle. The importance of housing type and immediate grounds would appear to refer unequivocally to young and middle sized children predominantly. While the detached home *does* provide at present a location for some teenage activities (indeed some builders are now constructing teenage rumpus rooms *in addition to* family rooms), when the teenager decides to pursue peer group activities outside his home, he finds the segregation of land uses a major obstacle. There is "nowhere to go" without an automobile and a good bit of travel. There is nothing exciting in a neighborhood designed for toddlers. The very same environment which is congruent for a style of life emphasizing the nuclear family becomes incongruent when, by virtue of a change in stage in the life cycle, a teenager *may* desire a life style different from that of his parents—at least temporarily. It is no wonder that cars and

---

15   Peter Rossi, *Why People Move*, New York: Free Press of Glencoe, 1955, Ch. 5.

motorcycles play such a part in the lives and problems of teenage suburbanites.[16]

The case of the teenager raises an intriguing issue. Not only do people at different life stages have different environmental needs, but these people may temporarily be part of the same family. Thus teenagers who typically live at home are often at odds with their families on how "good" a neighborhood they inhabit. But then when they enter young adulthood, these same people, with any degree of affluence, are more likely to split off from their parents and set up an independent household in a more hospitable location for a new stage in the life cycle to which they have been aspiring. This also very possibly changes the life cycle stage of their parents as well. Thus many of the centrally located high rise apartments now being built go not to alleviating housing shortages but to accommodate people who without independent means would still be living with parents.[17]

CHILDLESS ADULTS

Young childless adults, married and unmarried, share spatial needs to some extent with older, but not elderly, adults whose children have grown up and left home. Neither group need consider young

---

16 Herbert Gans, *op. cit.* In my own limited and biased contacts, I have yet to meet a teenager on Long Island driving *without* a revoked driver's license.

17 It is also intriguing to speculate on sex differences in accommodation to the environment, although, as anthropologists would tell us, male-female social differences are culture-bound. In any case, recent studies by some of my students show clearcut differences. For example, in a series of downtown Toronto high rise apartments, men typically live alone while women share with other female roommates. This might easily be chalked up to differences in their earnings but for other findings. In an unpublished study of student preferences in university housing, again in Toronto, the data showed that women prefer to share bedrooms with a roommate though they would rather have study facilities to themselves; among men, the pattern is reversed. In prison studies, researchers traditionally bring out the importance of having membership in a quasi-family grouping for women.

A recent market research study called Project Home conducted by Raymond Loewy/William Smith Inc. in New York brought out that men typically determine a couple's first home, while their wives maneuver them from place to place thereafter. At each step, each is attracted by different rooms in a new home: men by the foyer and livingroom, women by the bedroom and baths.

Fig. 3 The downtown section is a magnet, holding childless adults of various ages in close-in, high rise apartments. (Photo by the Toronto Star.)

children entering into their lives. Yet they are mobile adults, able to take advantage of what cities offer in the way of amenities.

The central part of cities has always been a stamping ground for young adults. Charles Abrams spoke of a waning but traditional function of downtowns as a location for the "quest for tryst" for young people.[18] It has been full of interesting locations where young adults could get together without elaborate pretenses or preparations (Fig. 3).

Others have argued in addition that apartment living in central locations should naturally be the optimal environment for adults whose children have left the family home. They no longer need the inside space provided by their suburban home; indeed they but rattle around inside. And maintenance of the house and grounds becomes an increasingly onerous chore. On the positive side, living in a downtown cliff provides, they say, much easier access to the restaurants and cultural activities that they now have the time and money to frequent, much like the younger adults.

Abu-Lughod studied the residents of newly constructed high rise apartments and rehabilitated town houses near the centers of

18 Charles Abrams, *The City Is the Frontier,* New York: Harper and Row, 1965, p. 339.

Man and his urban environment

several Eastern U.S. cities to see what kind of people were living there.[19] As expected, older couples were the group most overrepresented in these buildings, particularly the high rise. They didn't by any means *solely* occupy these buildings, but many more of them were there than one would have expected from their proportion in the population.

However, Abu-Lughod went on to ask them about their previous residences. What she discovered is that they had by and large always been apartment dwellers. Only 27% of them had lived in single family *or* duplex homes previously. Indeed they had moved for greater centrality, *not to substantially change their housing type.*

My own interviews on ideal environment,[20] discussed initially in Chapter 3, brought out more detail on this point. Older people, just like everyone else, expressed strong preferences for single family housing. But when they would specify where other land uses should be located, it became obvious that many would like to be close to a variety of nonresidential activities. The ideal for these older couples would be to have a small cottage, and the only one, on their local equivalent of Fifth Avenue. Inasmuch as this is patently impossible, some opt for the centralized location, since this *is* a crucial factor in the environment of older people, while others stand pat with the housing type they have come to appreciate.

To the extent that high rise buildings in central areas are built with only one or at most two bedrooms, this distribution of the childless, young and old, in the downtown will become pronounced almost by fiat. But its rationale goes deeper.

THE AGED

Special considerations mark physical environment for the elderly. Basic to this is a social stigma which younger people attach to the aged en masse. They typically recoil from contact with them and react with great impatience to their imperfections.[21] While many

19   Janet Abu-Lughod, "A Survey of Center City Residents," in Nelson Foote, *et al., Housing Choices and Constraints,* New York: McGraw-Hill, 1960, pp. 387-447.

20   Michelson, *Value Orientations and Urban Form*, unpublished doctoral dissertation in sociology, Harvard University, 1965.

21   See, for example, Bernice Neugarten and David Garron, "Attitudes of Middle-Aged Persons Toward Growing Old," *Geriatrics,* Vol. 14 (1959): pp. 21-24, and Jerome Tuckman and Irving Lorge, "Attitudes Towards Old People," *Journal of Social Psychology,* Vol. 57 (1953): pp. 148-153.

specific details of design are a function of the physiological problems of advancing age, other more general questions are raised by the matter of social stigma.

They boil down to whether housing planned for older people should be built in homogeneous concentrations (i.e., segregated) in neighborhoods or whether they should be scattered throughout areas with younger people (i.e., integrated). As described in Chapter 3, the "Mums" of Bethnal Green performed real services for their extended families and served as the symbol of family unity. They were aided in this by a housing pattern which allowed their integration throughout the neighborhood. But when "family housing," aimed at nuclear families, was constructed outside London to improve on Bethnal Green, it typically did not provide smaller accommodations suitable for people living alone or without children scattered throughout each area; this proved a barrier to the kind of life these older women had enjoyed, since proximity to the rest of the family had been essential to it.

In bygone periods when elderly people (if they lived so long) lived primarily with their children in homes that had three (and sometimes four) generations under a roof, a rather complete form of integration was the ideal.

Now residential independence from relatives is the rule. In 1960, 83% of American men aged 65 and over lived in their own households, 13% lived with others, and 4% lived in institutions. Among women, these figures were 70%, 25%, and 5%, strongly showing the same pattern despite the tendency of women to outlive their spouses and possibly seek other living arrangements.[22]

Furthermore, a survey of older people by Cornell University brought out that they *want* to have their own accommodations:

The persons studied were given a choice of three situations for elderly who can take care of themselves. These situations and the proportion of the total group responding to each, were as follows: (a) to live by themselves but **near** relatives, 52%; (b) to live by themselves **away** from their relatives, 31%; (c) to live with their families, 17%.[23]

Given that older people will predominantly have independent households, physical means exist to provide appropriate housing units in either segregated or integrated patterns. With respect to the

22 Glenn Beyer, *Housing and Society*, New York: Macmillan, 1965, p. 417.
23 *Ibid.*, p. 428.

former, there are now "proximate residences,"[24] developments with detached houses specifically for the elderly. There are forms of "congregate living,"[25] where older people live under one roof. There is "protected living,"[26] whereby institutional care is added to the foregoing. Indeed there is now the "geriatric complex,"[27] including all the previous three concepts as well as extensive recreational programs in many cases. To allow adequately for integrated housing, appropriate sized housing with proper facilities must be mixed in with the more orthodox housing in a neighborhood.

What must be asked is on what grounds one alternative might be chosen over the other. For example, the Scandinavians pioneered the idea of the old age *community* within a city.[28] Then observers began to feel a strong touch of pathos in the social life these people had with each other. The great events which transformed dull days into events were each others' *funerals*.

The pendulum then swung the other way. Apartments for the elderly were placed at appropriate locations throughout standard apartment buildings. Older people like to be near young children, and they can usefully serve as baby sitters. There is action to be seen even when the elderly are not involved with it. Yet, on the American scene at least, this pattern sets an old person in the open for the often unconscious, but nonetheless vicious, cuts that develop in contact with middle aged people and young adults.

Choice of one or another type of pattern is aided by the perspective of what old age means. Not only will a person's children have grown up and, normally, set up housekeeping elsewhere, but a second major source of interpersonal contact, the occupational world, is withdrawn. Thus an elderly person must find social contact either through relatives or elsewhere in the environment. The social relations of older people are crucial to understanding their welfare, and it is made even more salient by a rejection by other age groups. Rosow stresses that housing dissatisfaction among the elderly, regardless of its physical components, is exacerbated by loneliness and social isolation.[29]

---

24 *Ibid.*, p. 430.

25 *Idem.*

26 *Idem.*

27 *Idem.*

28 A prime example is De Gamles By, The Old Folks' City, in Copenhagen.

29 Irving Rosow, *Social Integration of the Aged*, New York: The Free Press of Glencoe, 1967, p. 336.

Social scientists now appear to agree, although with no feeling that they have solved all problems, that segregated age groupings provide a more complete social environment for older people despite potentially morbid aspects. It insulates them from external barbs, and it provides a significantly greater pool of age-mates from which to draw friends. Messer, for example, found lower *anomie* among older people in an age-segregated apartment complex in Chicago than in an integrated one.[30]

But while age-segregation and the physical details that support it provide sociability, they are not its exclusive agents. Several qualifications need be made to the necessity for it. First, Rosow points out that age segregation is a crucial force only among "locals."

People who want local contact are seriously disadvantaged if they live in areas of lower concentration of aged, but they have genuine opportunities which they effectively exploit when they live in high (age) density settings.[31]

People with cosmopolitan life styles ferret out their friends even without the aid of a high "density" of elderly nearby. This finding would, of course, support the importance of the local-cosmopolitan life style typology discussed in Chapter 3. Indeed, this particular case illustrates how two social variables that each relate to physical environment complement each other in optimizing the congruence between people and their physical environment.

The importance of the local-cosmopolitan typology in this context is underlined by a Vancouver study which demonstrated great fear of the unknown among older people when confronted with the possibility of living in an old age project at the periphery of the city. They knew their older, more central area, and they preferred run-down accommodations to anything better which would be more removed.[32] A home which is too quiet amid undisturbed grassy expanses could become a living cemetery.

---

30   Mark Messer, "Engagement with Disengagement," paper presented at the 1966 Annual Meeting of the American Sociological Association, Miami Beach, Fla.

31   Rosow, *op. cit.* p. 121. Reprinted by permission of Macmillan Co.

32   Arvey Hanowski, Ellen E. Hayward, Carla Reed, and Edward C. Teather, "Housing for the Aged: An Exploratory Study of Needs and Preferences," unpublished master's thesis, School of Social Work, University of British Columbia, 1962.

For a second qualification with respect to age segregation, Gillespie points out that people who already live in areas which are characterized by strong ties with neighbors do not lose these relationships as they age. This is particularly true among those in extended families. The people who can most benefit by age segregation are those living in less cohesive areas who by virtue of age "lose" their families and on-the-job friends. Some regular neighborhoods can provide these crucial social relations, while age concentration can do the same.[33]

This evaluation of physical environment in terms of its ability to bring sociability into the lives of the elderly came out in a general survey in North Carolina on "what makes a town an ideal place to live," as reported by Lamanna.[34] Older people were significantly more likely to rate aspects of sociability higher than younger people.

Therefore, on two grounds, age segregation, while positive for many people, is not *always* desirable.

What does all this imply in physical terms? It suggests that for at least part of the population of the elderly, housing units of appropriate types—not necessarily old age homes—must be grouped in sufficient number to provide the advantages of age segregation.

This does not mean, however, that they must be placed so as to be isolated from everything else. As I suggested in the previous section, older people have the time to enjoy some of the advantages of the city center, and placement of old age concentrations near hubs of action would facilitate their use—as a source of *activity*, not of *human contact*.

Willis, for example, discovered a favorable response among the elderly around London for location opposite a school. It gave them something to see and hear, and they had an interest in children at the start.[35]

In the Vancouver study, it was clear that older people wanted to live close to stores, as well as to transportation to other centers. Three times more respondents said that they considered stores and

---

33 Michael W. Gillespie, "The Effect of Residential Segregation on the Social Integration of the Aged," paper presented at the 1967 Annual Meeting of the American Sociological Association, San Francisco, California.

34 Richard Lamanna, "Value Consensus Among Urban Residents," *Journal of the American Institute of Planners,* Vol. 36 (1964): pp. 317-326.

35 Margaret Willis, *Environment and the Home,* London: London County Council, Architect's Department (mimeo.), 1954.

buses as important services than said the same for health services, churches, parks, community centers, libraries, and the like.[36]

Thus, apart from housing units for the aged and their measure of integration with other types of units, it is evident that proximity to sources of life and activity is important to older people.

Three categories of stage in the life cycle, then—the child raisers, the old and young childless, and the elderly—have marked implications for physical environment. The tentative conclusions which would stem from this chapter are as follows:

1. Direct access to the outside maximizes control in child raising under conventional parent-child relationships.

2. Self-contained housing units minimize parent fostering of children's inhibitions.

3. Adults, before and after raising children (as well as those who are childless), more frequently rate centrality (i.e., access to consumer goods and services) more highly than do families with growing children.

4. The aged find greatest satisfaction in a concentration of like-aged people, particularly when they have "local" life styles and previously lived in noncohesive neighborhoods.

5. Accessibility to lively activity is also beneficial for older people.

It is clear, therefore, that different aspects of environment are salient to people in different stages of the life cycle.

I shall turn in the next chapter to social class.

---

36   Hanowski *et al., op. cit.,* p. 108.

social class and the urban environment

Everyone knows about social class. Ranking is a game which people seldom cease playing. Their homes, neighborhoods, and automobiles all say something about their class standing. Even their speech conveys class connotations, however good a front is otherwise maintained.

Social scientists attempt to be more precise about class. They measure such intangible elements as power, prestige, respect, and honor primarily by means of occupation, education, and income, although housing and neighborhood conditions also play a part in some measures.[1]

Exact categories differ according to the researcher and the place researched. Some come up with six categories of social class: upper-upper, lower-upper, upper-middle, lower-middle, upper-lower, and lower-lower, each corresponding to some complex of characteristics, background, and behavior selected so as to differentiate

---

[1] See, for example, Lloyd Warner *et al., Social Class in America,* Gloucester, Mass.: Peter Smith, 1957. See also the "Chapin Social Status Scale," reprinted in Pauline Young, *Scientific Social Surveys and Research,* Englewood Cliffs, N.J.: Prentice-Hall, 3rd edition, 1956, pp. 343-345.

groups.[2] Another common scheme has five categories: lower, working, lower-middle, upper-middle, and upper.[3]

My own preference is for the latter set of distinctions, defined largely in terms of occupation, education, and income, although the importance of each element may differ by the particular class involved. When speaking of any single social class, I shall mean approximately the following:

a) *lower class:* low income; often no steady job or one subject to the whims of the employer; little education.

b) *working class:* regular blue-collar employment.

c) *lower middle class:* regular white-collar employment, usually for others; moderate salary at most.

d) *upper middle class:* high amount of education; comfortable salary or fees; sometimes self-employed but skills are transferable regardless.

e) *upper class:* great personal wealth either at present or within the family at some past date; at least moderate education; occupation, if any, is respectable.

There is no doubt that much finer distinctions in social class can be made in addition to these. Some people fit into special categories only. It is open to question what it means when the factors of occupation, education, and income are out of kilter in individual cases.[4] What, in relation to other people, is the place of the gambler, for example, who has great personal wealth, but little in the way of occupational and educational prestige? Indeed, even in the most homogeneous groups, such as are found on the campuses of prestige universities, distinctions are drawn between people on still additional grounds—dating prowess, clothing styles, academic achievement, and the like. And these distinctions are reinforced by a local jargon, which every organization maintains to some extent (e.g., armies, colleges, the civil service).

---

2   See, for example, Lloyd Warner *et. al., Yankee City*, New Haven, Conn.: Yale University Press, 1963, Ch. 2.

3   See, for example, the discussion of these differences in Herbert Gans, *The Urban Villagers*, New York: The Free Press of Glencoe, 1962. Ch. 11.

4   See, for example, Gerhard Lenski, "Status Crystallization. A Non-Vertical Dimension of Social Status," *American Sociological Review*, Vol. 14 (1954): pp. 405-413.

What, then, is the point of working with broad categories of social class, as in the following discussion? They may be meaningful indices for particular types of behavior which articulate with aspects of the physical environment.

Some may argue indeed that life style should have been included under the topic of social class. Do not life styles vary greatly between social classes? They certainly do. But life styles also vary greatly within classes on grounds of ethnicity, religion, and personal preference. Think, for example, of the different life styles found among working class men according to their background. In addition, recent research would indicate that many people now in lower middle class jobs still identify with the working class.[5] Hence, only a reduction of social class distinctions into an unmanageably large number of categories would permit treatment of both these phenomena under a single heading.

In this chapter, therefore, I shall investigate whether the broad distinctions in social class contain differences which are meaningful for the arrangement of the physical environment. While the environment may also serve as a source of *symbols* of social class, symbols are fickle; they change their meanings rapidly. Hence, I shall not treat class in its symbolic context. Second, I shall ask if the mere existence of these class differences articulates in any systematic way with environment.

In this context, social class must be viewed in two respects: where there is support for its relevance and where there isn't. Unlike some of the other variables, points where it lacks proven relevance may be worthy of note.

SOCIAL CLASS: ITS RELEVANCE
TO PHYSICAL ENVIRONMENT

Social class is one of the most utilized variables in sociology, and the attention devoted to it is justifed. It is relevant to numerous concerns. In this section, therefore, I shall be highly selective and single out three ways in which social class, without the explicit elements of life style, has been shown as relevant to certain aspects of the physical environment.

---

5   Richard Hamilton, "The Marginal Middle Class: A Reconsideration," *American Sociological Review*, Vol. 31 (1966): pp. 182-199.

Housing Quality

A series of studies based on aggregate data has pointed out that, with one qualification, the quality of people's dwellings is directly proportional to their social class, as viewed in terms of occupational prestige. Professionals, proprietors, and managers, for example, live in more expensive homes and maintain them better than do clerical workers, for another example, who in turn are ahead of unskilled workers in this respect.[6]

But the qualification is worth noting. There is a great similarity in the incomes of white-collar clerical workers and skilled blue-collar workers. Indeed, depending on how these groups are precisely defined, the latter may at times be more affluent. Yet the clerical workers are better housed than the blue-collar workers.[7] They live closer to the managers and professionals than they do to the blue-collar workers. To accomplish this, they spend a greater proportion of their income on housing. Skilled blue-collar workers, on the other hand, spend a greater proportion of their income on automobiles, television sets, and the like. The quality of their housing is simply less salient to them than it is to the white-collar people, for whom housing may well be a greater symbol of respectability.

This finding becomes more understandable in light of others which show that *education* is the aspect of social class which relates most closely to the quality of housing in which a man lives.[8] While income differences are often minimal between white-collar clerical

---

6   See, for example, O. D. Duncan and Beverly Duncan, "Residential Distribution and Occupational Stratification," in Paul K. Hatt and Albert J. Reiss, Jr. *Cities and Society*, New York: The Free Press, rev. ed. 1957, pp. 183-196, and James O. Wheeler, "Residential Location by Occupational Status," *Urban Studies*, Vol. 5 (1968): pp. 24-32. For a fascinating exception to this pattern under a vastly different system of housing allocation, see J. Musil, "The Development of Prague's Ecological Structure," in A. E. Pahl (ed.), *Readings in Urban Sociology*, London: Pergamon Press, 1968, pp. 232-259.

7   Duncan and Duncan, *op. cit.*

8   Charles Tilly, "Occupational Rank and Grade of Residence in a Metropolis," *American Journal of Sociology*, Vol. 67 (1961). pp. 323-330. Arnold Feldman and Charles Tilly, "The Interaction of Social and Physical Space," *American Sociological Review*, Vol. 25 (1966): pp. 877-884.

workers and skilled blue-collar workers, an educational difference is almost always present, just as this type of difference in turn separates the clerical workers from professionals, for example. Since education is a process that inevitably includes taste, standards of judgment, and the like—even if informally disseminated among students—it is no surprise to find that the quality of housing is a variable affected by degree of exposure to education.

This pattern has serious practical implications. Frequently, public authorities seek to upgrade the quality of housing in their area. Among the residents of condemned homes are blue-collar workers who could afford better housing according to objective scales that fix tolerable home rental or expense levels to a specific ratio of income. This ratio has typically been 25% although it has recently climbed to about 30%. The problem encountered is that these people are not in the habit of spending this much on housing, and they frequently find needed funds committed to other expenditures. Time payments and loans to which people are committed cannot be commuted merely because a public authority feels people should spend money on something else. This can therefore become the source of great misunderstanding and trouble. In a study of a new English development, for example, Morris and Mogey found that families used to low rentals (although in decrepit housing) often fail once faced with standard economic rent.[9]

Yet, no matter how salient social class is to the quality of housing demanded, as mediated by level of education, quality of housing is not really a component of physical form. All kinds of physical environment could *potentially* be kept up to perfect standards. All this says is that some people strive harder than do others to seek high standards of housing. This is important to know, but it does not help in suggesting what types of homes, neighborhoods, and cities need be provided.

Level of Environment Emphasized

Different levels of the environment are emphasized by people on different levels of the social class hierarchy. Among the lower class, it has been claimed, a safe home is an ultimate end. Rainwater argues

---

9   R. N. Morris and John Mogey, *The Sociology of Housing: Studies at Berinsfield*, London: Routledge and Kegan Paul, 1965.

that safety and security are the chief requirements of the lower classes in their homes.[10] They must provide safety from "both nonhuman and human threats,"[11] and a sense of autonomy from external exigencies. Among these threats, he lists the following:

Nonhuman

Rats and other vermin
Poisons
Fire and burning
Freezing and cold
Poor plumbing
Dangerous electrical wiring
Trash (broken glass, cans, etc.)
Insufficiently protected heights
Other aspects of poorly designed or deteriorated structures (e.g., thin walls)
Cost of dwelling

Human

Violence to self and possessions
Assault
Fighting and beating
Rape
Objects thrown or dropped
Stealing
Verbal Hostility, Shaming, Exploitation
Own family
Neighbors
Caretakers
Outsiders
Attractive alternatives that wean oneself or valued others away from a stable life.[12]

Rainwater feels that it is too much to expect that changes of physical environment can rout all or even many of the human threats from the life of the lower class person. Indeed it was in this

---

10 Lee Rainwater, "Fear and the House-as-Haven in the Lower Class," *Journal of the American Institute of Planners*, Vol. 32, no. I (Jan. 1966): pp. 23-31. Reprinted by permission.

11 *Ibid.*, p. 24.

12 *Ibid.*, p. 27.

specific context that Glazer made a remark which is now celebrated because of its more general connotations:

We must root out of our thinking . . . the assumption that the physical form of our communities has social consequences. . . . The truth is that social surroundings are more important in determining what happens to people than are physical surroundings.[13]

Yet Rainwater feels that many of the specific nonhuman dangers can be controlled by adequate housing, and that the average lower class person evaluates his home environment in terms of the adequacy of the *housing unit itself* in these terms. And this need for security colors the neighborhood as well, but in more general terms.

These conceptions of the house are readily generalized to the area around it, to the neighborhood. . . . The suburb, just as the village or the farm homestead, can be conceptualized as one large protecting and gratifying home.[14]

Lamanna's analysis in Greensboro, North Carolina, of what makes a town ideal supports this contention. His lower class respondents were significantly more likely to stress highly a need for *autonomy* than were the other class groups.[15]

Great differences appear about the level of environment emphasized between the upper middle class and the skilled blue-collar workers who buy homes, with the lower middle classes often split depending on the direction in which they are leaning in this hierarchy. Clark terms their orientations the *house-centered* orientation and the *community-centered* orientation, respectively.[16]

House-centered people at the lower end of this distinction are for the most part buying a detached home for the first time. They suffer at least to a degree the threats described by Rainwater. Their own house in a newly developing area appears the answer to problems of dirt, overcrowding and safety. They figure out just how

---

13   Nathan Glazer, "Slum Dwellings Do Not Make a Slum," *N.Y. Times Magazine,* November 21, 1965, pp. 57-59. © 1965 by the New York Times Company. Reprinted by permission.

14   Rainwater, *op. cit.,* p. 24.

15   Richard Lamanna, "Value Consensus Among Urban Residents," *Journal of the American Institute of Planners*, Vol. 36 (1964): pp. 317-323.

16   S. D. Clark, *The Suburban Society,* Toronto: University of Toronto Press, 1966.

much they can afford on a house and then buy it with great satisfaction. Later, they discover that commuting costs more than they expected, that the provision of community facilities raises their taxes intolerably, and that, more generally, the cost of living in and maintaining their new home is far higher than they expected. They have their house, but unanticipated demands are placed on them literally from all sides.

The Duncans' findings cited earlier would suggest that a small percentage of the working class depletes their income on housing in this way.[17] Yet the presence of concentrations of lower middle and working class people in suburban single family homes is increasing, suggesting a potentially widespread problem in the future.[18]

Community-centered people, on the other hand, tend to the upper middle classes. They seek not just a home (indeed they probably have one already) but a home that is within easy access to a series of shared recreation and civic facilities, yet within a scheme that protects them from unwanted encroachments from undesirable land uses or undesirable neighbors. They may not *use* these facilities much, but they *want* them. It is to this more elite grouping that the planned community holds appeal.[19] It is far from the thoughts of the house-centered purchasers. Community centers, libraries, and the like are important parts of the ideal communities of some people, but not others; social class makes a difference in this regard.

Community conflicts may ensue where a given municipality is divided among house-centered and community-centered purchasers. The latter are likely to demand services they particularly desire, while the former oppose them because they don't possess the marginal dollars to pay for them even if they *were* to appreciate their value. Gans describes a schism in Levittown based on school programs. The upper middle class and some lower middle class

---

17   Duncan and Duncan, *op. cit.* Wheeler, *op. cit.*

18   See, for example, Leo F. Schnore, *The Urban Scene,* New York: The Free Press of Glencoe, 1965, and Mary Powers, "Socioeconomic Heterogenity of Urban Residential Areas," paper presented to the 1964 Annual Meeting of the American Sociological Association, Montreal, as well as the excellent narrative in Clark, *op. cit.*

19   On the way that people respond to and comprehend planned communities, see Carl Werthman *et. al., Planning and the Purchase Decision: Why People Buy in Planned Communities,* University of Calif., College of Environmental Design: Institute of Urban and Regional Development Research. Reprint #10, July, 1965.

residents desired an enriched curriculum and extensive school facilities, while the working class and some middle class residents, confident that *new* schools were automatically *good* schools, rejected them as expensive frills.[20] "New town" activity and "community buildings"[21] are hence not as salient to some social class groups as to others.

In addition, the *existence* of class differences has potential implications for physical environment. In my study of ideal environment, for example, people who were highly class conscious, regardless of their own position in a class hierarchy, were significantly more likely to desire commercial and community facilities such as food stores and churches at a small, intimate scale. Those who did not make such a fuss about the existence of class differences among people, on the other hand, had no qualms about large scale facilities where, apparently, different kinds of people could mix at will.[22]

Mixtures of Social Class

A third consideration of social class is with respect to the geographic integration of social class groups. The foregoing section on housing quality indicates that large amounts of residential integration are not frequently found in America. In France, traditionally, the different social classes would be stacked vertically within the very same building. In the American South, until recently, there was a great mixture of class and racial differences within the same block. Yet, when the ideology supporting formal acknowledgment of class differences in society breaks down, then class differences are supported by other means, one of which is residential segregation. This is one explanation that has been tendered for the greater *racial* segregation in northern than in southern cities.[23]

---

20   Herbert Gans, *The Levittowners*, New York: Pantheon Books, 1967.

21   This is a recent and I believe very healthy trend in America, borrowed from Great Britain and Europe. See, for example, Clarence Stein, *Towards New Towns for America*, New York, Reinhold, 1956, and Edward Eichler and Marshall Kaplan, *The Community Builders,* Berkeley, Los Angeles: University of California Press, 1967.

22   William Michelson, "An Empirical Assessment of Environmental Preferences," *Journal of the American Institute of Planners,* Vol. 32 (1966): pp. 355-360.

23   See, for example, Gunner Myrdal, *The American Dilemma*, New York: Harper's, 1942.

Beshers[24] suggests that the erection of homogeneous, upper middle class suburban areas, with clear cut boundaries and great concern about the nature of the residents of the area, can be interpreted as ensuring that the daughters of the area marry within the same social class as that of their families. Citing studies that show that people by and large marry spouses who have lived quite close to them, Beshers stresses that casual neighborhood interaction in the course of growing up, in and out of schools, is what eventually specifies what young men will be chosen for marriage. Therefore people fight to keep their neighborhood "exclusive," and if that fails they create another one that might just last.[25]

Yet this is not considered democratic where an egalitarian ethos reigns. Designers are constantly admonished to produce neighborhoods that are socially integrated. The U.S. government, for example, gave $200,000 in 1966 to a private developer to find some way to work lower income residents into his new town.[26] One of the expressed goals of planned new towns is socioeconomic integration.[27]

Evidence on the complete intermingling of contrasting class groups is decidedly negative; Gans points to examples where a difference of about 20% in the cost of adjacent homes was successfully maintained, but stresses that developers have been stuck with unsalable homes once the differential got any higher.[28] People care about these differentials because they believe that the least valuable home in an area generally sets the public image of the area.[29] Even in Sweden, where new housing tracts are filled without reference to social class according to position on a lengthy waiting list, middle class tenants aspire to retreat into homogeneous communities as soon as they are able.*

---

24   James Beshers, *Urban Social Structure*, New York: The Free Press of Glencoe, 1962.

25   More discussion on the effects of propinquity will be found in Chapter 8.

26   *New York Times,* January 1, 1967, Sec. 8, p. 1.

27   See, for example, Eichler and Kaplan, *op. cit.*

28   Gans, *op. cit.*, p. 281.

29   Werthman, *et. al., op. cit.*

*   Göran Lindberg, *Social Omgivning: En Social-Ekologisk Undersökning av Tjugo Bostadsområden i Malmö,* Lund: Lunds Universitet, Sociologiska Institutionen, 1967.

Many positive consequences have been posited for successful residential integration. Perhaps the most crucial of them is that when placed within free and easy contact with status "superiors," people will shed their "undesirable" habits and adopt those they see around them at the same time that their more favored neighbors realize that they are human like anyone else and ignore differences in favor of common community goals. While some evidence supports this among social class equals who differ in race,[30] the evidence is decidedly contrary with respect to social class.

Gutman, for example, shows that working class wives had considerable trouble in adjusting to a mixed class suburb in New Jersey that he studied. They simply hadn't the social skills necessary to interact on a free and easy basis with the middle class women around.[31]

Gans claims that instead of forming friendships with their middle class neighbors in Levittown, working class residents "went their own way most of the time."[32] Just after the frenzied period of settlement had ended, when middle class residents had time to search past their neighbors for friends with similar interests, the working class residents withdrew into themselves, since they lacked the ability for or practice of this type of behavior.

Willmott and Young's study of Woodford, an English suburb, brought out that the working class residents of the area who had the strongest complaints about the "snobbishness"[33] of their neighbors were those most fully integrated geographically in the community.

Keller claims that both middle class and working class people have a fuller social life when they are among their own. In summing up an extensive review of studies on this subject, she concluded as follows:

The evidence as gathered from new towns and housing estates throughout the world suggests that mixing groups may actually lead

---

30   See, for example, Morton Deutsch and Mary Ellen Collins, *Interracial Housing. A Psychological Evaluation of a Social Experiment.* Minneapolis: University of Minnesota, 1951.

31   Robert Gutman, "Population Mobility in the American Middle Class," in Leonard Duhl (ed.), *The Urban Condition*, New York: Basic Books, 1963, pp. 172-184.

32   Gans, *op. cit.*, p. 170.

33   Peter Willmott and Michael Young, *Family and Class in a London Suburb,* London: Routledge and Kegan Paul, 1966, p. 121. See also Brian Jackson, *Working Class Community,* London: Routledge and Kegan Paul, 1968.

to hostility and conflict rather than to a more interesting and varied communal life; that the better off, no matter how defined or measured, refuse to live side by side, not to say co-operate in community clubs and projects, with those they consider inferior to them; and that those whose conceptions of privacy and friendship, sociability and neighboring are opposed will soon find themselves pitted against each other in resentment or withdrawing into loneliness. Social contrasts do not, apparently, automatically foster either creative self- or community development.[34]

Nonetheless, because a local area may be homogeneous with respect to social class does not mean that it will be monolithic. Gans describes his neighbors in Levittown, all of whom were earning about the same income, as follows:

Two were Anglo-Saxon Protestant couples from small towns, the breadwinners employed as engineers; one an agnostic and a gold buff, the other a skeptical Methodist who wanted to be a teacher. Across the backyard lived a Baptist white-collar worker from Philadelphia and his Polish-American wife, who had brought her foreign born mother with her to Levittown; and an Italian-American tractor operator (whose ambition was to own a junkyard) and his upwardly mobile wife, who restricted their social life to a brother down the street and a host of relatives who came regularly every Sunday in a fleet of Cadillacs. One of my next door neighbors was a religious fundamentalist couple from the Deep South whose life revolved around the church; another was an equally religious Catholic blue-collar worker and his wife, originally a Viennese Jew, she a rural Protestant, who were politically liberal and as skeptical about middle class ways as any intellectual. Across the street there was another Polish-American couple, highly mobile and conflicted over their obligations to the extended family; another engineer, and a retired Army officer. No wonder Levittowners were puzzled when a nationally known housing expert addressed them on the "pervasive homogeneity of suburban life. . . ."[35]

Gans goes on to dispute whether the average Levittowner has any less contact with (1) old people, (2) poor people, and (3) social problems than if he were to live in an appropriate (for him) local area of a city instead of a "homogeneous" suburb. Whether in small

---

34   Suzanne Keller, "Social Class in Physical Planning," *International Social Science Journal,* Vol. 18 (1966): p. 504. Keller's footnotes are eliminated in the text reproduced here.

35   Gans, *op. cit.,* pp. 166-167.

towns or cities, Gans claims, people have their own orbits which exclude dissimilar people.[36] A number of sociological studies indicate the class similarity of persons who socialize with each other.[37]

Yet what is homogeneity at one level contributes to heterogeneity at a higher level. What level of environment should remain homogeneous, and where should heterogeneity occur?

Gans, whose work in this area is invaluable, stresses that the block is the basic unit for homogeneity in social class. It is the block—two rows of homes facing each other across a street, perhaps no more than 12 homes in all—which at suburban densities forms a pool of people for neighbor relations and evaluations.[38]

One problem, however, with using the block as the basic unit of homogenity is that it leaves property values vulnerable to the effects of those on adjacent or nearby blocks, where home ownership is involved. Somewhat more popular among recent writers is the notion of keeping neighborhoods homogeneous, but articulating these neighborhoods with centers or facilities which people would *have* to use.[39] In so doing, it is hoped, they would rub shoulders with people of all types and achieve the desired effects.

The crucial factors are to specify the basis for homogeneity and to ensure that the mechanism that achieves it is not oppressive. There is, as should now be clear, much evidence for homogeneity in social class at the very local level. But even within a given class level, researchers have suggested stage in the life cycle, home ownership, and hence proprietary interests, life styles, and values—indeed mostly the very concepts stressed in this volume—as the bases for homogeneity. If one is to tailor neighborhoods or parts of neighborhoods for ultimate congruence with the people who might live in them, then it's possible that neighborhoods might be homogeneous indeed. But one must always balance this with

---

36   *Ibid.*, pp. 168-170.

37   See, for example, Edward O. Laumann, *Prestige and Association in an Urban Community*, New York: Bobbs Merrill, 1967.

38   Gans, *op. cit.*, pp. 172-174.

39   See, for example, Keller, *op. cit.*, John Raven, "Sociological Evidence in Housing (2: The Home Environment)," *The Architectural Review,* Vol. 142 (1967): pp. 236-240, and Bennett Berger, "Suburbs, Subcultures and the Urban Future," in Sam B. Warner, Jr. (ed.), *Planning for a Nature of Cities,* Cambridge, Mass: M.I.T. Press, 1966, p .162.

specification of where these areas fit into a larger pattern of heterogeneity, lest the real benefits to be gained from this arrangement be less than the detriments of an *over*concentration of like persons.

The art of arranging the mixture of people and the basis for their meeting is tricky, and there are no firm guidelines. In an area studied by Morris and Mogey in England, for example, groups differing in part in class were placed on opposite ends of the same block, but their subsequent interaction was worse than when they were completely intermixed.[40]

A followup on the class structure of areas within Britain's new towns, which were intended to be integrated with respect to class, shows that local neighborhoods became progressively *less* integrated through time. Individual subareas began to take on the coloration of one class level or another. Indeed in Crawley, a definite trend of middle class people to work in the town but to live in neighboring towns was noted.[41] This is, of course, the very antithesis of the new town concept, in which everyone who lives there works there and everyone who works there lives there.

Under what conditions do neighboring areas fail to integrate? There are no definitive answers at this point. However, a study in Toronto by Goldblatt indicated that facilities, to be shared jointly by two groups with a class difference, would accomplish their aim only if there were strong reasons why people from both areas should in fact use the facility. Facilities that can be done without promptly become the "turf" of one group or the other.[42]

Indeed, two distinguished observers of new town building stress that integration, as it is customarily done, is the one aspect *least* likely to attract people to new towns, let alone be a major accomplishment of them. They believe rather in the "trickle-down" theory, that of providing houses for the poor by creating new homes for the rich and encouraging the turnover of existing homes.[43]

In any case, whatever degree and form of segregation is involved must be entered into voluntarily and for a purpose:

---

40   Morris and Mogey, *op. cit.*

41   B. J. Heraud, "Social Class and the New Towns," *Urban Studies*, Vol. 5 (1968): pp. 33-58.

42   Sylvia Goldblatt, "Integration or Isolation," *Habitat*, Vol. 9 (Jan.-Apr. 1966): pp. 14-23.

43   Eichler and Kaplan, *op. cit.*.

it must not be coercive. If areas are properly designed physically so as to accommodate easily particular social characteristics, then the appropriate people will come *to them*. But what we definitely lack right now is any kind of mandate for complete integration of homes of markedly different price ranges *as a basis for* integrating different social class groupings.

SOCIAL CLASS: WHERE RELEVANCE LACKS SUPPORT

The above evidence has had to do with the housing quality sought, level of environment stressed, and social clusters suggested among different social class groups. This leaves untouched our basic concepts of physical environment. There does *not* appear to be evidence that rich people and poor people *by that criterion alone* have significantly different environmental needs.[44]

Two of my own analyses of housing preferences failed to provide the anticipated evidence of the connection between these two phenomena.

In the first study, the study on ideal environment originally detailed in Chapter 3, five "dimensions" of urban environment were assessed to see whether variations in preferred environment varied systematically with respondents' social class, as measured by occupation and education. The dimensions included housing type, lot size, accessible distance to selected land uses, conceptions of the neighborhood, and scale of nonresidential land uses. Although people made choices among environmental alternatives according to their values, to certain aspects of life style, and even, in one case, by degree of class-consciousness (independent of class level), neither occupational nor educational level was at any time a signficant factor in their choice.[45]

In the second study, the reanalysis of a nationwide survey conducted by the University of Michigan, I attempted to ascertain

---

44 Only their tastes in architectures and furnishings appear related to social class differences. See, for example, Werthman, *op. cit.*, Bennett Berger, *Working Class Suburb*, Berkeley and Los Angeles: University of California Press, 1960, and James A. Davis, "Living Rooms as Symbols of Status," doctoral thesis in Sociology, Harvard University, 1955.

45 For a full discussion of the social factors, see Michelson, "Value Orientations and the Urban Physical Environment, An Empirical Assessment," paper presented to the 1966 Annual Meeting of the Eastern Sociological Society, Philadelphia.

whether people desiring each of the following represented a distinguishable subgroup in any way, compared to the rest of the population:

1.   Those who now live in a single family home but who desire to move to some type of multiple dwelling.

2.   Those whose lot is larger than the median sized urban lot but who feel it is too large for them.

3.   Those who feel that their present dwelling area is uncrowded but who would like to live closer to the center of the city.

4.   Those who could travel to work by either public transit or private automobile and who, if cost and time were the same, would choose public transit.

There *were* distinguishable subgroups who had the above desires, at times identifiable with respect to stage in the life cycle and at times with respect to life style. Yet, again, neither occupation nor education was related significantly to conceptions of the desirable.[46]

These findings, however, run against the common notion that people of different classes have different conceptions of space and hence different ultimate needs in environment. There is evidence, for example, of a physically narrower range of social and economic activity among those towards the lower end of the status spectrum, as compared to those at the top.[47] This trend accounts for behavior which is largely local in character even beyond that which can be accounted for by some of the life style considerations of Chapter 3, such as the extended family (often related to ethnic group membership) and the local—cosmopolitan typology.

These class-based differences in the location of friends and facilities are illustrated dramatically by the study by Orleans cited in Chapter 2, in which the residents of only one area of Los Angeles, an affluent one, were found to have a comprehensive view of their metropolitan area. To assess images of the city, the researchers had

---

46   Michelson, "Potential Candidates for the Designers' Paradise," *Social Forces*, Vol. 46 (1967): pp. 190-196.

47   See, for example, Wendell Bell and Marian Boat, "Urban Neighborhoods and Informal Social Relations," *American Journal of Sociology*, Vol. 62 (1957): pp. 391-398, and Donald L. Foley, "The Use of Local Facilities in a Metropolis," in Paul K. Hatt and Albert J. Reiss, Jr. (eds.), *Cities and Society*, New York: Free Press of Glencoe, rev. ed., 1957, pp. 607-616.

asked their various respondents to draw maps of the city of Los Angeles (Fig. 1). In contrast to the broad-scale images drawn by the residents of Westwood, the much poorer Mexican-Americans of a section called Boyle Heights mentioned an area only several blocks in size, while those in a predominantly black section of the city near Watts, named Avalon, had an image only slightly more broad.[48]

How, then, is it possible to reconcile contemporary images and usages of the city which reflect class differences to the assertion that relationships between class and preferences for given arrangements of the environment are ungrounded? I think that the answer is to be found in the economics of social class.

For example, Caplovitz's now classic study, *The Poor Pay More*,[49] shows that the poorer people are, the narrower the physical scope of their shopping. This can reflect, among other things, a narrow point of view on the part of the purchaser which restricts him to stores which are near but "dear" or, on the other hand, a lack of funds with which to have the luxury of city-wide travel in order to make wise investments. Caplovitz opts for the latter type of explanation on the basis of additional data. These data tell him that when people are able to travel some distance to make a purchase, their tight financial condition forces them to make the purchase in a chain-store which emphasizes low down-payments and easy payments rather than discount stores which offer lower prices. *Immediate* financial considerations appear then to play a strong part in poor people's use of commercial facilities.

Economics is a large factor in the choice of jobs for poorer people. Travel to work costs money; indeed longer trips usually cost more than short ones. Nothing is new in these statements. What is relatively recent and relevant, however, is that just at the time that income and racial segregation are isolating increasingly large numbers of people in the centers of large American cities, many of the jobs that remain open to them (in perilously small number) are now to be found in the outer ring of the city.[50] This requires relatively high

---

48   Peter Orleans, "Urban Experimentation and Urban Sociology," paper presented at the 104th Annual Meeting of the National Academy of Sciences Washington, D.C., April 27, 1967.

49   David Caplovitz, *The Poor Pay More*, New York: The Free Press of Glencoe, 1963.

50   See, for example, Raymond Vernon, *Metropolis 1985*, Garden City, N.Y.: Doubleday Anchor Books, 1963.

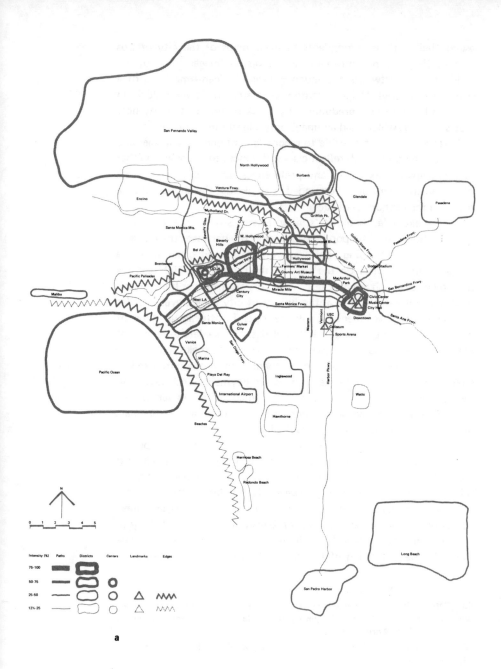

Fig. 1 Composite city images: (a) Westwood, (b) Boyle Heights. (Courtesy of the Los Angeles City Planning Department.)

Man and his urban environment

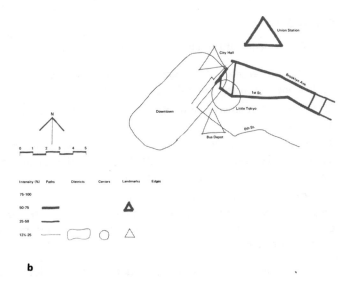

Union Station

City Hall

Brooklyn Ave.

1st St.

Downtown

Little Tokyo

6th St.

Bus Depot

N

0 1 2 3 4 5

Intensity (%)   Paths   Districts   Centers   Landmarks   Edges

75-100

50-75

25-50

12½-25

b

commuting costs among those with the lowest incomes. Literally, many people cannot afford to work, given transportation costs. Thus, mode of travel varies by social class, and public transportation is rightfully a public issue.[51]

Distribution of income will not change radically overnight, and therefore policy makers can't ignore decisions which ameliorate the plight of those whose mobility is restricted by income. However, the point of this section is that, *were* public policies to be comprehensive enough or to include a wide enough definition of the public welfare so as to make us able to treat income differentials as irrelevant to further decisions on the urban environment, then there is no evidence to show that rich people and poor people differ in their preference for many aspects of the environment, from housing to transportation and land use. Such differences in these preferences as have been documented are found in the other chapters of this section.

---

51   See, for example, "14,000 Reverse Commuters Buck the Tide and Their Ranks are Growing," *The New York Times*, September 10, 1967, p. 63.

SUMMARY

The evidence of this chapter, then, is as follows:

1. The percentage of income that people will spend on good quality housing varies primarily according to their education.

2. Different socioeconomic classes have different conceptions of housing adequacy.

3. Completely random placement of working class residents among middle class neighbors results in the isolation of the former rather than in any intended, positive result.

4. Although current usages and images of the city are restricted by personal resources, no significant differences in the *preferred* form of homes, neighborhoods, and cities have been shown related to social class differences.

Thus, where social class has been documented as relevant to the environment, it is of importance to planning and design officials, but the fact that our primary area of inquiry shows no proven relationship in this context should be of equal interest.

In Chapter 6, I shall assess the place of values.

values and the urban environment 6

There is probably no more meaningful concept in social science than values (or more precisely, value orientations). The term *means something different* to almost every observer!

Rarely do social scientists measure values the same way twice. Indeed, rarely do they even speak of the same phenomenon when they talk of values. Yet, values are themselves highly valued as human characteristics relevant to aspects of the urban physical environment.

Why are values thought of so highly? Why should one pursue the study of values in connection with the physical environment?

As part of the cultural system, values are conceptions of what ought to be. They are rules, guidelines for behavior. They are not group structures, nor life styles; they are the abstract goals which people seek to achieve via social groupings.

As such, values may get the aura of an *ultimate* factor. Parsons, for example, establishes a "hierarchy of control" between the cultural, social, and personality systems.[1] Although the variables of the respective systems interact, he feels that those in the cultural system take priority in the adjustment of variables with each other between systems. As they strain for consistency, variables in the other systems fall in line behind the cultural factors, of which values are crucial. Behavior, according to this point of view, is explained

---

1   Talcott Parsons, "An Outline of the Social System," in Parsons, Edward Shils, Kaspar Naegele, and Jesse R. Pitts (eds.), *Theories of Society*, New York: The Free Press of Glencoe, 1961, p. 38.

with reference to many variables in several systems, but the influence of value orientations permeates the others.

Parsons also suggests that societal groupings—groups as large as nations—share within themselves a limited number of value orientations in common, despite the internal differences which I have stressed in earlier chapters. Thus Parsons can trace values that he calls instrumental-activism as prevailing in all parts of American society now and throughout past history.[2]

Few social scientists take as extreme a stand on values as Parsons. Yet there is a feeling among many of them, as well as in people generally, that when they talk of values they are speaking of something basic. It is this aspect of values that recommends their scrutiny in the present context, for if they are closely tied to elements of physical environment, then knowledge of this relationship should be highly important to the understanding of environmental behavior.

Social scientists disagree about value orientations on at least five points: (1) their nature (are they orientations or objects, actions or internalized guides to action?), (2) their level of generality (do dominant value orientations prevail over all aspects of life?), (3) their amount of variation (to what degree do members of a cultural group share similar value orientations?), (4) their susceptibility to change (must it take a cataclysmic action from outside the group to change them?), and (5) the most basic unit for their study (what level of social system is most relevant to the formation and maintenance of value orientations, if any?).[3]

---

2   Parsons, *The Value System of American Society*, draft of forthcoming publication, Ch. 5.

3   Note the differing points of view in *American Behavioral Scientist*, "Value Inquiry," Vol. 7 (March, 1964): pp. 131-136; William R. Catton, Jr., "A Theory of Value," *American Sociological Review*, Vol. 24 (1959): pp. 310-317; John Gillen, "National and Regional Cultural Values in the United States," *Social Forces*, Vol. 34 (1955): pp. 107-113; Philip E. Jacob and James J. Flink, "Value Decision," supplement to *The American Behavioral Scientist*, Vol. 5 (May, 1962); Clyde Kluckhohn, "Have There Been Shifts in Values During the Past Generation?" in Elting E. Morison (ed.) *The American Style*, New York: Harper and Brothers, 1958, pp. 145-217; C. Kluckhohn, "The Study of Values," in Donald N. Barrett (ed.), *Values in America*, Notre Dame, Ind.: University of Notre Dame Press, 1961, pp. 17-45; Florence R. Kluckhohn, "Some Reflections on the Nature of Cultural Integration and Change," in E. A. Tiryakian (ed.), *Sociological Theory, Values, and Social Culture Change:*

I have my own prejudices,[4] but the term has been used in connection with the urban environment in so many ways (although without settling any of the theoretical problems) that I see no need to force it into any single, restrictive mold. I shall therefore use it quite eclectically in the review of literature to follow. *Caveat lector!*

One usage that I *shall* rule out in this discussion is that of economic value. I am not speaking of value in a dollar and cents context, as in land values.

Values can be seen in this context with respect to the point of view of at least two parties: the creator of urban environment and the user.[5] Obviously there is some overlap between creator and user; all creators are also users. However, it is equally obvious that some people have more say about the creation of physical environment than do most users. By what nonuser values are planners, architects, real estate brokers, politicians, and other creators guided? To what extent are they guided by the values and other characteristics of users? To what extent do they *try* to learn of user needs? Do they learn professional ideologies which guide their work? Do they have intense personal motives such as pride in creating the dramatic? Are they primarily guided by the almighty dollar?

For example, Gans describes the people who dictated the choice of Boston's West End for redevelopment as primarily interested in (1) improving the use of land on the fringe of the central business district, and (2) raising the city's tax level. The area was not by any means the city's worst slum, nor were considerations

---

Essays in Honor of Pitirim A. Sorokin, New York: The Free Press of Glencoe, 1963, pp. 217-247; Florence R. Kluckhohn and Fred E. Strodtbeck, *Variations in Value Orientations,* Evanston, Ill.: Row, Peterson, 1961; William L. Kolb, "Values, Determinism, and Abstraction," in Barrett, *op. cit.* pp. 47-54; Charles Morris, *Varieties of Human Value,* Chicago: University of Chicago Press, 1956; Talcott Parsons, *The Value System of American Society,* publication forthcoming; Arnold M. Rose, "Sociology and the Study of Values," *British Journal of Sociology,* Vol. 7 (1956): pp. 1-17; William A. Scott, "The Empirical Assessment of Values and Ideologies," *American Sociological Review,* Vol. 24 (1959): pp. 299-310; and Otto von Mering, *A Grammar of Human Values,* Pittsburgh: University of Pittsburgh Press, 1961.

4   See William Michelson, "Value Orientations and the Urban Physical Environment: An Empirical Assessment," paper presented to the 1966 Annual Meeting of the Eastern Sociological Society, Philadelphia.

5   I am indebted to Herbert Gans for stressing this point.

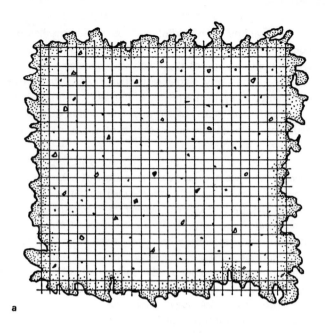

a

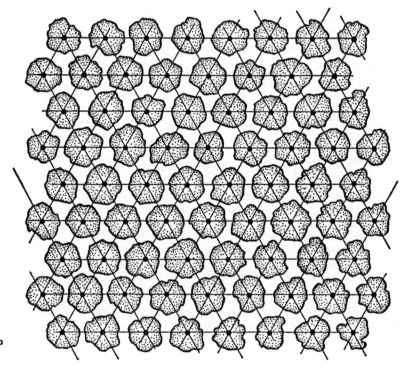

b

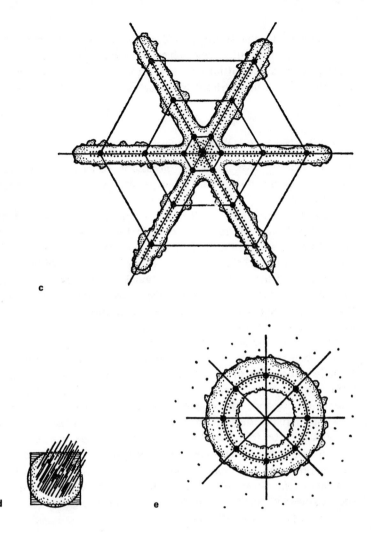

Fig. 1   Designs of macroscopic urban forms: (a) dispersed, (b) galaxy, (c) star, (d) core, (e) ring. (Courtesy of *Daedalus.*)

of the meaningful residential environment for either the old residents or the new cliff dwellers ever a major factor in the decision.[6]

---

6   Herbert Gans, "The Human Implications of Current Redevelopment and Relocation Planning," *Journal of the American Institute of Planners*, Vol. 25 (1959): pp. 15-25.

Answers to the above questions are vital but not currently on hand, and much future research could be fruitfully applied to the ideology and sources of information of the shapers of urban areas.[7] This chapter will be restricted to the values of rank and file users of environment.

VALUES AND MACROSCOPIC FORM

Several writers have suggested necessary connections between particular values and large scale urban patterns such as were sketched in Chapter 2.

Lynch, for example, on the basis of the concepts listed on page 42, designed five different macroscopic forms which cities might take. As illustrated in Fig. 1, they are: (a) complete dispersion, (b) galaxy of centers, (c) the star, (d) the core city, and (e) the ring.

Several of these patterns have rationales that are at least partly valuative in nature. Complete dispersion, for example, maximizes stability and conservation of resources according to Lynch. The galaxy of centers emphasizes spontaneous communication. The core city stresses communication over privacy.[8]

Grebler compared the spatial aspects of postwar reconstruction in Italian cities with those of British cities. In the former, residences were located above stores, so that a great mixture of land uses ensued. In England, the planners took great pains to separate the land uses. Grebler suggests than an explanation for these divergent patterns is to be found in the cultures of the respective countries (i.e., in their values).[9] One could easily single out British privatism, on the one hand, and Italian value on conviviality, on the other, although Grebler does not elaborate this point. Meyerson, however, goes somewhat further than Grebler in tying together specific arrangements of space with culture:

Is it any accident that the Piazza San Marco in Venice is the focus of urban activities that it is—the playground of the urchin who would

---

7   There has been recent interest in approaching these questions. See for example, Robert Gutman, "The Questions Architects Ask," *Transactions of the Bartlett Society,* Vol. 4 (1965-66): pp. 49-82.

8   Kevin Lynch, "The Pattern of the Metropolis," *Daedalus* (Winter 1961): pp. 79-98.

9   Leo Grebler, *Europe's Reborn Cities,* Washington, D.C.: Urban Land Institute, Technical Bulletin No. 28, 1956.

use the streets in other societies, the protective fold where one meets friends and enemies, where business is transacted, where exercise is obtained. Where needs for cultural activities, religious activity, and numerous other activities are assuaged? I suggest that there is in Italy a parallelism between the urban square and a particular kind of gregariousness.[10]

He contrasts this to what happened in Paris, where the French "twisted" the pattern to meet their own cultural requirements.

The great boulevard in France is consonant with a characteristic affinity for display. The boulevard offers a socially sanctioned opportunity for the promenade where one can see and be seen. Some of what Italy focuses into a square, France elongates into a linear system.[11]

VALUES AND LOWER LEVELS OF ENVIRONMENT[12]

Firey brought the whole notion of values into view with respect to the environment, as stressed in Chapter 1.[13] Yet, in the sense in which he used them, values were an instrument which blocked change, not a concept which specified how the environment should be shaped. Beacon Hill could well have looked like the Piazza San Marco, I believe. It was its traditional character that the historical values held by Bostonians were upholding. Similarly, the old burial grounds had a symbolic, not a spatial reference for these people; and the Boston Common was simply one of a kind, not the possessor of a particularly valued set of spaces.

It was his disciple Jonassen who first entertained the notion of a *particular* environment articulating directly with *specific* values, when he studied the Norwegian colony in New York City,[14] as

---

10   Martin Meyerson, "Natural Character and Urban Development," in Carl J. Friedrich and Seymour E. Harris (eds.), *Public Policy*, 1963, p. 87.

11   *Ibid.*, p. 89.

12   Valuable work assigning values to people's preferences in home interiors has been conducted by Glenn Beyer, "Housing and Personal Values," Ithaca, N.Y.: Cornell University Agricultural Experiment Station, Memoir 364, July 1959. Although interiors are not a subject of discussion here, this research is worth noting.

13   Walter Firey, *Land Use in Central Boston*, Cambridge, Mass.: Harvard University Press, 1947.

14   C. T. Jonassen, "Cultural Variables in the Ecology of an Ethnic Group," *American Sociological Review*, Vol. 14 (1949): pp. 32-41.

Fig. 2 Street scene in Crestwood Heights. Seeley *et al.* claim that housing like this reflects given values in the population. (Photo by the author.)

described also in Chapter 1. Since then, several authors have used value orientations in this view, some explicitly, some implicitly.

Seeley and his colleagues found values helpful in understanding the physical environment of *Crestwood Heights*, an enclave of Toronto. This area is characterized by massive single-family homes (Fig. 2), which have little surrounding land or setback from all-residential streets which wind at times. These authors assert that the environment reflects certain value orientations shared by the residents. They are, basically, (1) individualism, (2) an orientation to the present and the future, *not* the past, (3) a belief in mastery over nature, and (4) an orientation to achievement on the part of the men, to becoming better persons on the part of the women, but to simply enjoying life as it is on the part of neither.[15]

---

15   John R. Seeley, R. Alexander Sim and Elizabeth W. Loosley, *Crestwood Heights*, New York: Basic Books, 1956.

Man and his urban environment

Fig. 3 A typical street scene in Jane Jacobs' beloved Greenwich Village, showing the relationship among stores, dwellings, and streets. (Photo by Richard Brause.)

Jacobs used values more implicitly in a popular and widely read book on the optimal design of urban areas.[16] She advocates, among other things, a general dwelling pattern which places apartments above stores, to rise to a total of about four stories. This pattern would, as in her own Greenwich Village in New York City, be found on both sides of narrow streets. Large open spaces, such as parks, would be avoided.

What reasons are advanced for these proposals? They all boil down to safety. Running like a *leitmotiv* through this work is the unstated value that men are evil and that they will maul each other without restraining forces which can be aided by arrangements of physical environment. The housing patterns of Greenwich Village *do* provide surveillance over the streets. Jacobs describes in detail how

---

16   Jane Jacobs, *The Death and Life of Great American Cities*, New York: Random House, 1961.

the careful eyes of shopkeepers and of residents hanging out of their apartment windows can, if they desire to, patrol the streets against those who would abduct or molest the area's children or perpetrate worse crimes (Fig. 3). As for parks, everybody knows what happens at night when they're deserted, according to Jacobs. Her concern for safety is best exemplified by her own words:

Great cities are not like towns, only larger. They are not like suburbs, only denser. They differ from towns and suburbs in basic ways, and one of these is that cities are, by definition, full of strangers. To any one person, strangers are far more common in big cities than acquaintances. More common not just in places of public assembly, but more common at a man's own doorstep. Even residents who live near each other are strangers, and must be, because of the sheer number of people in small geographical compass. The bedrock attribute of a successful city district is that a person must feel personally safe and secure on the street among all these strangers. He must not feel automatically menaced by them. A city district that fails in this respect also does badly in other ways and lays up for itself, and for its city at large, mountain on mountain of trouble.[17]

Therefore, an emphasis on safety can quite rightly become the basis for particular spatial arrangements which involve housing type, density, access to open space, and mixture of land use, although there is no saying that Jacobs' plans would really achieve this goal if widely implemented. Nonetheless, an emphasis on one value does not mean that other values are necessarily finding expression in an environment. One might argue that other values such as beauty and convenience which are emphasized by a goodly number of people, are ignored in this case in a single minded pursuit of safety. In a review of Jacobs' book, Lewis Mumford stressed this quite forcefully:

Her simple formula does not suggest that her eyes have ever been hurt by ugliness, sordor, confusion, or her ears offended by the roar of trucks smashing through a once-quiet residential neighborhood, or her nose assaulted by the chronic odors of ill-ventilated, unsunned

---

17 *Ibid.*, p. 30.

housing at the slum standards of congestion that alone meet her ideal standards for residential density.[18]

That beauty, order, spaciousness, clarity of purpose may be worth having for their direct effect on the human spirit, even if they do not promote dynamism or reduce criminal violence, seems not to occur to her.[19]

But the case is illustrative of the relationship between values and urban environment regardless of its desirability for widespread application.

Young and Willmott show a change in the values of their ex-ghetto residents after exposure to Greenleigh, their low density suburban tract.[20] Two values stemmed from this environment. First, since, as described in Chapter 3, the setting led to each family "keeping up with the Joneses," a certain amount of money became a prerequisite. This in turn required that the men start to emphasize their jobs much more. In general, people began to value other people less as a basis for behavior and started to value "things" more. They became object-oriented in the low density setting, whereas they had previously been person-oriented.

Hand in hand with object orientation came more of a future time orientation. Unless people planned ahead, for catching trains to work, for making purchases, etc., they could not achieve the accumulation of possessions that became such an important part of life. Although spontaneous decisions on use of time could be managed in Bethnal Green, they were not feasible where great amounts of space had to be covered.

Values are implicit among the reasons people advance for moving from one part of a city to another. Ross, for example, contrasts the rationales of those who moved from a peripheral area to the central city with those of people making the opposite move.

---

18   Lewis Mumford, "The Skyline: Mother Jacobs' Home Remedies," *The Urban Prospect,* New York: Harcourt, Brace & World, 1968. This essay originally appeared in *The New Yorker,* Vol. 38 (Dec. 1, 1962); the quotation is from p. 167 of the original version.

19   *Ibid.,* p. 168.

20   Michael Young and Peter Willmott, *Family and Kinship in East London,* London: Routledge and Kegan Paul, 1957.

The centralizers make their move most frequently on the grounds of *convenience*. Their new location is closer to work, school, etc. Decentralizers stress *aesthetic* reasons most frequently, a major difference.[21] One of the most basic value dichotomies, instrumental-expressive, is involved in this choice of environment in cities as they are now structured.

Much the same finding emerged from my study on ideal environment.[22] The more that people could be characterized as high on instrumental values as a result of their interviews, the closer they ideally wanted to be to various kinds of activities and facilities, such as stores, schools, physicians, and churches. Conversely, the lower a person's score was on instrumental value orientations, the further away he preferred these land uses. There is certainly nothing surprising about this.

Instrumentalism was, in addition, found related to desires for ideal lot size. The more instrumental a person's values turned out to be, the smaller he wanted his lot to be. This has a plausible explanation. The larger the lot, the more upkeep. The larger the lot, the greater the distance built in which must be overcome in reaching neighbors and nonresidential land uses. It is therefore to be expected that people with strong instrumental values would prefer smaller spaces surrounding them. The other side of this coin, of course, is

---

21   H. Lawrence Ross, "Reasons for Moves to and from a Central City Area," *Social Forces*, Vol. 40 (1961): pp. 261-263.

22   William Michelson, "Value Orientations and the Urban Physical Environments." See Chapter 3 for a fuller description of the study.

The value orientations to which I refer in this context are based on a content analysis of open-ended statements in the interviews from questions having to do with various aspects of urban habitation. Coding was conducted by two researchers independently, with reliability over the normal standard of 90%. These value orientations characterizing people are thus of a lower level of generality than those assessed by the Kluckhohn scheme. The Kluckhohn scores, derived on a general level from all aspects of a person's life, turned out to be unrelated to any individual's choices of urban form. Since the Kluckhohn theory posits that the value orientation emphasis utilized in any instance by a person may vary according to the substantive behavior involved and that dominant value orientations are hence not exclusive, this finding is consistent with the theory. It does show, however, that the considerations underlying choices of urban environment may be independent of dominant value orientations, thus forcing the scrutiny of value orientations at lower levels of generalization for the guidance gained from knowledge of such empirical relationships as exist.

Table 1 Percentage of Citation of Particular Value Orientations When Evaluating Four Different Housing Types

	Housing type evaluated			
Value orientation cited	Single family house	Two family or row house	Walkup apartment	High rise apartment
Instrumentalism	6.6	9.2	11.3	26.6
Expression	6.9	49.7	49.2	48.0
Group-mindedness	7.9	2.1	2.8	4.8
Individualism	63.4	34.4	29.4	12.7
Doing orientation	15.3	4.6	7.3	7.9
Total	100.1%	100.0%	100.0%	100.0%
N=	366	195	248	252

that people desiring a large amount of space around their homes are low in this value.

Those desiring large lots are, not surprisingly, high in individualism. An arrangement of space which works to keep people at a distance is most congruent with this particular value. The reverse follows by definition: People who don't value their privacy as highly tend to idealize smaller private open spaces.

In this study it was also possible to see what values people themselves used to evaluate specific physical environments. Did substantially different types of housing or open space get weighed with a common measure or did relevant values change according to the arrangement involved?

People used very different valuative grounds to assess single family houses at the one extreme, and high rise apartments, at the other. A detached home, for example, is evaluated on the basis of its ability to provide privacy for a family—as well as for family activity to a lesser degree. (Fig. 4a). Regardless of whether or not they like the house, people speak according to criteria of individualism. Regardless of whether or not they themselves are high in individualism, people bring this measure to bear on single family housing. The association between the two is paramount in the public mind. Note Table 1.

High rise apartments, however, are evaluated in terms of beauty and convenience, not privacy (Fig. 4b). Again, whether or not they like them, people look for the instrumental *and* expressive qualities

More than just a house!

In Monmouth Heights at Marlboro, you'll enjoy the kind of satisfying life you've always dreamed of. A quiet country life with clean fresh air, green fields, an unhurried atmosphere—all the peace and privacy you need so badly at the end of a busy day. And what a great place for children to grow!

All around you are a variety of things to do, places to go. There are golf courses, state parks, picnic groves, playgrounds. The famous resorts of the Jersey shore are but a half hour drive away. The new Garden State Arts Center is nearby. The important everyday things, too: good schools, convenient shopping, houses of worship.

Take your choice of many different homes in Monmouth Heights at Marlboro. Prices start at $29,500—complete! Included in the prices are General Electric central air conditioning, G.E. kitchen and laundry appliances. Landscaping, too. And remember: There are no closing costs when you buy a Levitt home!

A beautiful home in a beautiful community...a social life as varied as you wish...the comforts and conveniences of an urban area plus the pleasures of country living. Yes, there's more to life than just a new home in Monmouth Heights at Marlboro. Come take a look around! Decorator-furnished models are open for your inspection every day until six-thirty at night. You'll be a welcome visitor any time.

The Jamestown—4 bedrooms, 2 baths—$33,500 Central air conditioning included.

From New York: N. J. Turnpike south to Exit 11 "Woodbridge-The Amboys" to U.S. 9 south, fifteen miles to exhibit. *From Bklyn & L.I.:* Verrazano Bridge thru Staten Island on Interstate Rte. 278. Cross Goethals Bridge to N.J. Turnpike south to Exit 11. Proceed as above. *From New Jersey:* Garden State Pkwy south to Exit 123. Rte 9 fifteen miles to exhibit.

Pay only 5% down on most homes—no mortgage money problems here!

COPYRIGHT ©1968 LEVITT AND SONS INCORPORATED

Monmouth Heights *by* Levitt and Sons
at MARLBORO
Englishtown, N.J. 07726 Tel: (201) 462-8800
INCORPORATED
SINCE 1929

a

BREATHTAKING...

the panorama of the Hudson and Manhattan's skyline ... the circular tower for the luxury life ... and the minutes-to-midtown convenience of it all

An exclusive one-of-a-kind apartment residence featuring:
• Central air cond • 24-Hour Doorman • Large private terraces • FREE CHANNEL 3 FOR GIANT FANS • Free Swimming Pool • Free Health Club—Sauna • Free Gas & Electric • Hotpoint Dishwasher.

Dynamic Studios & One Bedrm Apts. From $185.
Fantastic Duplex Penthouse
2 & 3 Bedroom Apartments, from $350
Immediate Occupancy

FURNISHED MODEL APTS BY Greenbaum Bros. of Paterson, N.J./Builders: Starret Bros & Eken, Inc. Luciani Construction Corporation./Renting office open daily and Sunday 10 to 8 PM/Phone (201) 868-0100

Take either George Washington Bridge or Lincoln Tunnel or Port Authority Bus #165 or #166 stops directly at door.

The **Stonehenge**
ON THE PALISADES
8200 Boulevard East, North Bergen, N.J.

MANHATTAN EXHIBIT HALL at 667 Madison Ave., N.Y.C. Open Every Day—10 A.M. to 8 P.M. Renting Agent J. I. SOPHER & CO., INC. Phone (212) HA 1-4835

Fig. 4 Newspaper advertisements for high rise apartments and single family homes. Note the difference in values emphasized in these two advertisements. (Part (a) courtesy of Levitt and Sons, Inc., and The Strathmore Agency. Part (b) courtesy of J. I. Sopher and Co., Inc., and Newmark's Advertising Agency, Inc.)

b

Values and the urban environment

in them, or those which they think *should* be in them. Is it any wonder that developers pile opulent lobbies and architectural frills on top of efficient living space, with barely a mention of privacy?

Building types intermediate in size and in "impingement potential" (our basic elements of environment operative in housing type) are evaluated by value patterns intermediate to those discussed above. Thus the two family and row houses, for example, as well as the walkup apartment, were discussed at times with respect to individualism and at times with respect to expression. It took high rise, however, to really bring out instrumental values.

On the other hand, with respect to amounts of space separating homes, people's rationales vary hardly at all. Whether people want a great deal of land or whether what they want is very small indeed, they want it for what they can do on the land as individuals or as families. Responses dealing with activity and accomplishment (what I categorized as the "doing" value orientation) were forthcoming as rationales for the choice of all sizes of lot. This finding complements the material in Chapter 3 with respect to activity pursued around the home by men and with respect to the frustrations of those without private open space.

Many architects and other vocal intellectuals fail to understand why so many people clamor for postage-stamp-sized lots. Why don't people give up their measly scraps of land, they ask, and combine them into a piece of public open space really worth having.[23] The answer seems beguilingly simple: Public open space, no matter how large, does not allow activities that people want to perform on private open space, no matter how small. These activities are supported by both people's values and their life styles.

Thus we have a case—that concerning private open space—in which people utilize particular values situationally regardless of what their dominant values might be.

SUMMARY

In short, there are a number of discrete findings and insights on the relation of values to the urban physical environment. None contradict, and a few dovetail neatly. However, like the field of values in general, these findings remain more as a suggestion of what

---

23 William F. Whyte, "Cluster Development," in F. W. Eldredge (ed.), *Taming Megalopolis*, Garden City, N.Y.: Anchor Books, 1967, pp. 462-477.

might potentially be learned from the systematic pursuit of values than as a firm documentation which can immediately serve as a basis for large-scale intervention. Although much more work in this area of study is advisable, certainly some of the findings, like those more general in values research, are fruitful for carefully delimited undertakings:

1. National and cultural values frequently transform the type and the use of urban spaces in any place.

2. People who highly value convenience are likely to prefer more mixed land uses and small lot sizes. People who highly value individualism prefer larger lot sizes.

3. People evaluate housing with different yardsticks according to the type of housing.

4. People associate private open space with active family pursuits, regardless of the size of the space.

pathology and the urban environment

7

As numerous authors have pointed out, there has traditionally been an anti-urban bias among intellectuals and indeed among serious students of the city.[1] Men have been attracted to its study because of the lurid fascination of evils which demanded explanation. It is ironic that one of the most pronounced phenomena of our time, the overwhelming concentration of the citizens of modernized countries in cities, is accompanied by an ethos that glorifies rural virtues.[2]

The outstanding faculty in urban sociology, for example, grew up in Chicago in the first half of the 20th Century, a time when Chicago was enduring all the birth pangs of a large, industrial metropolis whose citizens streamed in from all parts of the world. As I suggested in Chapter 1, student after student of the great masters selected social pathologies as subjects for study—delinquency, mental illness, prostitution, skid rows, slums, etc.—utilizing both ecological theory and method.[3]

---

[1]   Morton White and Lucia White, "The American Intellectual versus the American City," *Daedalus* (Winter 1961): pp. 166-179.

[2]   See, for example, the discussion in Maurice Stein, *The Eclipse of Community*, Princeton, N.J.: Princeton University Press, 1960, Ch. 1.

[3]   See this lineup in Ernest Burgess and Donald Bogue (eds.) *Contributions to Urban Sociology*, Chicago: University of Chicago Press, 1965.

Three major statements stand out as illustrative of the pathological effects which *cities*, as entities, were supposed to have on individuals—above and beyond the kinds of explanations which stemmed from ecological theory.

THE CITY ITSELF AND PATHOLOGY

Georg Simmel, a German sociologist whose writings straddled the turn of the century, spoke of the *intensification of nervous stimuli* as the crucial feature of urban life.[4] Lights, noises, signs, and movement were all more part of urban life than its simpler, more leisurely, rural counterpart. As a result, people were forced to adopt a more calculating and rational approach to their daily routine; they were guided by *mind*, not *heart*. To get along, they were forced into a stable and impersonal time schedule. They were forced to be exact in everything done, lest ill consequences occur. With all the bustle amid profusions of people, they were forced into a perennial state of distrust and reserve. Another man was not automatically accepted as good; you had to carefully scrutinize his symbols of propriety. This forced people into differentiating between people, quite a contrast from the village ethos where one man is as good as any other.

What emerged more generally out of these adjustments to urban life, according to Simmel, was the *blasé attitude.* Urbanites appear not to care. They lack spontaneity. They have withdrawn behind a critical facade. Many people interpret this as pathological. In glorifying the assumed open, trusting, and spontaneous posture of nonurban peoples, they treat what may well be a *different* pattern in cities as a *harmful* one. And harmful it may be, both absolutely and in certain circumstances, but labeling it as pathological is nonetheless a value laden decision, which may say as much about the labelers as those labeled.

A second illustrative statement came from a Chicago sociologist, Louis Wirth, in the late 1930's.[5] Suggesting that there was a way of life which was typical of urbanites, Wirth stressed three global

---

4   Georg Simmel, "The Metropolis and Mental Life," in Paul K. Hatt and Albert J. Reiss, Jr. (eds.) *Cities and Society*, New York: Free Press of Glencoe, rev. ed. 1957, pp. 635-646.

5   Louis Wirth, "Urbanism as a Way of Life," *American Journal of Sociology*, Vol. 44 (1938): pp. 1-24.

characteristics of cities which accounted for its diverse elements. They were: large size, high densities of population, and heterogeneity among the population.

Not all of the elements in Wirth's urban way of life are negative. In fact, Wirth's concepts are by and large less value laden than Simmel's. Yet elements deemed pathological found their way into his list. For example, Wirth claimed that large numbers of people in a city led to "the relative absence of intimate personal acquaintanceship"[6] and "the segmentalization of human relations which are largely anonymous, superficial, and transitory."[7] High densities were responsible for "accentuated friction,"[8] among other things. Heterogeneity was said to bring about instability and insecurity.

A third writer, this one a psychologist writing during the same period as Wirth, addressed himself to the poverty and crowding that were so typical of cities at that time.[9] As people lived in tightly packed quarters, they could not help but see undesirable behavior all around them: muggings, wife beating, alcoholism, etc. This led, first, to a process of hardening; people feel badly the first time they see or commit an act which they know is deviant, but they feel easier about it each successive time it occurs until they are hardened to it. Nonetheless, they would begin to feel insecure and inferior with knowledge of what was going on, and they lacked self-sufficiency, according to Plant. All this tended to destroy whatever illusions young people might have had about life; it's hard for a young girl to idealize marriage when the couple next door does nothing but fight.

Just as Simmel posited the blasé attitude as a cumulative result of different aspects of urban life, so psychologist Plant stressed *mental strain* as a general characteristic of those exposed to these urban stimuli.

It was arguments of the above type that typified an early feeling that physical aspects of the whole city were acting

---

6   *Ibid.*, p. 1.

7   *Idem.*

8   *Idem.*

9   James Plant, "The Personality and an Urban Area," in Paul K. Hatt and Albert J. Reiss, Jr. (eds.), *Cities and Society*, New York: The Free Press of Glencoe, 1957, pp. 647-665.

pathologically on its residents. These feelings may remain, but research has turned to consider more specific aspects of the city and their relation to pathology.

HOUSING CONDITION

Although not related directly to basic differences in types of housing, neighborhoods, or cities, housing *condition* has nonetheless been studied at great length for its relation to pathology. There was a great deal of faith in the 19th and early 20th centuries, for example, that if reformers could only wipe out slum housing physically, they would wipe out the social and health problems of the people living there.

"Once upon a time," says a close student of New York's slums, "we thought that if we could only get our problem families out of those dreadful slums, then papa would stop taking dope, mama would stop chasing around, and junior would stop carrying a knife."[10]

An exhaustive review by Schorr suggests that improvement of the *condition* of housing has a marked effect on physical health when it goes past a critical threshold of decency. The provision of a roof, some heat, or sanitary facilities when there were none, for example, makes a huge difference in health, while additional, less spectacular improvements have inconclusive results. As Schorr puts it:

. . . although the evidence is scattered, taken as a whole it is substantial. The type of housing occupied influences health, behavior, and attitude, particularly if it is desperately inadequate. In the terms that we use today, "desperately inadequate" means that housing is dilapidated or lacks a major facility such as running water. In these terms, 13 million homes in the United States were inadequate in 1956.[11]

---

10 Daniel Seligman, "The Enduring Slums," in William H. Whyte (ed.) *The Exploding Metropolis,* Garden City, N.Y.: Doubleday, 1957, p. 106.

11 Alvin Schorr, *Slums and Social Insecurity,* Washington, D.C.: U.S. Government Printing Office, p. 31.

The most sophisticated study in this tradition was conducted in Baltimore by Wilner and his associates.[12] Comparing 300 black families who had just moved from substandard private housing to new and sanitary public housing, with a like number of families who continued to live in substandard housing, the researchers assessed the social and physical influence of improved quality of housing. They found some mild improvements in the social relations of these people as a result of their moving to better housing. For example, they had better relations with neighbors, and their self esteem rose. But their social pathologies did not appreciably lessen; for example, they did not substantially change their family life or lack of aspiration for upward mobility.

But one improvement did ensue. Children's illness were less severe and not as prolonged in the new housing. As a result their school attendance records and their grades improved.

Improvements in the condition of housing, therefore, do not revolutionize the lives of people, particularly when they start with severe problems that are primarily social in origin. Nonetheless, changes in condition may affect particular aspects of health (i.e., *severity* of illness), which may have a limited effect on social effectiveness. Furthermore, housing condition, despite its extent of study, is by no means the only aspect of environment which can potentially articulate with pathologies. Other elements of environment are relevant as well. I shall therefore turn to a few of them that have been studied in this context.

PHYSICAL ENVIRONMENT AND PATHOLOGY

Density

Interested citizens have traditionally included high density as one of the leading factors in the environment which brings about breakdowns of all kinds. Throughout early history, this may have had a basis in fact, as sanitary conditions, never under scientific control, became truly dangerous in densely settled areas. Epidemics took a severe toll. Even today, when health regulations are more far reaching, studies report that people with mental and physical ailments are concentrated in areas of high density. But is

---

12 Daniel Wilner, *et. al., The Housing Environment and Family Life,* Baltimore: Johns Hopkins Press, 1962.

there *meaning* in this relationship? Or is this relationship instead a result of the clustering in areas left to them by others and which just happen to have high densities of those most likely to experience pathological conditions? Is this finding true for all societies?

Martin, for example, after reviewing British materials, states that any conclusions about a relationship between health and environment must take into consideration the specific social and medical context in which it is found. Nonetheless, he feels justified in claiming a "clear association"[13] between health and both overcrowding and air pollution.

Density, as was suggested in Chapter 2, has different meanings. Schmitt,[14] for example, investigated the alleged effects of two of them: *overcrowding* (many persons per room) and what he calls *high density* (many persons per acre). He took measures of both concepts for the census tracts comprising the greater Honolulu area and correlated them, while holding income and education constant, with nine measures of pathology: (1) death rate from all causes, (2) infant death rate, (3) suicide rate, (4) tuberculosis rate, (5) venereal disease rate, (6) mental hospitalization rate, (7) illegitimate birth rate, (8) juvenile delinquency rate, and the (9) imprisonment rate.

Schmitt found that *both* measures of density varied systematically with the measures of pathology, consistent with his expectations. However, he then went on to discover that the more relevant of the two in this context was high density. Holding constant the particular density of persons per acre, the degree of crowding within living quarters didn't show any relation to the incidence of pathology. On the other hand, however, given a specific level of internal crowding, external densities nonetheless "explained" variations in pathology.

Overcrowding within quarters is hence a variable whose effects are uncertain at best, even though it would on face value appear extremely relevant to pathology. Biderman, for example, studied historical incidences of overcrowding in slave ships, in prisoner of war camps, in the steerage of immigrant ships, etc. He concluded that pathologies were a result of overcrowding when the populations involved lacked optimism or group organization. When, however,

---

13   A. E. Martin, "Environment, Housing, and Health," *Urban Studies*, Vol. 4 (1967): p. 18.

14   Robert C. Schmitt, "Density, Health and Social Organization," *Journal of the American Institute of Planners*, Vol. 32 (1966): pp. 38-40.

overcrowding was a necessary condition to a desired end, then people survived it without severe repercussions. This was best illustrated by the survival of voluntary immigrants to the New World, in contrast to the slaves.[15]

Nonetheless, densities of persons per acre aren't invariably associated with pathologies. Schmitt spotlights the case of Hong Kong.[16] The density of some residential areas of Hong Kong is more than four times that of the most densely populated census tracts in American cities. Thirteen census tracts in Hong Kong have over 2,000 persons per acre of ground space,[17] while the highest densities in American tracts are "450 persons per acre in both Boston and New York, 163 in Chicago, 150 in Philadelphia, 132 in Honolulu, and 62 in Seattle."[18]

Yet, Hong Kong is anything but a behavioral sink.

Death and disease rates, except for tuberculosis, are relatively low. There were 5.9 deaths per 1,000 inhabitants in Hong Kong in 1961, a rate well below the comparable United States figure (9.3). Infant mortality in the Colony amounted to 37.7 per 1,000 live births, higher than the U.S. rate (25.2) but far below the levels in many other parts of the world. Maternal deaths totalled 0.45 per 1,000 births, compared with 0.32 in the United States. Patients hospitalized for psychiatric disorders as of the end of 1961 amounted to 0.3 per 1,000 population, a rate less than one-tenth as great as that reported for America. "The major public health problem facing Hong Kong" (according to an official report) was still tuberculosis, with a new case rate in 1961 of 4.0 per 1,000 and a 1961 death rate of 0.6 per 1,000, both of which were ten times the corresponding U.S. levels. Juvenile delinquency and adult crime rates are likewise lower than in many other areas. Cases of murder and manslaughter in Hong Kong numbered 0.8 per 100,000 residents in 1961, or about one-sixth of the U.S. rate. The rate for all "serious crimes" combined, 478 per 100,000 was less than half the American rate, despite inclusion of some types of offenses omitted from available U.S. statistics.

---

15   Albert Biderman *et. al., Historical Incidents of Extreme Overcrowding,* Washington, D.C.: Bureau of Social Science Research, Inc., 1963.

16   Robert C. Schmitt, "Implications of Density in Hong Kong," *Journal of the American Institute of Planners,* Vol. 24, no. 3 (Aug. 1963): pp. 210-217.

17   *Ibid.,* p. 211.

18   *Idem.*

Juvenile delinquency and teen-age violence increased during 1961 but were still far from reaching U.S. dimensions.[19]

I have stressed continually that standard measures such as density per se are less keen and helpful in this context than other concepts that could potentially convey how the individual might experience the components of density. In addition, there is no underestimating the fact that the people of Hong Kong are not leading the lives of proper Philadelphians in their high density settings. They have evolved their own styles of life consistent with a unique culture, that are at least reasonably congruent with the exigencies of such high densities.

The Japanese exemplify successful adjustment to very high densities. Faced with huge urban masses in a country with no room in which to expand, and without the precedents for high rise construction, the Japanese have made their dwellings small, and private open space is minimal. The Japanese have reacted to this pressure by "turning inward." They strongly distinguish between what is private and what is public in physical as well as social terms. Interiors of homes are personal, and their lack of size is compensated for by an intensity of detail. Every inch is open for utilization through physically undifferentiated use of interior space. Every room may potentially be used like any other, with only the movement of portable partitions as prerequisite. Furniture is at a minimum, and ornamentation is in miniature—a flower setting, not a collection of antique ale jugs. Perhaps the Japanese garden most exemplifies the intensive use of personal space; it portrays meaning and detail while occupying little space (see Fig. 1).

In contrast, exterior space is unkempt and unorganized to an extent unknown in American cities. Having turned inward to adjust to their great local densities, the Japanese have ignored what goes on outside their personal shells.

Meyerson summarizes this situation as follows:

That which reflects the individual's domain and responsibility is painstakingly cared for. But the public, the secular, the foreign exists without apparent concern from any master. Tokyo sprawls over a vast area with little coordination of its streets. Streets and public places are likely to be dirty. No one feels any compunction or

---

19 *Ibid.*, pp. 215-216.

Fig. 1 Intensive Japanese use of indoor and outdoor space. (Courtesy of the Consulate General of Japan, Toronto, Canada.)

Man and his urban environment

suffers loss of face in throwing slops into the street or otherwise abusing public areas . . . In no other large country is so much private beauty surrounded by so much squalor.[20]

Loring puts the strengths and weaknesses of the several kinds of density in perspective. Although he found in Boston significant differences in family disorganization (defined in standard social work terms) according to measures of both overcrowding and high density per acre, on further analysis of his data, he concluded that the densities resulted in pathological results *only* when the seeds of pathology had already been sown among his respondents. Some people are more likely to react pathologically, and high densities may aggravate the existing condition to bring it about. Densities are the straw that breaks the camel's back. As Loring put it:

. . . the over-density presented by usage of housing or neighborhood space may aggravate or accelerate, not cause or motivate, any tendency to disorganization in a personality or group.[21]

Therefore there are at least two major reasons why arbitary standards of density are not meaningful with respect to pathologies. First, density figures bear only indirect relations to the actual spatial situations that confront individuals. It is not inconceivable that innovations in design technology can enable comfortable living in hitherto unheard of densities. It is not the number of people per acre but rather the nature of separation of these people from each other and from nonresidential land uses that comprises the physical agent of health or pathology.

Second, the relationship between space and pathology is mediated by variables such as culture. This is a case in which the Parsonian hierarchy of control among systems appears to be borne out. Disruption to the individual and his psyche in a particular environment is very much dependent on the definitions and rules specified by the cultural system, at the top of the hierarchy, and by his relations within the social system.

---

20   Martin Meyerson, "Character and Urban Development," *Public Policy*, Vol. 12 (1963): pp. 94-95.

21   William C. Loring, "Housing and Social Organization," *Social Problems*, Vol. 3 (1956): p. 167.

Some additional light on densities and adaptations to them came from a study of elementary school children in Toronto.[22] This study accumulated information on the school achievement of a cohort of students from kindergarten through third grade through teacher ratings and standardized tests. Home interviews were subsequently held with parents of a nonrandom but nearly representative sample of 710 of them, which included a large amount of information on family characteristics, attitudes, and physical accommodations.

One analysis of this body of data[23] asked whether the various types of achievement measures varied significantly in a statistical sense with different physical aspects of students' homes after controlling for social characteristics normally thought to explain student achievement. Consistent with Schmitt's findings on the several measures of density, internal overcrowding was not related in any significant way to achievement, while the number of families on the block was, in several instances. The pattern of this relationship was not linear, however, inasmuch as achievement scores of students did not decline appreciably until the number of families on the block exceeded 100.

Another largely insignificant environmental factor was whether or not a child shared the room in which he did his homework. Much more important in this context than physical crowding and lack of personal privacy is the use that people make of the space they have (i.e., the adaptation factor). Significantly higher scores were found among children whose homework was done in rooms devoted *at that time* to only quiet pursuits. Where space was arranged so that children had to force their attention away from more active pursuits, such as television or conversation, in order to concentrate on work, their scores fell. Within certain limits, then, adaptation within a given set of spatial constraints so as to provide *functional privacy* is a

---

22   Student Achievement Study conducted by Dr. Edgar Wright, Research Department, City of Toronto Board of Education.

23   These data were first described in William Michelson, "The Physical Environment as a Mediating Factor in School Achievement," paper for discussion, 1968 Annual Meeting of the Canadian Sociology and Anthropology Association, Calgary, Alberta. I am grateful to the Research Department of the City of Toronto Board of Education for making available their data for supplementary analysis.

very real phenomenon. But a real question is the *extent* that a member of a particular cultural group can adapt without the benefit of several generations of adjustment.

Noise

Consistent with Simmel's dictum on the importance of nervous stimuli, noise has been often selected as a crucial element of high density or mixed use areas which could be the effective agent of pathology. This selection has usually been on the basis of a hunch by an observer trying to ferret out crucial aspects of the environment. For example, it is now common to explain some black children's lack of attention to what teachers say by reference to their home environment. In a setting thought to be filled with noise, children are said to "tune out" all but what they specifically want to hear. It is therefore thought part of a syndrome originating at home for these pupils to tune out their teacher.

Direct evidence on the relation of residential noise to pathology is hard to come by. Farr, however, found that noise levels affect the incidence of diseases that are related to tension, such as duodenal ulcer, but not all diseases. Noises can be upsetting emotionally even at the same time that they are not such as to disturb normal hearing. Noise is defined in this case as "unwanted sound," characterized by its unexpectedness, interference, inappropriateness, intermittency, and reverberation. Furthermore, it originates elsewhere, since a person has a high tolerance for what noise he creates. In this regard, cacophony can be as bad as loudness.[24] This finding is supported by testimony given to a New York State Legislature committee in 1966 by a psychologist and a psychiatrist. They argued that they had discovered evidence of mental disturbance among residents of the area surrounding New York City's Kennedy Airport, caused by the interruption of nighttime dreams by jet noise. A minimum number of dreams is a necessary part of good mental health, according to the testimony given the committee, and disturbance of them is the first step to serious problems.[25]

---

24   Lee E. Farr, "Medical Consequences of Environmental Home Noises," *Journal of the American Medical Association*, Vol. 202 (1967): pp. 171-174.

25   "Jet Noises Linked to Psychiotic Ills," *The New York Times,* March 13, 1966, p. 66.

Thus, while humans have a great ability to screen off their consciousness from unwanted sounds, they may not be completely able to screen them off from their emotions. This may be exhibited in unexpected pathological responses.

Housing Type

Back in the 1930's, Faris and Dunham put a spotlight on housing type as a possible source of pathologies by finding that manic-depressive mental illness was related (via ecological correlations) to residence in rooming houses and apartment hotels, in middle class areas as well as poorer areas.[26]

They explained this phenomenon in terms of an absence of social contacts enjoyed by people living there. Wirth described dense living as promoting physical proximity and social distance.[27] These people were thought to be isolated, and many of them contracted mental illness because of this isolation.

Firey, however, viewed this relationship of short-term multiple dwellings and pathology in a far different light. Far from the physical components causing pathological behavior, he argued that people with pathologies seek out particular residential quarters so that their pathologies might be maintained. To be specific, Boston's South End contained a number of subdivided rooming houses, where transients could have shelter at low cost, for short-term periods, and without any household accoutrements of their own. Furthermore, the turnover of residents was so rapid that people did not know or care about each other. Thieves, prostitutes, alcoholics, and the like situated in this area because they would not be conspicuous there. Their comings and goings would not be under surveillance.[28]

In viewing these two positions at this point in time, it is easier to see that in the former case, the relationship might be explained by a special self selection of residents to rooming houses and apartment hotels that wasn't amenable to investigation via the ecological method. People most open to breakdowns were the kind seeking this housing. In the latter case, it may well have been the subdivision and

---

26   R. E. L. Faris and Warren Dunham, *Mental Disorders in Urban Areas*, Chicago: University of Chicago Press, 1939.

27   Louis Wirth, *op. cit.*, p. 55.

28   Walter Firey, *Land Use in Central Boston*, Cambridge, Mass.: Harvard University Press, 1947, Ch. 8.

rental policies of landlords that accounted for the match between the environment and the pathology.

Yet there is some evidence that the link between multiple dwellings and pathology may be more than incidental.

Fanning compared the health of wives and children of British armed service personnel in Germany who live in self contained houses with the health of those living in three and four story apartments.[29] All 558 families studied were those of noncommissioned ranks falling within the same occupation category, and all had been assigned their house or apartment by chance, not choice. All were equally close to community facilities and to a doctor's office, and they all came under the care of the same medical group. All had either two or three bedrooms and central heating.

Yet the morbidity rate of the apartment dwellers was 57% greater than that of those living in houses, as measured by first consultation rates for any ailment.[30] While the seriousness of their illnesses did not differ by housing type, there was only one type of illness which house dwellers suffered more than apartment dwellers: low back-strain syndrome. Differences were particularly marked in respiratory infections and psychoneuroses. Within apartment buildings, rates of neuroses varied directly with the height of the apartments.

Fanning attributes these differences to the cramped space and greater isolation of women in apartments removed from the ground. While they may have gardens below, these are not part of the normal living space of the family. It takes some degree of effort to reach them, unlike the gardens of families housed "on the ground." He traces respiratory difficulties to the lessened physical activity created by this lesser amount of utilizable space. He traces the psychoneurotic difficulties to the fact that, given greater distance from outdoor spaces where women can conduct social intercourse with their neighbors, women in these apartments were more socially isolated. This conclusion is accented by his finding that those women in flats who did not have young children, who were able to

---

29   D. M. Fanning, "Families in Flats," *British Medical Journal*, Vol. 18 (1967): pp. 382-386. I am indebted to the London Observer Service for their kind assistance in tracing this study.

30   *Ibid.,* p. 383.

come and go from their homes more freely, did *not* follow the general pattern; their mental health was excellent.

This study is open to many interpretations. One, for example, is that even physical health, as measured here, may be part of a mental health syndrome.[31] Women who are isolated may think much more of their ills than those in the mainstream of social activity. First consultation rates may reflect just hypochondria among these women, but this is not an insignificant datum, as it hits directly at the relation of mental health to housing.

In our own study of suburban Toronto housewives, we found that those who had a clearly outlined place of their own where they could meet others without the need for an excuse to stay had the most local friends *and* were satisfied with their situation. That is, women with open space defined as their own (even if not owned as "property") knew significantly more people than did those women without it, and they were far less likely to want to move. Women who predominantly met neighbors in the no-man's land of an interior hallway may have been closer to them for contact, but the auspices for contact made that situation quite undesirable to them. [*]

Indeed, Rosenberg speaks of high density housing as promoting *loneliness* rather than crowding. [†]

In general, it might be possible to speak more specifically of pathology as a function of a degree of access to where people do things or receive others (which isn't necessarily where they live). But in so doing, one must take care to specify for what type of people (i.e., by life style, stage in the life cycle, social class, values) this might be true. In any case, reports such as this leave open the possibility of some direct relationship between pathology and housing type.

To this point in this chapter I have outlined a few of the elements of physical environment that have been suggested as relevant to pathology. In general, past findings have been suggestive,

31   "Living in Flats," editorial, *British Medical Journal*, Vol. 18 (1967): 376.

*   William Michelson, "Analytic Sampling for Design Information: A Survey of Housing Experience," paper to be published in the proceedings of the first annual meeting of the Environmental Design Research Association, held at Chapel Hill, North Carolina, June 8-11, 1969.

†   Gerhard Rosenberg, "High Population Densities in Relation to Social Behavior," *Ekistics,* Vol. 25 (1960): pp. 425-427.

but far from conclusive, about direct relationships of environment and clear cut pathologies. There is one aspect of intervention in the manmade environment, however, that has been shown to have a direct connection with a specific pathology.

FORCED CHANGE AS A VARIABLE

When people have been forced to change their residence, the result under certain circumstances has been what psychiatrists call a "grief syndrome."[32] Forced change is not by any stretch of the imagination a concept of physical environment. Yet it comes into play even at times when public officials intervene to supposedly upgrade the quality of environment, for urban renewal, condemnation of deteriorated housing, etc. Grief is a psychosomatic syndrome that may include intestinal disorders, nausea, vomiting, and crying spells, for example, over an extended period of time. It is similar to reactions among people who have had kin or close friends die, but who have not availed themselves of normal channels of expression of grief such as funerals.

It comes into play among people who have for one reason or another formed an attachment to an area and are now compelled to leave it. They feel, psychologically, that they are losing something. In the West End of Boston, for example, among those women who had previously reported liking living there "very much," 73% later gave evidence of extreme grief. Among those who "liked" living there, 53% demonstrated this syndrome, and even 34% of those who were ambivalent or negative about the area showed it.[33]

There is thus an emotional charge at times linking people with a house and an area. And this charge is not irrational, for its existence is based on a positive function which the neighborhood performs in the lives of people. In Chapter 3 I suggested at some length how the arrangement of physical environment often found in urban ghettos is congruent with a particular style of life, one which Fried equates with working class status, although I do not exclusively. Fried argues that immigrants ultimately face two transitions, a cultural change in going from one country to another, which is felt immediately, and a

---

32   See Mark Fried, "Grieving for a Lost Home," in Leonard Duhl (ed.), *The Urban Condition*, New York: Basic Books, 1963, pp. 151-171.

33   *Ibid.*, p. 155.

change upward in social class some time after arrival, which makes a person fully mobile in his new society.[34] The latter change, Fried feels, includes a change in life style.[35] Living in a neighborhood conducive to the group's original life style enables its members to overcome their cultural change without forcing them to alter their style of life before increased education and occupation makes this seem desirable.

A forced move among such immigrant groups, however, requires that people make both changes at once, according to Fried. To reach this conclusion, Fried makes two major assumptions, both of which may be justified. The first is that a duplicate of their former physical environment is not available into which all the people who want may freely move. If it were available, and given adequate financial arrangements, no major adjustment would have to be made. The second assumption is that there is indeed a congruence between a life style and a physical environment. Fried assumes (correctly, according to the data of this volume) that a given life style cannot as easily be assumed in some settings as others. Indeed, data from the West End study brings out convincingly that those who adjusted most successfully in their forced change were those who were prepared before the move for a change in life style and hence environment.[36]

What could ideally be done to minimize these pathologies of dislocation, given the assumption (and a major one) that redevelopment is inescapable in some cases? One solution, which meets both of Fried's assumptions, is the assumption of responsibility by a municipal authority for the provision of replacement housing which not only meets requirements of cost, health, welfare, and safety, but which also re-creates by improved and more efficient methods the

---

34 Mark Fried, "Functions of the Working Class Community in Modern Urban Society: Implications for Forced Relocation," *Journal of the American Institute of Planners*, Vol. 33 (1967): pp. 90-103.

35 Fried's point of view is at variance with mine expressed earlier. He feels that changes in style of life are inevitable concomitants of changes in economic circumstances. Much of the evidence cited earlier would indicate that this is not the case. He also equates intense kinship interaction with membership in the working classes.

36 Mark Fried, "Transitional Functions of Working-Class Communities: Implications for Forced Relocations," in Mildred B. Kantor (ed.), *Mobility and Mental Health*, Springfield, Ill.: Charles C. Thomas Publishers, 1965, pp. 123-165.

basic components of environment which accommodated the life style of these people previously and which serves to soften the impact of the great changes they undergo as a result of immigration. There is no need to question whether it would be a creation with limited time value, since immigrant areas of cities never seem to suffer from a lack of customers.

It is difficult to assess how much of the impact of a forced move stems from the loss of a financial investment. But in any case, elderly owners of homes in older areas of cities are struck particularly hard in this respect. They usually suffer a loss in quality of residential environment, since what they receive in *market* or *condemnation* value for a home long since paid off cannot buy an adequate *replacement* in today's market.[37] In addition, the added amount of rent or capital costs for housing in the fixed budget of a pensioner is either unmanageable or difficult to manage. Only the payment of the replacement value of a home would mitigate literal subsidization of municipal undertakings by elderly citizens who can least afford it.

Furthermore, there is some evidence that people form attachments to an area simply because they have had extended exposure to it. Experimental studies in psychology have brought out that what is known and experienced is rated highly no matter how unfavorable it may be to an outside observer. As a report put it:

. . . men and animals do not so much stay near what they love, as they love what is near and familiar.[*]

My argument, of course, is that they do both.

Nonetheless, while the pathological results of forced change must be anticipated where relevant, they are by no means part of any urban change. Wolf and Lebeaux, for example, documented (before the 1967 riots) that many blacks in Detroit openly welcomed demolition of their neighborhoods through urban renewal. They had little of the attachment to their area described by

---

37 See Toronto Real Estate Board, *A Study of Expropriation for Urban Renewal in the City of Toronto*, 1967, and Herbert Gans, "The Human Implications of Current Redevelopment and Relocation Planning," *Journal of the American Institute of Planners*, Vol. 25 (1959), pp. 15-25.

* John Leo, "Nearness Termed Key to Fondness," *The New York Times*, May 18, 1969, p. 58.

other authors.[38] Their neighborhood couldn't be destroyed quickly enough.

Studies by Tilly and others show, for example, that much of the "in-migration" from rural areas to large cities is not accompanied by pathologies because it is managed with the aid of personal ties that existed before the move. This is true in such diverse places as Wilmington, Delaware,[39] Paris, France,[40] and Ciudad Guayana, Venezuela;[41] everybody "knew" somebody in the city even though elaborate kinship networks were not necessarily transported from country to city. It is a common finding that it takes several generations before migrants assimilate "up" to the pathology rates of natives.[42]

SUMMARY

In short, other than providing totally ramshackle housing, the surest way to induce pathological responses in people through environmental manipulation is to force their move from a neighborhood which is congruent with their life styles without either a substitute life style desired on their part or a physically acceptable neighborhood open for their mass relocation. Such conventionally pursued causes of pathology as housing condition, high density, noise, and housing type reap uncertain results due to (1) very limited effects documented, (2) ambiguity of the physical referent, (3) the salience of intervening variables, and (4) the lack of precise

---

38   Eleanor Wolf and Charles W. Lebeaux, "On the Destruction of Poor Neighborhoods by Urban Renewal," paper presented to the 1966 Annual Meeting of the American Sociological Association, Miami Beach, Florida.

39   Charles Tilly and C. Harold Brown, "On Uprooting, Kinship, and the Auspices of Migration," *International Journal of Comparative Sociology*, Vol. 8 (1967): pp. 139-164.

40   Guy Pourchet, *Le Peuplement de Paris*, Paris: Presses Universitaires de France, 1964, see esp. p. 182.

41   John Stuart MacDonald and Leatrice MacDonald, "Chain Migration, Ethnic Neighbourhood Formation, and Social Networks," *Milbank Memorial Fund Quarterly,* Vol. 42 (1964): pp. 82-97.

42   See, for example, Leonard Savitz, *Delinquency and Migration*, Philadelphia Commission on Human Relations, 1967, and Judith Kenman and Everett S. Lee, "Migration and Crime," *International Migration Digest,* Vol. 3 (1966): pp. 7-14.

definition of dependent pathologies. But they remain potentially meaningful. As they stand today, however, these results are as follows:[43]

1.   Housing condition leads directly to social and physical pathologies only where it is desperately inadequate. Marginal improvements in housing condition have been found markedly related to few expected benefits, the most pronounced of which is shorter children's illnesses.

2.   High neighborhood densities seem more related to social pathologies than crowding within dwelling units, but their effect is mediated by personal and cultural factors.

3.   High noise levels are related to the incidence of diseases that involve tension.

4.   Lack of ability to meet people in a place where contact can become meaningful (such as can now be found in certain types of apartment buildings) is related to an increased incidence of reported medical problems, possibly reflecting induced introversion.

5.   A forced change of residence induces a psychiatric syndrome more directly than many other aspects of environment. This is particularly acute among people whose cultural or occupational traits (or both) are different from middle class norms.

---

43   See also George M. Carstairs, "Overcrowding and Human Aggression," in H. D. Graham and T. R. Gurr, *The History of Violence in America,* New York: Bantam Books, 1969, pp. 751-763.

determinism by the urban environment

8

There is an unwritten rule that anyone writing on the social influence of architecture must quote Winston Churchill's statement upon reopening the House of Commons after its wartime destruction: "We shape our buildings, and afterwards our buildings shape us."[1] While in other chapters I have pursued the question of the extent to which selected social characteristics make a difference in the planning of housing and neighborhoods for cities, at this point I should like to explore the extent to which buildings and neighborhoods shape the lives of the people there *regardless* of their personal characteristics.

The question asked here is how much the physical environment influences who comes together with whom. Assuming for the moment that some people are going to have more friends living in their local neighborhood than others, depending on their personal characteristics, to what extent are the people with whom they spend time determined by the arrangement of physical space?

---

[1] Quoted by R. K. Merton, "The Social Psychology of Housing," in Wayne Dennis (ed.) *Current Trends in Social Psychology*, Pittsburgh: University of Pittsburgh Press, 1948, p. 204.

Planners and architects daily draw site plans which specify where people will live with respect to other people. Do they at the same time specify social groupings of the same people? Can designers, if they so desire, intelligently plan "healthy" social lives for people as part of an overall master plan for an area?

Many previous researchers have responded in the affirmative. William H. Whyte, Jr., after studying one prototype suburb, stated:

Given a few physical clues about the area you can come close to determining what could be called its flow of 'social traffic', and once you have determined this, you may come up with an unsettlingly accurate diagnosis of who is in the gang and who isn't.[2]

The principle involved here has been applied to space within buildings as well. It has been widely adopted by office planners and by others whose job it is to satisfactorily arrange people in large interior spaces, such as offices and barracks. For example, I am writing this chapter from an office on the tenth floor of a modern office building, all of whose interior walls are portable and are rearranged yearly, according to current demands. During the most recent reorganization, my office door ceased to open out onto a busy reception area and instead faces a quiet hallway of offices, of which mine is the last. I now find that I see a great deal of one or two people, of whom I previously saw only a moderate amount; but on the other hand, I've almost totally lost contact with other people whom I used to see regularly.

Similarly, a very careful study of army barracks brought out that the installation of partitions at regular intervals within barracks influenced the formation of strong friendship groups within the areas bounded by the partitions while at the same time it lessened the formation of social relationships over a wider area—a pattern characteristic of barracks without partitions.[3] Other studies have been conducted with similar results on school libraries, cafeterias, and residences.[4]

---

2   William H. Whyte, Jr., *The Organization Man*, Garden City, New York: Doubleday, 1957, p. 366.

3   Robert R. Blake, Clifton C. Rhead, Bryant Wedge, and Jane S. Monton, "Housing Architecture and Social Interaction," *Sociometry,* Vol. 19 (1956): pp. 133-139.

4   See the work of Robert Sommer. For example, *Personal Space,* Englewood Cliffs, N.J.: Prentice-Hall, 1969.

To many white-collar workers and G.I.'s, this phenomenon is at least recognized, if not understood. To assess the extent to which it is valid with respect to the home environment, I shall draw on a number of case studies of appropriate areas.

THE CASE FOR SPATIAL DETERMINISM

After World War II, when faced with an avalanche of returning veterans, many of whom were now married, universities commonly produced extensive planned residential developments. One such university was the Massachusetts Institute of Technology. M.I.T. prepared two adjacent areas for married veterans. One of these, called Westgate, contained very small prefabricated single family and detached homes grouped around an ordered series of courtyards facing away from a central access road. The site plan of Westgate is illustrated in Fig. 1. The other facility at M.I.T., called Westgate West, consisted of a number of buildings which had previously been wartime barracks. These buildings were subdivided so as to provide five apartments on each of two floors within each building; access to each apartment was from an outdoor balcony or porch rather than from any central hallway. The arrangement of apartments in Westgate West is illustrated in Fig. 2.

Westgate and Westgate West not only served the residential needs of returning veterans, but they also served as the setting for a significant research project.[5] The researchers wished to determine the extent of environmental influence on the friendship patterns and opinions of the residents of these areas. Different influences work in Westgate and Westgate West. Let us examine them separately.

In Westgate, the factor most clearly influencing friendship formation was the physical distance between the front doors of housing units. The fewer the number of feet separating the front doors, the more likely it was that the people behind these doors would become friends. People were likely to make friends with others in the same residential court, and within each court they were likely to be friendly with those living closest to themselves.

In retrospect, such a finding does not appear at all unlikely. The men and their families all arrived at Westgate independently and

---

5   Leon Festinger, Stanley Schacter, Kurt Back, *Social Pressures in Informal Groups,* Stanford, Cal.: Stanford University Press, 1950. Figures 1 and 2 are from pp. 14 and 36 of this work.

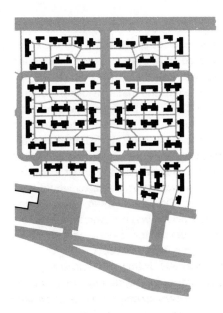

Fig. 1 Site plan of Westgate. (Courtesy of
the Stanford University Press.)

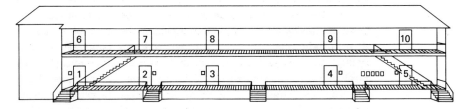

Fig. 2 Schematic diagram of a Westgate West building. (Courtesy of the
Stanford University Press.)

from all parts of the world. They had no choice in the selection of
dwelling units. It is not surprising that their personal contacts were
with those with whom they were most easily put into contact.
Nonetheless, one must pay full tribute to the influence that space
played in this context.

There were few people without close ties to the others in their
court, and the majority of these people represented exceptions to
the factors operating to produce spatial determinism. They were in

part people whose front doors looked out on the access road rather than onto the footpath in the interior of the courts. They were also couples in which the wives worked during the day and hence were not around to participate in the daily social life of the court.

The authors discovered, in addition, that friendship patterns were not the end of the process started by spatial determinism. Friendship patterns had *consequences* in the life of the Westgate community. The opinions that people held on issues that were important locally were a function of the particular clique. Indeed the more inbred the friendships of members of any court were, the less likely it was that any of the residents of that area would have deviant opinions on a given issue. Deviation would occur in any given location only inasmuch as a person was not primarily intimate with the others in that court or to the extent that he held membership in a diversity of groups outside the court.

Another consequence of spatially influenced friendship networks is consumer behavior, according to Whyte. *Fortune* magazine studied the purchase of air conditioners among residents of an area of row housing in Philadelphia, most all of whom were white-collar workers in the same age and salary brackets. While 20% of the homes had air conditioning, these homes were not randomly distributed. They were located in tight clusters along the sides of streets, which in this case were the physical equivalent of the courts in Westgate. Rows of housing were conspicuous by either the presence or absence of air conditioners, as well as other types of purchases such as awnings and initialed doors, a consequence of communication and social pressures among neighbors. Whyte argues on the basis of this that younger families sell *each other* on major appliances, eliminating part of the need for salesmen who convince or who need to know about the products they sell.[6]

One of my own students reports a "quiet crescent" in a Toronto suburb in which six of the seven homes now have electric organs. One can only wonder what the odds are that this could have happened by chance alone.

In Westgate West, space was equally deterministic. It was, however, a different unit of distance that led to the formation of friendships in Westgate West. On the basis of physical distance alone,

---

6   William H. Whyte, Jr., "The Web of Word of Mouth," *Fortune*, Vol. 50, no. 5 (Nov. 1954): pp. 140-143, 204-212.

one would expect that people who lived in the "same" apartment on the first and second floor as viewed from left to right would be approximately equally popular and would be friendly with the people in the corresponding apartments on their respective floors. Furthermore, on the basis of physical distance alone, one would not expect differences in the total number of friendships made by all those on the first floor as opposed to all those on the second floor.

But residents of the second floor could not exit from the building in any direction they wished. They were forced to exit via one of two possible paths—by the stairways at either end of the balcony. These stairways brought residents of the second floor directly by the doors of just certain residents of the first floor. This meant that a *few* of the residents of the first floor were well known to those of the second. Thus the patterning of people's movement, as opposed to the simple separation between their doors, led to distinctions in the friendship patterns of residents of the first and second floors in Westgate West. This kind of distance, the researchers call *functional distance*; it is an aspect of what I labelled as manipulated distance in Chapter 2.

In short, the MIT studies brought out two kinds of distance, physical and functional, which determined friendship patterns and consequent opinions except in unusual circumstances among a large number of families.

A more detailed illustration of functional distance stems from a recent study of dormitories at Princeton University.[7] Case studied student friendship patterns from entry to entry and from floor to floor in four story buildings which are divided into separate entries to vertically defined sections of buildings. In both buildings, the crucial element literally contributing to functional distance was the placement of lavatory facilities, as they were not decentralized throughout the building.

In one square building with an open courtyard, there were four entries, separated internally by fire doors. There were, however, but two washrooms per floor. One was located next to the fire door separating entries one and two. The other was in a similar position with respect to entries three and four. In this situation, friendship

---

7   F. Duncan Case, Jr., "The Influence of Architecture on Patterns of Social Life," unpublished Junior Paper, Princeton University Department of Sociology, 1967.

patterns followed the lines of where students traveled by necessity. There was much contact between the residents of entries that shared lavatory facilities and little between the entries that didn't. In addition, there was relatively little contact between floors of this building.

In a second dormitory, however, every entry had a washroom, but they were located only on alternate floors. In this situation, the more frequent pattern of contact was between floors, particularly between the floors that shared washrooms. Contacts between entries were much less frequent.

Case concludes that 70% of the friendship relations held by residents of the former building were influenced by architectural sources, while 76% of those in the latter building were so influenced.[8]

Case thus explores both the horizontal and vertical dimensions of manipulated distance.

Another major effort on the subject which built upon the MIT studies, was Leo Kuper's survey of postwar housing outside Coventry in England.[9] Kuper studied semidetached housing built along a standardized plan. Each two attached houses were oriented to each other as illustrated in Fig. 3. Thus each home was a mirror image of the other, and the rooms were arranged such that the residents frequently found themselves on opposite sides of a relatively flimsy center wall, both day and night. Impingements of party neighbors on each other were the source of a great deal of annoyance and embarrassment.

However, only one set of immediate neighbors was on the other side of a party wall. The other set of neighbors was on the other side of a small walkway. A crucial question to be raised in this context, then, is whether there was any regular difference between the pattern of contact that people had with their party neighbors—with whom they were in contact most hours of the day and night—and that which they had with their side neighbors—with whom contact was far less continuous.

Despite the fact that party walls drew people together regardless of their volition, people had the most frequent and intense

---

8   *Ibid.*, p. 57.

9   Leo Kuper, "Blue Print for Living Together," in Leo Kuper *et. al., Living in Towns,* London: The Cresset Press, 1953, pp. 1-202.

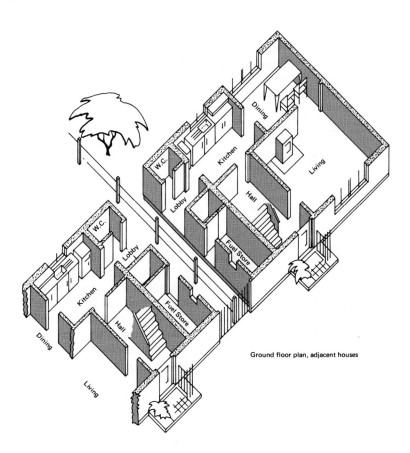

Fig. 3 Ground floor plan, adjacent houses, Coventry, England. (Courtesy of The Cresset Press, Ltd.)

relations with their side neighbors, not their party neighbors. This was as true of really friendly relations as it was of hostile relations.

The mechanism that brought this about was the placement of doors. One entrance to each dwelling unit was from the walkway, and the doors of side neighbors faced each other across this narrow strip. The nearest doors of party neighbors were more widely separated.

Thus the placement of doors brought people together all on their own "turf," where they could talk, wave to each other, and eventually initiate more complicated forms of social relationships. Such a means of turning neighbor relations into something more definite wasn't present to the same degree with the party wall neighbors in this instance. Even though the party wall neighbors were almost always known to the residents of this subdivision, they were considerably less likely than side neighbors to be either best friends or the objects of "sociable" relations.

Nonetheless, it should be noted that the proximity created by strategic placement of doors could lead just as easily to feuding as it could to friendship. Such spatial proximity, in short, brought about intense relationships, both positive and negative.

Kuper points out, in addition, that the placement of doors and windows had a still greater effect on the lives of people in various parts of the subdivision. A more general site plan of the development can be found in Fig. 4.[10] Residents of cul-de-sacs were generally less satisfied with their housing than were those who lived in a longer straight line on the side of an external roadway. On the basis of his studies, Kuper attributes this difference to the lack of privacy which residents of cul-de-sacs undergo as a function of the placement of their windows and doors. They feel that they cannot enter or leave their homes without being observed. For normal daily activities, this is not such a hardship. But when people have unusual errands or trips taken at unusual times, they resent feeling that their movements are well known to their neighbors. This was much less a factor in the lives of those living in long lines along the roads.

Thus Kuper develops the influence on people's social relations of the outlook of doors and windows.

Much of the same findings emerged from another study of a postwar university community, this one at the University of Minnesota. Working at the same time as Festinger and his associates, but independently of them, Caplow and Foreman traced the friendship patterns of the married veterans living in a subdivision called University Village, the layout of which is illustrated in Fig. 5.[11] Like the homes that Kuper described, housing in University Village was all semi-detached, with party walls in the center and front doors on the extreme opposite sides of the housing unit.

Like Kuper, these researchers found that friendships followed along the lines dictated by the orientation of the front doors.

---

10 Kuper, *op. cit.*

11 Theodore Caplow and Robert Forman, "Neighborhood Interaction in a Homogeneous Community," *American Sociological Review*, Vol. 15 (1950): pp. 357-366.

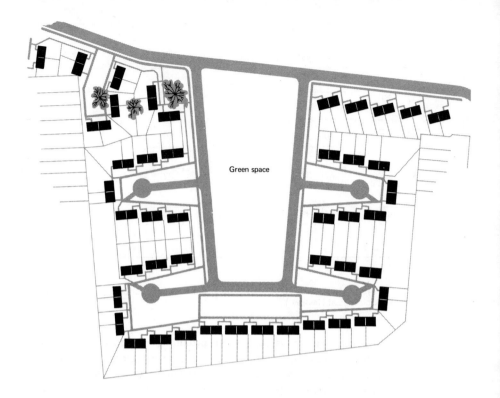

Fig. 4   General site plan of Braydon Road residential unit, Coventry, England. (Courtesy of The Cresset Press, Ltd.)

Everyone sharing a given sidewalk was extremely likely to know everyone else whose front door looked out on that same sidewalk. People were much less likely to know others whose homes and even doors may actually have been closer to theirs but whose front door did not *look out* on the same sidewalk.

    Additional evidence comes from a study by Robert K. Merton and his associates of a carefully planned industrial town in the U.S., called Craftown.[12] Seven hundred families are housed in Craftown, four families to a building. Although Kuper's findings might appear to be contradicted by Merton's findings that 19% of the Craftown residents' friendships are with people living in the same building, compared to only 5% with people in an adjacent building, these

12   Merton, *op. cit.*, p. 188 ff.

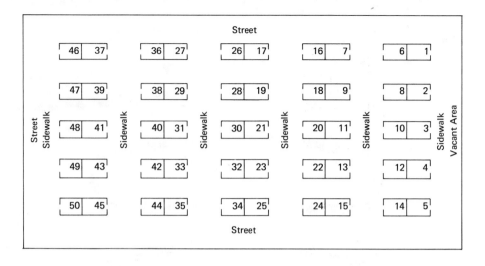

Fig. 5 University Village: plan of a sample block. (Courtesy of the American Sociological Review.)

findings nonetheless reflect the proximity of doors. In Craftown, doors of residents of the *same* building are closest each other.[13] Thus, although the *pattern* of friendship in Craftown differs from that in Coventry, the constant determining factor is the placement of doors.

This is brought out strongly by Merton's analysis of friendships that people maintain with others who live across the street from them. Out of these types of friendships, 74% are among people who have doors facing the street. Only 22% of them are among people only one of whom has a door facing the street, and only 4% of them are among people who do not have doors which face the street.[14]

Very simply, then, people can be aware of each other's existence in a number of ways, but specific elements of their physical environment, particularly doors, can be designed and oriented so as to expand people's *awareness* of other people into *contact* with them.

The potential influence of proximity, whether intentionally planned or not, cannot be overemphasized. As hinted in Chapter 5,

13 *Ibid.*, p. 204.
14 *Ibid.*, p. 207-208.

studies on the choice of marriage partner have traditionally shown that people have tended to marry someone who lived very close to their parental home.[15] Even today, a time when more and more young people are receiving training at the post high school level, residential propinquity remains a major factor in choosing a mate. Although advanced training offers the possibility for people to meet potential marriage partners with interests very similar to their own to a much greater extent than was formerly possible, the similarity of occupational interests is no more likely to predict this crucial choice than is proximity of residential location. Each is strong, and there is no way of predicting accurately beforehand which one will be the determinant crucial to any particular marriage, even with knowledge of a person's social class.[16]

The principle involved, of course, is pretty simple. In these days, when few marriages are arranged by anyone other than the participants in Western society, people have to meet before they marry. And two of the most common places to meet are in local neighborhood institutions, as stressed in Chapter 5, and at the job.

A final study to be mentioned in this context strongly suggests that the patterns created by spatial determinism last over relatively long periods of time. William H. Whyte, Jr., studied the town of Park Forest, Ill. over several years.[17] Located approximately 25 miles south of the center of Chicago, Park Forest is a booming town for the up and coming young executive and the professional, the type who has been dubbed by Whyte "the organization man." Such people are generally mobile, both socially and in their place of residence. Of the 17,600 dwellings in Park Forest, approximately 3,000 changed hands every year at the time Whyte was studying this town.[18] There was thus a continual turnover of residents in Park Forest, and therefore it was possible to study the physical aspects of friendship patterns independent of the particular people who happened to be involved in any single point in time.

Some of the Park Foresters lived in two story garden apartments grouped into courts. Each court developed through time

---

15   See the review of this in James M. Beshers, *Urban Social Structure*, Glencoe, Ill.: The Free Press, 1962, Ch. 6.

16   Natalie Rogoff Ramsøy, "Assortive Mating and the Structure of Cities," *American Sociological Review,* Vol. 31 (1966): pp. 773-785.

17   Whyte, *op. cit.,* Ch. 25.

18   *Ibid.,* p. 335.

a particular culture of its own. One would be known for its wild parties; another, for its emphasis on church going; a third would be actively involved in community affairs, while in a fourth the residents would be typified by their constant complaining. As Whyte observes this situation, the particular interest of any court seems to remain active regardless of the real fact that many residents are being replaced.

Other Park Foresters live in single family homes on individual lots. Whyte performed an ingenious experiment on one of the single family home areas. He mapped out which homes participated in various kinds of get-togethers during the period of January to July 1953. As can be seen in Fig. 6, the activities were predominantly among those who lived very close to one another. Whyte then returned and obtained the same information for the same months three years later, in 1956. By that time a great number of the original residents had moved away from Park Forest and had been replaced by other people. Nonetheless, practically the same homes were involved with the same other homes in social activity at this later date. As can be seen in Fig. 7, the activities had changed in the three year period but whatever force was at work in bringing together the original residents of this area also appeared to be at work after these people had been replaced by others.

There were several factors which helped to bring people together, in Whyte's estimation. First, the presence of children and their need to play with other children close at hand would acquaint parents with other adults who happened to be living nearby. In addition, the siting of driveways and stoops, and the presence and situation of lawns (both factors manipulating proximity) helped to bring people together.

Whyte also makes some acute observations about the social life of people living in different locations on the city or suburban block. People living on corners, he asserts, are much more likely to be isolated from other people than are those who live in the middle of blocks. By the same token, the residents of the middle of the blocks are likely to be inundated with friends and friendships just because of the placement of their houses with respect to other houses. This leads Whyte to some overwhelmingly deterministic conclusions. The gregarious person who by ill fortune winds up living on a corner will end up with extremes of frustration and will figuratively wither on the vine; the odds are great that he will want to move to a more "friendly" neighborhood or town. On the other hand the man who

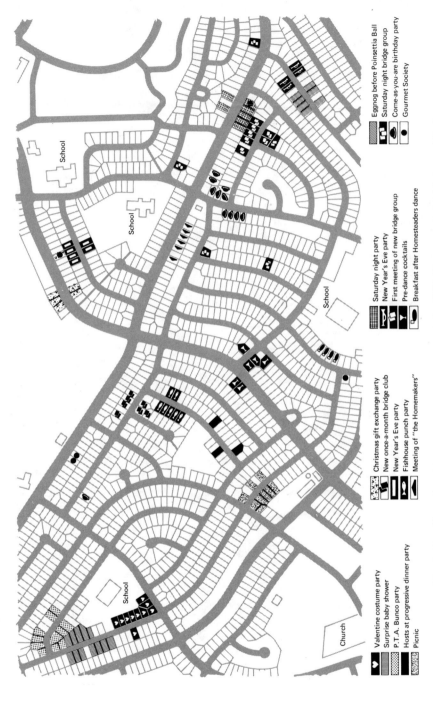

Fig. 6   Sampling of social groupings in Park Forest, Ill., in 1953. (Courtesy of Doubleday and Co.)

Legend (right side):

Eggnog before Poinsettia Ball
Saturday night bridge group
Come-as-you-are birthday party
Gourmet Society

Saturday night party
New Year's Eve party
First meeting of new bridge group
Pre-dance cocktails
Breakfast after Homesteaders dance

Christmas gift exchange party
New once-a-month bridge club
New Year's Eve party
Fishhouse punch party
Meeting of "the Homemakers"

Valentine costume party
Surprise baby shower
P.T.A. Bunco party
Hosts at progressive dinner party
Picnic

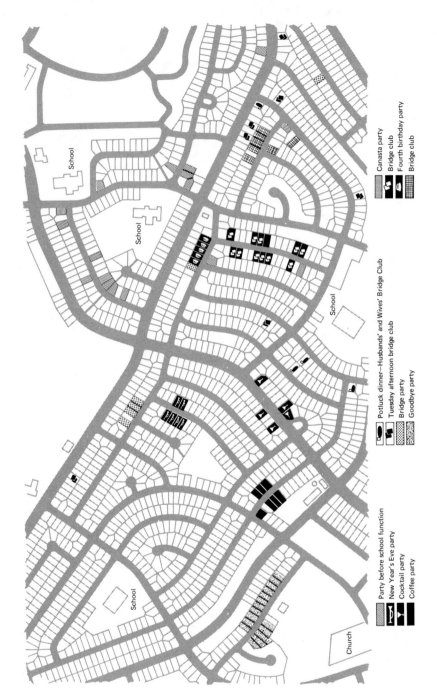

Fig. 7 The same area three years later. (Courtesy of Doubleday and Co.)

Party before school function
New Year's Eve party
Cocktail party
Coffee party

Potluck dinner—Husbands' and Wives' Bridge Club
Tuesday afternoon bridge club
Bridge party
Goodbye party

Canasta party
Bridge club
Fourth birthday party
Bridge club

wishes extremes of privacy, who likes to keep his neighbors at a distance, will be beset with problems from living in the middle of a block; life for him will be a constant war to fend off unwanted but persistent intruders.

The city planner, according to Whyte's conception of determinism, therefore has the power to *determine* the nature of intensity of people's social lives, or the problems they face from resisting the ascribed intensity. He can shape on his drafting board the length and shape of city blocks, as well as the number of homes that will be found at different locations on that block.[19]

CONDITIONS WHICH MODIFY SPATIAL DETERMINISM

We have thus seen that there have been a number of strong statements which support spatial determinism of who neighbors with whom and with what intensity, backed by painstaking and at times ingenious research. Nonetheless, these findings of spatial determinism are now being strongly challenged.

Gans' study of Levittown, New Jersey, for example, repudiates any notion of strict spatial determinism of friendship patterns, particularly that based on positioning of front doors.

If the front door had been significant, owners of the Cape Cod and ranch houses should have chosen their right-hand and across-the-street neighbors most often; those of the Colonial houses should have chosen their left-hand and across-the-street neighbors. The data show that the Cape Cod owners visited most often across the street, but equally between right-and left-hand neighbors; the ranch owners chose left-hand neighbors twice as often as their other neighbors; and the Colonial owners showed a slight preference for left-hand neighbors.[20]

Dennis, moreover, while in the process of rejecting the possibility that there are social consequences of physical proximity, adds an ideological rejection. He feels that those who advocate neighborhoods planned with interaction in mind in fact act as agents of social control for the "establishment" of the area. If people

---

19   *Ibid.*, Ch. 25.
20   Herbert Gans, *The Levittowners*, N.Y.: Random House, 1967, p. 158.

interact happily with neighbors, they will not try to change basic aspects of societal structure.[21]

Since examples which negate notions of strict spatial determinism are current, then the question of spatial determinism turns into one of a slightly different nature. *Under what conditions* can we find an element of spatial determinism of human friendship patterns?

There is a wide agreement on one such condition: *homogeneity*. The residents must be socially homogeneous or think themselves so. A look at the people who were the subject of the studies that were cited to show the case *for* spatial determinism will show that within each study they were extremely homogeneous. The students of Westgate, for example, were all married veterans who were studying engineering at a highly prestigious and intellectually demanding university. Those at Princeton were all single freshmen carefully selected on the basis of past accomplishments. The people whom Kuper studied were largely members of the British working class who badly needed housing following the second World War. The students at the University of Minnesota were so homogeneous that the researchers were unable to find any significant status differences among them in statistical tests;[22] even the most popular residents of that area were indistinguishable in socio-economic status from the least popular. The residents of Craftown resemble those of Coventry in many ways. Park Foresters fit still another mold so well that Whyte felt justified in assigning them a common label. Homogeneity, then, is singularly common to the examples which support spatial determinism.

Gans suggests how homogeneity, even when not naturally great, can be *induced* by other circumstances. Above and beyond any apparent homogeneity among home buyers in Levittown, for example, Levitt's salesmen had a clear policy of stressing to prospective buyers that everyone in town was approximately the same respectable class and that everyone got along with everyone else extremely well. It was, they said, a friendly town with friendly people. People also tended to think that Levittown was homo-

---

21 Norman Dennis, "The Popularity of the Neighborhood Community Idea," in A. E. Pahl (ed.), *Readings in Urban Sociology,* London: Pergamon Press, 1968, pp. 74-92.

22 Caplow and Forman, *op. cit.*, p. 365.

geneous because all the eventual buyers had to pass a searching credit check conducted by the Levitt organization; as a result, they felt secure against the potential presence of people with significantly lower status. Finally, the homes were priced at levels similar enough to induce a feeling of homogeneity among their buyers.[23]

In an analysis based on a Detroit Area Study conducted by the University of Michigan, Tomeh showed that the greater the perceived homogeneity of residents in a neighborhood, the greater was their participation within that neighborhood.[24]

But why does homogeneity serve as a condition which helps bring about spatial determinism of friendship? When people first arrive at a new home, they are unlikely to know many or any of their fellow residents. With whom, then, do they establish cordial relations? If all people within a wide area are felt to resemble one another, then the path of least resistance is to strike friendships with those who are closest.

Residential propinquity throws people together. When doors are relatively close and people have no reason to hurry inside (as from a hallway), people are more likely to have sustained eye contact with each other. When people don't think they have to go further out in an urban area to find compatible friends, casual relationships with neighbors can turn into more deeply held friendship relations.

Contact with those in surrounding homes usually comes about through one or more of several ways. First, children often form friendships with other children which subsequently bring their respective pairs of parents together. Some families actively search for children the same age as theirs as potential playmates. In other homes, the children bring home these friends themselves. In any case, given a feeling of homogeneity, possessing children the same age, and having easy access to each other, neighbors strike up friendships. Being in the same stage in the life cycle and, beyond that, sharing similar ideas of childraising, are crucial aspects of suburban homogeneity, even when people differ in, say, religion or ethnicity.

---

23 Gans, *op. cit.*, pp. 13-14. See also his "Planning and Social Life," *Journal of the American Institute of Planners*, Vol. 27 (1961): pp. 134-140.
24 Aida K. Tomeh, "Empirical Considerations in the Problem of Social Integration," *Sociological Inquiry*, Vol. 39 (1969): pp. 65-76.

Secondly, when people occupy new residences, they often find themselves faced with numerous manual tasks, both inside and outside. Few people have either the knowledge or the tools to undertake all the jobs facing them completely on their own. So they ask their neighbors, who are usually doing much the same thing. Again, when there is a feeling that the neighbor is just as good a man as anyone else in town, casual contact has a chance to turn into something deeper.

Furthermore, people moving into new quarters are generally so hyperactive in organizing their own nests that they really don't have much time to go off and find friends among people other than their immediate neighbors. Once people assume that homogeneity is the case, they allow propinquity to specify their immediate choice of friends, almost by default.

As time goes by, however, many of the factors which permitted homogeneity to serve as a condition of spatial determinism cease to be as all-consuming as they once were. Children find friends in institutions such as schools and clubs. Neighbors cease to be as important once their initial advice and aid in emergency situations has been received. People start to meet many other people once they have time to venture forth from their now organized homes. Thus, once people have become relatively settled in a particular area, the more common it becomes for friendships with neighbors to become only a much smaller part of the total friendships the people hold.

Gans, for example, points out that after two years in Levittown, about a third of the residents said that none of the couples they spent most of their time with came from the same street. About another third said that less than half of these couples came from the very same street as they. Only 31% of Gan's respondents had the majority of their friendships still located on the same street.[25]

Therefore a second condition is necessary in order that spatial determinism of friendship patterns may work. There must be a strong or continued need for mutual assistance or contact, such as that among newly arrived homeowners (particularly those with children) lacking time to seek out friendships elsewhere.

This is the pattern in areas of new housing (for purchase). It is also the case that Whyte describes in the organization man's suburb, where the turnover of population is constant and where almost the entire town might be expected to have changed hands within a

25   Gans, *The Levittowners*, p. 182.

period of say, five years. Once people have remained stationary for a period of time they may be in less need of assistance, their children will have found other friends or indeed grown up, and they are able to perceive differences among themselves, which violates conditions of homogeneity.

Shulman presents evidence from Ottawa and Toronto that mutual assistance among selected neighbors *grows* with the length of time a family has lived in one place.[26] This is not incompatible with the foregoing inasmuch as those acquaintanceships that do ripen through time into deeper friendships should show more emotional and functional dependence among the participants than those which are more newly formed. Nonetheless, friendship patterns which are a microcosm of the physical layout of a neighborhood are more likely to be a function of newly arrived status, when immediate needs are present. The *intensity* of contact with particular neighbors may be less at the moment than it will be later on, but the *concentration* of contact in the local area will be greater when these needs are current and are not ameliorated either by other means or by people already known.

What about the situation when one family moves in and may need help but whose neighbors are long established? Is this mutual or, in fact, unilateral need? According to Shulman's observations, this is still mutual aid as long as the recipient is capable of reciprocating at some future time if necessary. If he isn't, then neighboring contact, despite the need of one party, is more likely to be minimal.[27]

As was suggested in Chapter 5, there is a social class difference in what happens next in the search for friends.

NEIGHBORING IN RENTAL SETTINGS

Two conditions thus have been isolated throughout the literature under which proximity becomes a factor in friendship: the first is

---

26 Norman Shulman, "Mutual Aid and Neighboring Patterns: The Lower Town Study," *Anthropologica,* Vol. 9 (1967): pp. 51-60, and "Urban Environment and Social Interaction," unpublished term paper, University of Toronto, Department of Sociology, August, 1968. See also E. Pfeil, "The Pattern of Neighbouring Relations in Dortmund-Nordstadt," in R. E. Pahl (ed.), *Readings in Urban Sociology,* London: Pergamon Press, 1968, pp. 136-158.
27 *Ibid.*

homogeneity (or at least perceived homogeneity) and the second is the need for mutual aid.[28]

Several settings are popularly known for the lack of neighboring in their confines. One is public housing, and another is the high rise apartment. The above two conditions may shed some light on behavior in these settings.

First, public housing under most circumstances fails to meet either condition for intense proximate friendship. Several studies agree that prospective tenants of public housing perceive great differences between themselves and other people living in public housing.

Young and Willmott, for example, found that residents of nearby and similar ghetto areas in London consider each other as members of different cultures when placed side by side in a new suburban housing development.[29] They act *with reference to* other people rather than *with* them.

Hartman discovered that Boston's West Enders thought that residents of public housing were not at all like themselves. He found that the environment of the few who subsequently moved to public housing had greatly improved in *condition.* However, those few still did not like living there because, perhaps not surprisingly, they then found their neighbors uncongenial.[30]

Among a sample of Puerto Ricans, Hollingshead and Rogler discovered much the same distrust of fellow tenants (or *potential* fellow tenants) in public housing.[31] Only 7% of the husbands in public housing think it is a good place to raise children, while 38% in a matched sample of slumdwellers think this of their area.[32] 86% of the men and 71% of the women dislike their public housing, while

---

28   For a theoretical discussion of utopias whose conclusions strongly support my current assertions, see Rosabeth Moss Kanter, "Commitment and Social Organization: A Study of Commitment Mechanisms in Utopian Communities," *American Sociological Review,* Vol. 33 (1968): pp. 499-517.

29   Michael Young and Peter Willmott, *Family and Kinship in East London,* Baltimore: Pelican Books, 1962 (orig. ed. 1957), pp. 121 ff.

30   Chester Hartman, "The Limitations of Public Housing: Relocation Choices in a Working-Class Community," *Journal of the American Institute of Planners,* Vol. 24 (1963): pp. 283-296.

31   August B. Hollingshead and Lloyd Rogler, "Attitudes Toward Slums and Public Housing in Puerto Rico," in Leonard Duhl (ed.), *The Urban Condition,* New York: Basic Books, 1963, pp. 229-245.

32   *Ibid.,* p. 239.

only 35% of the slumdwellers feel this way.[33] At the root of these feelings in this case is the belief that their neighbors will report any slip they might make with respect to the myriad of rules which badger the resident of public housing in Puerto Rico (and elsewhere).

Thus there is a decided *feeling* of heterogeneity among residents of public housing in many places, even if objective data could prove otherwise.

Moreover, even though there may be turnover in the units, there is little to bring people together for mutual aid. They must not make repairs or alterations to their apartments themselves, and their dependence on the city or other level of government is underscored by a welter of regulations. Indeed it often takes promotion of a conflict situation by professional community organizers to bring out a common goal to serve as the basis for organization.

One exception sheds light on this generalization. Bellin and Kriesberg discovered in Syracuse, New York, that husbandless mothers have three to four times the neigboring in public housing as outside it. These are people who *have* a well defined need for mutual assistance, and there are more likely to be people within the same building who are in the same boat in public than in private housing. Significantly, in the four projects studied, an appreciably higher number of husbandless mothers than regular mothers (55% to 40%) put a value on friendliness in neighbors.[34]

In what are normally termed luxury apartments, proximity appears to have little effect on friendship patterns. Again, perceived homogeneity and a need for mutual aid are lacking. While residents may appear homogeneous with respect to superficial economic criteria, they do not perceive this. They are more likely to be cosmopolitan in their urban contacts, and they seldom have even the common possession of children as interests shared with neighbors. They also pride themselves on their *lack* of dependence on neighbors, often a function of newlywed status or, later in life, economic affluence. They *desire* to be on their own.

---

33 *Ibid.*, p. 238.

34 Seymour Bellin, and Louis Kriesberg, "Informal Social Relations of Fatherless Families: A Study of Public Housing and Social Mobility," paper delivered to the 1965 Annual Meeting of the American Sociological Association, Chicago.

Only among young singles or families with children in private rental accommodations have I heard reports in North America of any significant neighboring in high rise buildings, and this is very much a function of perceived homogeneity and certain mutual needs. Reports from Australia strongly support the necessity of perceived homogeneity and mutual need as a function of active neighborhood interaction in such settings.[35]

SUMMARY

In short, spatial proximity often based on the position and outlook of doors may determine interaction patterns, but this normally occurs only under conditions of real or perceived homogeneity in the population and where there is a need for mutual aid, which is in many instances caused by population turnover where residents themselves cope with repairs and like problems.

This Chapter concludes this section on evidence of the relationships between social phenomena and the urban physical environment. In the concluding chapter, which constitutes Section III, I shall first take a short look back at the conclusions found throughout Section II and evaluate briefly the state of knowledge on this subject. Then I shall look ahead to the possibilities and some strategies for increasing knowledge of man and his urban environment.

35   A. Stevenson, E. Martin, and J. O'Neill, *High Living: A Study of Family Life in Flats,* Melbourne: Melbourne University Press, 1967.

section III
where we stand

a short look back, and then ahead

9

Throughout the six chapters of Section II, I presented evidence concerning the relationship of selected aspects of the physical environment to particular social characteristics and activities of people. The literature was diffuse and the research was not always conclusive. Nonetheless, a number of tentative conclusions emerged.

Collated from the various chapters, these findings are as follows:

1. Intense, frequent association with a wide range of relatives thrives in areas in which many people have easy physical access to each other, while the same people find that this style of life diminishes involuntarily in areas of low density.

2. An emphasis on the nuclear family and its joint activities is most congruent with the access of people to each other and to various activities now provided by the typical housing, open space, and land use patterns of the suburbs.

3. Active, traditionally masculine pastimes are part of home life only when the environment is structured so as to minimize the impingement of neighbors on each other.

4. Specialized interests which require co-enthusiasts are difficult to satisfy in low density areas. Adaptive behavior, often expressed in terms of kaffee klatching or organizational participation, is essential for those whose lives have previously included other people and activity but who are suddenly relatively isolated.

5. People with "cosmopolitan" life styles desire more physical separation from neighbors and place less emphasis on proximity to facilities and services than do people whose interests are "local".

6. Direct access to the outside maximizes control in child raising under conventional parent—child relationships.

7. Self-contained housing units minimize parent fostering of children's inhibitions.

8. Adults, before and after raising children (as well as those who are childless) frequently rate centrality (i.e., access to consumer goods and services) more highly than do families with growing children.

9. The aged find greatest satisfaction in a concentration of like-aged people, particularly when they have "local" life styles and previously lived in noncohesive neighborhoods.

10. Accessibility to lively activity is also beneficial for older people.

11. The percentage of income that people will spend on good quality housing varies primarily according to their education.

12. People in different socio-economic classes have different conceptions of housing adequacy.

13. Completely random placement of working class residents among middle class neighbors results in the isolation of the former rather than in any intended, positive result.

14. Although current usages and images of the city are restricted by personal resources, no significant differences in the *preferred* form of homes, neighborhoods, and cities have been shown related to social class differences.

15. National and cultural values frequently transform the type and the use of urban spaces in any place.

16. People who highly value convenience are likely to prefer more mixed land uses and small lot sizes. People who highly value individualism prefer larger lot sizes.

17. People evaluate housing with different yardsticks, according to the type of housing.

18. People associate private open space with active family pursuits regardless of the size of the space.

19. Housing condition leads directly to social and physical pathologies only when it is desperately inadequate. Marginal improvements in housing condition have been found markedly related to few expected benefits, the most pronounced of which is a shorter duration for children's illnesses.

20. High neighborhood densities seem more related to social pathologies than crowding within dwelling units, but its effect is mediated by personal and cultural factors.

21. High noise levels are related to the incidence of diseases that involve tension.

22. Lack of ability to meet people in a place where contact can become meaningful (such as can now be found in certain types of apartment buildings) is related to an increased incidence of reported medical problems, possibly reflecting induced introversion.

23. A forced change of residence induces a psychiatric syndrome more direct than most other behavior responses to environment. This is particularly acute among people whose cultural or occupational traits (or both) are different from middle class norms.

24. Spatial proximity, often based on the position and outlook of doors, may determine interaction patterns, but this normally occurs only under conditions of real or perceived homogeneity in the population and where there is a need for mutual aid, which is in many instances caused by population turnover in situations where residents themselves cope with repairs and like problems.

What do these tentative conclusions add up to? What are the strengths and weaknesses of this body of knowledge? In the individual chapters, comments and criticisms were directed at the strength of research in specific areas. Here I shall discuss the research as a whole.

On the positive side, first, these findings provide some measure of support for the notion that particular arrangements of physical environment are congruent with some social conditions and incongruent with others: that different systems do in fact interact with one another. For example, the data on the physical settings of given life styles are particularly revealing. Yet this information goes only so far as to suggest the interrelation of a selected few variables in the systems of social science with those of the environmental system and to detail the nature of the interaction connected with this limited number of factors. It does *not* even begin to indicate the total range of social variables which are involved in interrelations with the environment.

Also on the positive side are some of the practical applications of some of these findings to the concerns of physical planners. A variety of *issues* (such as urban renewal), *principles* (such as the cluster concept), and *standards* (such as density) are put in a new light by social research. For example, planning for urban renewal must take into consideration both the relation of life style to its setting and the effects of forced change. The cluster concept must be evaluated for any proposed application with respect to how potential residents regard the use of private and public open space. Absolute density standards as they now stand are vacuous, since they lack consideration of both the actual spatial arrangement of people with respect to each other and the extent that cultural factors ameliorate or deteriorate a given spatial situation. Therefore, at least partially on the basis of findings such as these, some planning decisions are being made differently than they were before the research took place.

On the other hand, much of what has emerged is limited in scope and in time. Let me elucidate.

First, with respect to scope, people can be characterized in an infinite number of ways, each of which at least minimally affects what you otherwise know about them and can use as a basis for practical planning. Although, as suggested above, there is presently no inventory of *all* social factors that are relevant to the environment, even the broad factors reviewed in Section II give us substantially different variables which, one by one, tell us something additional about a family and its potential needs. For example, what you may assess about a particular family's housing on the basis of its life cycle stage *may* be altered to some degree when you learn of its values or its social class.

In some cases, the combination of a given condition on each of two factors represents a significant social state with respect to the environment. For example, as detailed in Chapter 4, the combination of life style and life cycle stage among the elderly with local orientations is important to practical decisions in physical environment.

Nonetheless, most of the findings now available are restricted in scope to one social factor at a time. Inasmuch as these social factors are major ones and reflect the prominent features of specific situations which sociologists and physical designers may encounter, the limited scope of the individual bits of knowledge does not render them valueless. One would expect that the mosaic would not look otherwise once the more subtle details are combined with these highlights, but this is an empirical question. In any case, the scope gained by viewing social factors severally is virtually missing from this body of knowledge.

With respect to limitations in time, much current research tying together social problems and physical environment relies on a snapshot image at one point in time. What has mainly been ignored is the dynamic process of adjustment between the two. Some problems may vanish with exposure to new surroundings; others may appear. Exactly how people adapt to a variety of specific changes in their environment, as opposed to their first confrontation with them, is valuable but scarce information.

These limitations in scope and time are illustrated by mention of just a few questions that stem directly from the findings sketched above. It is difficult to put a value on one piece of knowledge as opposed to another, but it is obvious to me that the unanswered questions are no less important than those which now have answers. They point to urgent research efforts which must make sense out of what we now know just as they identify potential social problems in planning.

1.   What happens to the North American father's image and activities when "frontier" housing conditions cease to be even unrealistic expectations? Is there a new, sedentary, indoor life style? What effect does this have on the raising of future generations? What extra-residential substitutes are used if a person can't play an expected role in his own dwelling?

2.   Can't a family unit contain within itself contradictory residential needs? For example, aren't the lacks in suburban residence a partial impetus for young adults to split off from their families at the earliest opportunity?

3.   What changes in the concept of "family accommodation" are occasioned by the mother who works every day?

4.   To what extent would high rise improve as a location for family living with (a) expensive sound insulation, (b) children's facilities within control distance from the parent, and/or (c) more tenant responsibility for maintenance and remodelling.

5. What is the "tipping point" in class difference between neighbours such that on one side they will interact and, on the other, ignore each other?

6. Taking as an assumption current notions that neighborhood integration should properly involve residentially separate groups of people who meet on the common turf of facilities and schools, what sizes should each of the separate blocs be, and at what ratio should they mix?

7. To what extent does the threshold of housing aspiration *rise* with exposure to improved housing?

8. Do people *learn* to seek certain *ends* from their housing (apart from their overt housing preferences)? Can they learn to achieve these ends through *other means*? For example, can public open space accumulate functions traditionally performed on private lots?

9. What is the ability for humans to adapt to higher densities? What form does a positive response take?

10. Will people suffer a psychiatric syndrome if the local group with whom personal ties are strongly established moves *en masse* to a new and viable but functionally equivalent environment, despite being forced to move?

An *ultimate* need is to be in a position to weigh social problems inherent in planning with economic, political, technological and other problem areas impinging on decision-making, but each area must have its own house in order as a prerequisite. This is obviously not yet the case on the social side.

THE FRONTIERS OF ACTION AND RESEARCH

It is this relative state of knowledge of social problems in planning within the context of important unanswered questions that led a recent correspondent to bemoan to me that "The frontier of action is moving much faster than the frontier of social science thinking."

My correspondent is undoubtedly correct. Departures from past practices in physical development are increasing. A great deal of money, private and public, is staked on the appropriateness of innovations. Given the state of knowledge on man and his urban environment, however, these decisions have had to be made largely on the basis of concerned observation and good guesses.

Let me mention a few examples of bold ventures fraught with question marks which coincide with some of the gaps apparent in our analysis of social science knowledge. First, to continue with a concept from an earlier discussion, it is fashionable for new communities, both privately and publicly financed, to utilize the cluster concept: minimal, if any, open space under private control in exchange for extensive public open space. For example, Reston, Virginia uses this concept. Kanata, near Ottawa, was built on this plan, and Edgely, on the fringe of Toronto, will be so built. Yet little is known about how people (of many descriptions) regard and use this space as compared to more common chunks of private open space. The well-heeled, intellectual residents of Reston speak glowingly of their surroundings, but their numbers to date have been disappointingly small.

Satellite communities, with a balance of land uses are strongly championed by some. It is assumed, as a basis for tranquil and efficient living, that people who live in a satellite community also work there, and vice versa. Yet, except where there is a strong central control over both, such as in Great Britain, this rule seems honored in the breach. Some of my students found the overwhelming majority of residents of Bramalea, a new "suburban city" with plentiful industry near Toronto, to be commuters, although judgment on that venture is undoubtedly premature.[1] But it raises the question as to what meaning satellite towns in North America have for their residents, other than as a source of needed housing.

A third bold venture near Toronto alone is in the field of transportation: the GO Transit System, supplying fast, regular, suburban rail service both East and West of the city center. It is an example of a new rapid transit facility run with government subsidy to alleviate commuting pains among suburbanites working in the central city. A large volume of research is being conducted on what impact such a system has on commuters' choice of mode of transportation and on land values in metropolitan Toronto and vicinity. To assess the potential reception of additional GO systems, however, one would need to know what are the interests and characteristics of people induced to move near and use GO transit. Not every resident of Toronto necessarily associates the benefits of far suburban residence with the pleasant but not markedly inexpen-

---

1   Term papers by Henry Lammers and Kathy McCormick.

sive nor fast ride on the GO train. It is an open question as to whether the "social market" for a GO system is fully tapped by one, two, five, or ten GO systems.

I have no bones to pick with Reston, Kanata, Edgely, Bramalea, or GO. I'm glad to see the frontier of action advance. We can not stop needed development to wait for research to catch up. However, since understanding the effects of innovations depends in part on *social* research, there is no excuse for the frontier of social thought to be a yard removed from the frontier of action. No matter how daring any new development may now seem, it will not be the last frontier of action, and the others have every right to benefit from it. Moreover, the same vehicle can serve to advance the states of both action and research.

A MARRIAGE OF FRONTIERS

What I suggest is that basic research must become an integral part of ongoing planning and development. There is probably no argument these days about research accompanying large-scale public demonstration projects such as GO transit, although this research is now largely confined to pragmatic, operational questions.[2] However, while these types of project are ideally suited for evaluation, planning programs do not have to be large or dramatic to contain unproven assumptions and the raw material from which to learn about the adjustment of people to environment for both theoretical and practical gain. Our efforts to simply keep up with the population, performed with care but under duress, contain the stuff to help us avoid making the same mistakes twice; what suggestions for improvements in the design of physical accommodations for a given clientele can be gained from a study at one point in time can be "fed back" into the design of the next development and then tested to see if they were correct.

We must simply turn our attention to a thorough and regular followup analysis of current physical developments. And I feel that this should be guided by the intersystem congruence model.

---

2   See, for example, Michel Chevalier, "A Programme of Adaptive Performance," *Community Planning Review,* Vol. 14, no. 2 (1964): pp. 18-22. As this book goes to press, more than a year from the time this paragraph was first written, additional research on GO is under way.

Yet now, particularly in architecture, there is precious little followup of all but the largest scale developments. The "architectural experiment" is typically a mental search—based on individual creativity, architectural trends, and casual insight—for the best solution to a given set of problematic social, economic, and physical circumstances. The experiment ends once the solution is proposed; it seldom continues after the building is built, so as to see if the solution in fact works. A rather extreme statement of this situation emerged from a recent conference:

"I have never," said Mr. Doblin, "seen an architect go into a building he designed to do an analysis of it, to see how it was functioning after it was up."[3]

The knowledge to be gained from such experimentation must cease to appear as a potential source of indictment to individual architects and planners. It can be viewed more positively as a source of knowledge that would further their creation of better products. It is a tool working *for* them in the long run.

There is one implicit assumption running through this argument as well as through all of Section II: that *what a researcher can learn of the relationship of man and environment in the present and through the past is of some relevance to the future.* This assumption must be made explicit and more detailed. Of what relevance is *current* research to *future* urban design?

CURRENT RESEARCH FOR FUTURE CITIES[4]

The basic concepts to represent the physical environment, which I stressed in Chapter 2 need to be developed according to six criteria and faithful to the ego-centered point of view, are intended to be meaningful physical units, the *end process* of design. But if spatial units are the ends of design, then technology is the means.

---

3   Cited by Eric Larrabee, "Summary of the Proceedings," in Laurence B. Holland (ed.), *Who Designs America?*, Garden City, N.Y., Doubleday Anchor Books, 1966, p. 331.

4   This section of Chapter 9 is based in large part on my interpretation, "Urban Sociology as an Aid to Urban Physical Development: Some Research Strategies," *Journal of the American Institute of Planners*, Vol. 34 (1968): pp. 105-108.

At any given time, the ways in which people know how to create spatial separations are limited. For example, most people can conceive of freedom from many kinds of unwanted impingements only in terms of a single-family home on a large lot in an all-residential neighborhood. Yet, there is no saying that this is the only means of producing spatial separation. At a future time, the same kind of spatial unit may be created by a vastly changed technology. Moshe Safdie *claimed* to have created it by quite different means in Habitat 67 in Montreal, although some will disagree as to whether or not he succeeded. Hence, while arrangements of space are created by particular technologies, they exist independent of any one technology—present or future.

The phenomenon that I believe social scientists can study productively is how various kinds of people adjust to the various kinds of spatial separations that abound today. This will carry meaning for the planning of future cities because a huge variety of spatial separations that are likely to represent the overwhelming majority of spatial separations that future technologies will create can be found *today* in bits and pieces throughout the world. What *new* developments offer is significant *concentrations* of patterns of space designed today for modern social ends. To this extent they are worthy of special research emphasis but not to the total exclusion of other, existing developments.

What the future will bring is a multiplicity of new ways of *creating* spatial separations. For, even if the apparent promise of unlimited technological progress is only minimally fulfilled, we can expect great changes in the way designers shape space in cities. New building techniques abound. New types of transportation make fairly recent science fiction seem outmoded. There is certainly no basis for suggesting that our current stock of buildings should remain in toto the yardstick for future policies.

Thus our ends are predominantly with us now, but our means will change. Social scientists can aid the development of housing by identifying the spatial separations that current research shows most easily accommodate various subsectors of the population. They can and should study the success with which physically different homes and neighborhoods accommodate different social groups. Section II indicates a bare beginning to the achievement of these two goals. Then, inasmuch as the rudimentary evidence now on hand indicates that physical surroundings do make a difference as a limiting and

Man and his urban environment

encouraging factor in people's lives, a product of this work, as applied to any city in particular, would be a distribution of types of desirable spatial separations for the city's residents, which designers could use as a starting point for their plans.

Note that the social scientists are not determining the design or construction of homes, neighborhoods, or cities from their research. They are, rather, offering suggestions for optimal spatial arrangements with consideration for stated criteria of mental health, family and community organization, and the like. The physical designer, on his part, must now come forward with the most efficient physical means to produce the requisite spatial units. He is no longer required to play amateur sociologist, psychologist, or the like, but he is taxed with the challenge of creating a given spatial structure by means that he or his city can afford and which are politically acceptable. In making his role explicit, the division of labor I suggest puts a greater—not a lesser—burden of innovation on the designer than he has now.

In short, social scientists can produce informed estimates of the spatial needs of future construction as a result of their present studies, providing that they study human behavior in conjunction with the most basic concepts of space. This will aid experts in design by enabling them to concentrate on the most desirable means to the spatial ends.

Such a concentration of the social scientists' efforts will change the usual conception of their role in the design field from conservative to more neutral researcher. Sociological studies relating to design commonly demonstrate, among other things, attachment of people to their present environment, be it urban ghetto or suburban home. The sociologist, therefore, appears to be defending the continued existence of a physical situation that many designers don't happen to like. It is a much happier service for the sociologist to be able to point to spatial components of a ghetto or an estate which, created by more "acceptable" means, could accommodate the same people as well or better.

The thrust of this argument, then, is that it is profitable to study what now exists in order to benefit what will be built in the future. As the preceding discussion suggests, to be successful, such research must include sites chosen carefully for their relevance in both social and spatial terms; innovative developments are, as stated, highly relevant in this regard. But, in addition, the methodology of successful research in this area must be carefully considered. While there is no single foolproof method, some approaches may be more promising than others. I should like to outline below a few selected research techniques which appear to have some degree of potential, discussing them with respect to the two complimentary approaches to study described at the end of Chapter 1—experiential congruence and mental congruence.

Experiential congruence of people and environment is the research approach that is basically needed to form specific physical plans for the future. Nonetheless, a knowledge of mental congruence is necessary to assess the public's predisposition to accept and make successful whatever may be proposed; to ignore this factor is to invite failure, no matter how objectively correct future plans may be. I shall outline a few research strategies that I believe are particularly well suited to the empirical study of the interrelations of social and physical phenomena.

STUDYING MENTAL CONGRUENCE

Research on the mental congruence between people and their urban environment has centered around survey research. The gathered opinions of large numbers of individuals differs from the types of data used to describe spatially determined aggregates in traditional ecological research. What do people *think* about aspects of their housing and cities? What are their preferences? Past surveys have shown both the problems and the promise of this approach.

The problems stem from the difficulty of obtaining information through a finite series of questions which shows how a respondent rates many variables in a complex substantive area in relation to each other. In one study, for example, respondents were asked to rate the importance they attached to specific elements of the environment on a three-point scale (1 = unimportant, 2 = somewhat important, and 3 = very important); every element suggested was rated on the average at least somewhat important, and most of them received a plurality of ratings as very important.[5] How should one establish "real" importance? Or comparative importance?

---

5   Richard A. Lamanna, "Value Consensus Among Urban Residents," *Journal of the American Institute of Planners,* Vol. 30 (Nov. 1964), pp. 317-323.

The semiprojective game situation offers a fruitful approach to mental congruence. Within the context of the intensive interview it is possible to set up hypothetical situations in which people can get involved. When playing the game, people are forced to make a limited number of choices among elements whose relative importance the researcher is attempting to judge; the reasons given for the decisions made are of interest to the researcher, who wants to see if many people make the same choices in order to gain the same goal.

Wilson, for example, conducted a game in studying two southern cities in which respondents were supplied with a limited amount of play money and were forced to spend it judiciously among a variety of elements which constituted the nature of a neighborhood and were present or absent, distant or close, as determined by the respondent's expenditure.[6] He forced people, through a familiar medium, to declare the relative importance to themselves of various aspects of the environment. In this game, they couldn't declare themselves in favor of everything; they had to weigh the elements carefully in order to demonstrate their preferences.

In my own research, as a part of intensive interviews, I had each respondent draw a sketch map of his ideal environment, from housing type to lot size to block and on outwards to the placement of activities in appropriate places through what they later designated as their neighborhood and the rest of the city. Examples of these maps were shown in Chapter 3. One question that I set out to answer was the relative importance to people of these different *levels* of environment. Hence I asked the respondents to rank aspects of the sketch (home, block, neighborhood, and city), in which they had invested time and thought, with respect to their relative values to them. But rather than to ask for simple rankings, which are difficult for an honest respondent if the alternatives are many or complex, I had them choose between pairs of all the dichotomous combinations of the four levels ("If you could have *either* the (e.g., *home*) you want *or* the (e.g., *neighborhood*), which would you choose?") By this technique the continuing importance of the neighborhood (though not any single conception of it) in urban areas was brought out, a finding that agrees with Wilson's.

---

6   Robert L. Wilson, "Livability of the City: Attitudes and Urban Development," in F. Stuart Chapin, Jr., and Shirley Weiss (eds.), *Urban Growth Dynamics*, New York: John Wiley & Sons, 1962, pp. 359-399. See also Chapin's game on allocation of time in F. Stuart Chapin, Jr., *Urban Land Use Planning* 2nd ed., Urbana: University of Illinois Press, 1965, pp. 250-252.

In short, in a realm where opinion is important but where traditionally straightforward questions may be inadequate, the semiprojective game situation may be a source of needed data.

This volume has not emphasized perception. Yet it is worth noting that serious efforts to assess what people notice and use as guides about their cities have used one type of a projective test—mapping—in a number of instances.[7] Mapping gives respondents the opportunity to select or emphasize one or more elements of the environment as they see fit and to place these elements on paper in the order in relation to one another that they "know" them. The result, in addition, is a permanent record suitable for analysis in comparison with other maps. Mapping, nonetheless, is a relatively unrefined technique, and there are many options available that seek to cope with variations in the respondent's ability to draw maps.[8]

STUDYING EXPERIENTIAL CONGRUENCE

The study of experiential congruence by its definition involves activity and not opinion. Hence, research into this aspect demands straightforward but comprehensive accounting of behavior asserted to be congruent with particular types of spatial arrangements under conditions of exposure to those environments. Research design and techniques are both critical in this context.

The design of the research must specify that the systematic relationships recorded are related to the environment and not to some spurious factor.

As Parr put this crucial matter of study design:

We must look for situations and methods of inquiry that will allow us to compare empirical field observations on the assumption that a single factor—or at most only a few—has so predominated in the

---

7   See, for example, Peter Orleans, "Urban Experimentation and Urban Sociology," paper presented to the 1967 Annual Meeting of the National Academy of Sciences, Washington, D.C.; Kevin Lynch, *The Image of the City*, Cambridge, Mass.: The M.I.T. Press, 1960; Charles Tilly, "Anthropology on the Town," *Habitat*, Vol. 10, no. 1, (1967): pp. 20-25, and Carl Steinitz, "Meaning and the Congruence of Urban Form and Activity," *Journal of the American Institute of Planners*, Vol. 34 (1968): pp. 233-248.

8   See the discussion of this in Peter Orleans, "Sociology and Environmental Planning: A Scalar Perspective," paper presented to the 1968 Annual Meeting of the American Sociological Association, Boston, Mass.

determination of the recorded phenomena that the infinite diversity of other, and minor, influences may be omitted from quantitative consideration in the first approximation. And we must design experiments that enable us to confine the variability of environment to one feature at a time, while bearing in mind that changes in the variable feature may also alter the response to the constant elements.[9]

All this argues for the relevance of the classic experimental design for research bearing on the environment. What this involves is the study of more than one group at a time, with the only difference between them (or at least, the only significant one) being the factor whose effect is to be measured. For example, to assess the effect of a new form of cul-de-sac on people valuing privacy, one might study two groups: one of which would be living in or moving to the new cul de sac arrangement, while the other would not. Otherwise the people would ideally be in the same social class, share similar life styles and values, have the same stage in the life cycle, be moving for the same reasons, etc. Given sufficient *control* over all variables other than exposure to the new cul de sacs, one would then attribute such differences in adjustment as are found between the groups to exposure to the new cul de sac.

The ideal experimental situation would be the one involving movers, since it incorporates before-and-after observations. It is not surprising that some of the most suggestive research in this area comes from before-and-after studies of urban renewal "victims."[10]

A diagram of this research design is as follows:

Before	Stimulus	After
A	↓	A^1
B		B^1

Stimulus effect = $A^1 - B^1$

$(A = B)$

---

9 A. E. Parr, "Environmental Design and Psychology," reprinted from *Landscape*, Vol. 14 (Winter 1964-65): re-print, p. 2.

10 See, for example, Chester Hartman, "The Consequences of Relocation for Housing Welfare," in James Q. Wilson (ed.), *Urban Renewal: The Record and the Controversy*, Cambridge, Mass.: M.I.T., 1966, pp. 293-335; Marc Fried, "Grieving for a Lost Home," in Leonard Duhl (ed.), *The Urban Condition*, New York: Basic Books, 1963, pp. 151-171; Michael Young and Peter Willmott, *Family and Kinship in East London*, London: Routledge and Kegan Paul, 1957; and Daniel M. Wilner and Rosabelle P. Walkley, "Effects of Housing on Health and Performance," in Leonard Duhl (ed.), *The Urban Condition*, N.Y.: Basic Books, 1962, pp. 215-228.

It is assumed on the basis of as much information as can be gathered that A is equal to B at the onset. Both may, for example, be residents of the same area who are about to move. Only A, however, is subjected to the stimulus—moving to the particular cul de sacs. Then, when measured after the stimulus has occurred or begun, the difference between the groups $(A^1 - B^1)$ is that attributed to the stimulus.

Somewhat less than ideal is the case in which two groups deemed originally equal are viewed only at the "after" point in time. In this case, one must *assume* that A equaled B originally, since this cannot be observed empirically. Given this assumption, the rest of the research approach is similar to the ideal design. But even in the ideal scheme it is always an open question as to whether it *really* was the stimulus that accounted for the inter-group differences and not still an untapped variable; in the incomplete design the tentativeness of conclusions is even greater.

	Stimulus	After only	
(A)	↓	A^1	Stimulus effect = $A^1 - B^1$
(B)		B^1	$(A) \stackrel{?}{=} (B)$

Newly built developments are well suited to natural experiments according to this design. They assume the part of Group A in the above diagrams, inasmuch as they are likely to contain physical features that are innovative and whose effects are to be measured. Since it should be possible to match the population moving to the new development with those in surroundings that contrast with respect to one or two major aspects, then the makings are available for the natural experiment.

In this approach, the types of people are held constant and the environment is controlled. Sampling would be overtly based on the physical factors under study, given matching on the social factors. However, the opposite approach is also feasible. To study the congruence or incongruence of social and physical factors, one may study people who are in exactly the same type of environment but differ in one or two respects on social variables. This latter approach, though, may be more difficult to carry through, since there may be fewer appropriate cases available for study as housing is now allocated in North America.

Obviously, research designs utilizing natural experiments may be even more complex. For example, the effects of *two* factors can be explored by the study of four groups both before and after. In any case, the major point to be emphasized is that there may be found right now, in new and existing developments, the raw materials for knowledge that will be useful for the future, which can be refined by the classical experimental method without the necessity to depart from real life into the laboratory or to build developments merely for study. What's needed for study is *there* and *happening*.

While observations before and after the onset of a stimulus or a condition are valuable, viewing these phenomena over a significantly long time period and gathering data at many different times is even more fruitful for the study of experiential congruence. This is called the longitudinal (or panel) study. For example, longitudinal studies of movers can potentially answer a number of questions crucial to planners and sociologists alike:

1.   To what extent does a particular residential environment tend to attract a particular type of resident? When selecting a new home, do people envisage how they will lead their lives after moving?

2.   To what extent do people carry out the lives they intended to lead in their new environments? What factors prevent the execution of preconceived plans? Could these factors be modified by the provision of appropriate facilities or services?

3.   To what extent does a particular way of life become pronounced in a particular physical setting? Do aspects of the environment influence what people do, with whom they do it, and where they do it; or, all else being equal, do they merely repeat the round of life that they formerly pursued in a physically different environment? What consequences do answers to the foregoing questions have for the differential provision of facilities and activities?

4.   If a typical way of life emerges in a particular setting, what happens to the new resident who fails to adopt it? Does he tend to

Time (am)	What doing?	Who else?	Where?	Doing anything else?	Typical
6:00					
6:15					
6:30					
6:45					
7:00					
7:15					
7:30					
7:45					
8:00					
8:15					
8:30					
8:45					

Begin by asking the respondent the time he (she) got up that morning and what he did first. Ask how long this activity took and then record it on the sheet at the appropriate times. Ask whether or not anyone was with the person when he did it; determine whether the presence of the other individual(s) was incidental or whether he was asked to accompany the respondent so that it was really an interaction process. Ask where the activity took place and whether or not the respondent was doing anything else at the time. If a person goes to a store or somewhere, be sure to check the time to store, shopping, and home again. Finally, ask the respondent what he did next and then repeat the above line of questioning. **Do not attempt to record what was being done at each time given on the sheet;** rather use the sheet simply as a method of calendaring the day's activities.

The minimum time span to be considered for an activity is 15 minutes. Record start and stop time to the nearest quarter hour. Do not record for any activity that is less than a quarter hour.

Time spent travelling to or from an activity is a separate activity and should not be included with that activity.

Fig. 1 A sample time budget.

move? Does he tend to develop problems of varying degrees of seriousness? Or, on the other hand, are some typical patterns only a statistical phenomenon, unrelated to successful adjustment to the residential environment? Is there any way to identify the potential malcontent before his move?

5. Does it take longer for people to adjust to some settings than to others? What problems typically emerge in specific settings during particular time periods after settlement, and could they be remedied if anticipated?

Thus the natural experiment utilizing a longitudinal perspective may be a design well suited for environmental studies, one not generally part of the ecological repertoire.

Since I am suggesting the relevance in this context of survey methods within imaginative study designs, it is evident that I consider a very wide and also very standard range of sociological and psychological research techniques to have potential value.

This is certainly not a methodology textbook, and it is not possible to discuss the details of survey research in these pages.[11] Yet one type of survey gives evidence of great relevance to experiential congruence. Since it is underutilized, it deserves special mention. Like panel design, the *time and activity budget* focuses on time; only in this case the focus is on use of time, rather than on its progression.

The time budget is a technique for eliciting accurate descriptions of behavior, not opinion. The researcher asks his respondents for an account of *what* they did on the weekday before and in finely divided periods of time, *where*, and *with whom* the activity took place (see Fig. 1). By such relatively straightforward means, the researcher can ascertain the qualitative *and* quantitative aspects of social activity as well as its spatial distribution, together with the

---

11 See, for example, Leon Festinger and Daniel Katz (eds.), *Research Methods in the Behavioral Sciences*, New York: Holt, Rinehart, and Winston, 1953; William J. Goode and Paul K. Hall, *Methods in Social Research*, New York: McGraw-Hill, 1952; Fred N. Kerlinger, *Foundations of Behavioral Research*, New York: Holt, Rinehart, and Winston, 1965; Matilda White Riley, *Sociological Research*, New York: Harcourt, Brace, and World, 1963; Claire Selltiz *et al, Research Methods in Social Relations*, New York: Holt, Rinehart, and Winston, rev. ed. 1964; and Pauline Young, *Scientific Social Surveys and Research*, Englewood Cliffs, N.J.: Prentice-Hall, 3rd. ed., 1956.

necessary information to construct interaction networks and other aspects of social structure.[12] While participant observation and poll-type interviewing can give *glimpses* of the same data, time and activity budgets can serve as the basis for extremely fine environmental comparisons in time and space which can be greatly aided by contemporary computer technology. Diaries, such as have been used in traffic studies, are similarly helpful; but cooperation may be more difficult to obtain in their use, particularly if longer periods of time are covered or if they are used on repeated occasions.

Researchers have also used existing maps and reproductions of aerial photographs as surfaces on which people can detail their daily activity patterns.[13]

But although I have stressed survey techniques used in sociological and psychological research, I do not wish to ignore the insights offered by some anthropological techniques. These techniques are largely nonreactive; the researcher does not *formally*

---

12   See, for example, Chapin, *Urban Land Use Planning*, and some examples of the use of this tool in Albert J. Reiss, "Rural Urban and Status Differences in Interpersonal Contacts," *American Journal of Sociology*, Vol. 65 (1959), pp. 182-195, and F. Stuart Chapin, Jr., and Henry C. Hightower, *Household Activity Systems—A Pilot Investigation*, Chapel Hill: University of North Carolina, Center for Urban and Regional Studies, 1966. In this study, the authors apply fruitfully the concept of activity systems to physical planning, but in a different context than the above suggestion, namely that it could be used to compare the "effects" of contemporary physical environments which differ physically. An expert implementation of this tool can be found in the current "Boston Housing Study" of Charles Tilly. This technique has recently been accorded increased interest, as evidenced by the worldwide studies of time coordinated by Dr. Alexander Szalai of UNITAR which were presented at the 1966 meeting of the International Sociological Association at Evion, France and published as the December 1966 issue of *The American Behavioral Scientist*.

13   Great amounts of research utilizing some of the most advanced versions of these techniques are under way in Scandanavia at, among other places, Institutionen for Byggnadsfunctionslära in Lund, Sweden, Statens Institut for Byggnadsforskning and Generalplaneberedningen in Stockholm, Norges Byggforskningsinstitutt and Norsk Institutt for By-og Regionforskning in Oslo, and Statens Byggeforskningsinstituttet in Copenhagen. The need for such an approach is stressed by R. E. Pahl, in "A Perspective on Urban Sociology," in his *Readings in Urban Sociology*, London: Pergamon Press, 1968, pp. 3-44.

request anything of his respondents.[14] Tilly, for example, points out several types of observation that say something about how people live in given settings:

Count the proportion of door-buttons pushed down in automobiles in the street in order to see how willing people are to leave their cars unlocked;

notice how many backyards in a neighborhood contain grass, how many flower gardens, how many trash piles, and how many vegetable patches, to get an idea of the local style of life;

check the percentage of blinds which are drawn, to judge how much people are shutting themselves off from others on the street;

notice how many liquor bottles are thrown out on trash day, and what kind, to guess the home drinking patterns;

record how many houses have outside Christmas decorations, and how elaborate they are, to gauge how much it is an occasion for public display.[15]

What the anthropologist contributes to the study of experiential congruence is not "hard" data (i.e., quantitative and systematic) like that from time budgets and some other types of surveys. But the insights this "softer" type of data afford are valuable as complementary information. They help the researcher to interpret and understand the trends stemming from large scale survey coverage of an area with which he may not be personally acquainted.

In some cases it is possible for researchers to themselves live in the urban quarters under study, so as to share many of the personal experiences of residents of the area as well as to maintain 24-hour surveillance over the streets and their people. Their observations are thought more complete, detailed, and accurate than those of the average man in the street due to the rigor introduced by anthropological points of view and methods. But in the many cases in which residence in the study area is impossible for a researcher, nonreactive techniques are worth pursuing on their own.

---

14 See, for example, Eugene J. Webb et al, Unobtrusive Measures: Nonreactive Research in the Social Sciences, Chicago: Rand McNally, 1966.
15 Charles Tilly, "Anthropology on the Town," Habitat, Vol. 10, no. 1 (1967): p. 24.

In any case, some of the more insightful studies have *combined* "hard" and "soft" types of data[16]—an ideal parallel to having a complete natural experimental design.

TO ORGANIZE FUTURE EFFORTS

To this point, I have suggested the following state of affairs:

1.   The research on hand and synthesized in Section II supports the intersystems congruence model of man and environments, and it has valuable practical applications.

2.   Nonetheless, this research is extremely limited in both time and scope.

3.   While the frontier of action is now ahead of the frontier of research, the same developments can be used as the vehicle for the advancement of both.

4.   Current and past research *is* relevant for future design.

5.   Specified research strategies and techniques appear fruitful for the necessary study of both mental and experiential congruence of man and environment.

I have not said anything about *who* could most profitably conduct the needed research. Yet even the most strongly supported ideas may fail to be implemented if the organizational context is inadequate.

I do not believe that the present research task can be accomplished solely under the present organization of social science research with respect to physical design. There are several reasons for this.

First, most research in this area is done on an *ad hoc* basis. Researchers within planning agencies must normally function on a firefighting basis, responding to hurried calls for help. Longer range research, when done, is hampered by the constant and valid need to put out fires. Academics, on the other hand, rarely have research budgets. They must justify their efforts to granting agencies on a

---

16   For example, see the myriad of publications stemming from the West End Study (of Boston) and the study of Levittown, New Jersey—in both of which Herbert Gans participated. See his references in the bibliography as well as those of Marc Fried, Chester Hartman, and Edward Ryan.

year-to-year basis, with demonstrated results at frequent intervals; this process serves to limit the comprehensiveness of research undertaken.

Second, for social scientists to undertake research on planning topics, they almost always have to work with an agency other than their own. This tends to restrict initial contact, inadvertently prevent the communication of needed information, and in any case stand in the way of long term commitment to these subjects. Social researchers within planning agencies, on the other hand, are generally more expert in planning than in any given social science and are less likely to envisage the needed research, even if free to pursue it.

Third, research which delves into questions of man and his urban environment must, as stressed in this chapter, involve the study of large numbers of people in carefully chosen situations over significant periods of time in order to be sensitive and accurate. Such conditions are under the span of control of large scale developers in both the public and private spheres, but not of the usual social scientist.

Finally, it is ultimately desirable to isolate situations of incongruence and their suspected physical and social sources from studies in one location and then to test whether suggested remedies work from study of the next new site. But this feedback process is beyond even the hope of the social scientist at present.

To maximize the gains to both social science and to practical design, I would urge the creation of a group within each appropriate planning and design staff, whose sole function is the *review* of social consequences of developments in operation. This *social review board* would examine the functioning of housing, transportation, commercial, industrial, and other relevant developments both through time and in comparative perspective. It would see if the assumptions guiding their planning were correct. It would assess social problems developing in their wake. It would propose lines for future development. It would follow up these phenomena continuously with every wave of decision. And in so doing it would accumulate theoretical evidence on the interrelations of the environmental system with the systems of traditional social science.

There is no question that a social review board on every staff making large scale environmental decisions would have a wealth of materials from which to draw crucial knowledge. Somewhat more problematic, however, is the funding and staffing of such boards.

Social scientific research, properly done, can be expensive. At a time when support for such research is relatively low, the cost of a large-scale onslaught appears tremendous. But it is dwarfed by the amount spent on the construction of the facilities in question and even their operating deficits at times. When a transit system, for example, loses a million dollars a year *more* than expected, can not one consider bearing the much lower cost of researchers who stand a chance of discerning the system's problems? One approach commonly used to put research costs in perspective to development costs is to budget the former at a regular percentage of the latter; somewhere around 1 to 3% has been shown to be more than adequate elsewhere.

Staffing a social review board is difficult since the skills involved are generally in short supply. But there has never been a well-known *demand* for them, nor any traditional training ground for such personnel. I do not believe the past is an accurate index of the future, though, for anyone close to universities (or who reads the mass media, for that matter) can document the growing excitement among students for training in urban affairs. Enrollments in such courses have skyrocketed, and additional courses as well as interdisciplinary graduate curricula on urban affairs have become part of university offerings. Given coordinated attention by present specialists and sufficiently publicized recruiting of young people, social review boards should not suffer from lack of personnel.

Unlike some, I am not pessimistic about the future of cities. I am confident that they will flourish in the future as they do at present, despite all the ills which they've always had. They may, however, take on radically different shapes and forms as technology advances and human demands change.

What exists at present is an unprecedented opportunity to *control* the development of the future city. Both the design professions and the social sciences have advanced to the point that talk of design for the optimal combination of urban environments for the divers individuals populating any particular city is no longer idle chatter, given a continuation of recent public interest in the control over physical chaos.

Park, Burgess, McKenzie, and their colleagues in Chicago added a new chapter to the book of social science when confronted with the enormity of the initial growth of a typical North American metropolis. Now these metropoli face a comparable watershed: they must *cope with* the results of this huge growth and maximize the quality of the life of the people who are there. A new chapter in social science remains to be written.

We must not exaggerate the importance of physical environment by itself to quality of life. Yet it is by now evident that the nature of physical environment is by no means irrelevant to people, their characteristics, and their activities. Cities can only gain by minimizing "planned incongruence" in future designs. And social science can only gain through the heightened understanding of social phenomena afforded by the additional perspective of physical setting.

To gain this knowledge, however, a new perspective on environmental research, such as outlined in Section I, may be required. Although there is both precedent and evidence in Section II for the required research, a future investment in research of task force dimensions is in order. It has been my endeavor in this concluding section to point out some promising lines of design, techniques, and organization for the study of man and his urban environment in the hope that they will hasten the advance of this research.

bibliography

bibliography

Abrams, Charles, *The City is the Frontier,* New York: Harper and Row, 1965.

——, *Forbidden Neighbors,* New York: Harper and Bros., 1955.

——, "The Uses of Land in Cities," Editors of the *Scientific American.* New York: Alfred A. Knopf, 1965, 122-132.

Abu-Lughod, Janet, "The City is Dead—Long Live the City: Some Thoughts on Urbanity," in Sylvia F. Fava (ed.), *Urbanism in World Perspective,* New York: Thomas Y. Crowell Company, 1968, 155-165.

——, "A Survey of Center-City Residents," in Nelson Foote, Janet Abu-Lughod, Mary Mix Foley, and Louis Winnick, *Housing Choices and Constraints,* New York: McGraw-Hill, 1960, 387-447.

——, "Testing the Theory of Social Area Analysis: The Ecology of Cairo, Egypt," *American Sociological Review,* Vol. 34, (April, 1969): 198-212.

Adams, Bert N., *Kinship in an Urban Setting,* Chicago: Markham Publishing Company, 1968.

Alexander, Christopher, "The City as a Mechanism for Sustaining Human Contact," in William R. Ewalt (ed.), *Environment for Man,* Bloomington: University of Indiana Press, 1967, 60-102.

——, *Notes on the Synthesis of Form,* Cambridge, Mass.: Harvard University Press, 1964.

American Public Health Association, "An Appraisal Method for Measuring the Quality of Housing," New York: The Association, 1946.

Arensberg, Conrad M., and Solon T. Kimball, *Family and Community in Ireland,* Cambridge, Mass.: Harvard University Press, 1940.

Back, Kurt, *Slums Projects and People,* Durham, N.C.: Duke University Press, 1962.

Barker, Roger G., *Ecological Psychology,* Stanford, Calif.: Stanford University Press, 1968.

_____, "Ecology and Motivation," *Current Theory and Research in Motivation,* Vol. 8 (1960): 1-49.

_____, "On the Nature of the Environment," *Journal of Social Issues,* Vol. 19, No. 4 (1963): 17-38.

_____, and Herbert F. Wright, *Midwest and its Children,* New York: Harper and Row, 1955.

Bell, Wendell, "The City, the Suburb, and a Theory of Social Choice," in Scott Greer, Dennis L. McElrath, David W. Minar, and Peter Orleans (eds.), *The New Urbanization,* New York: St. Martin's Press, 1968, 132-168.

_____, "Social Choice, Life Styles, and Suburban Residence," in William M. Dobriner (ed.), *The Suburban Community,* New York: G. P. Putnam's Sons, 1958, 225-247.

_____, and Maryanne T. Force, "Urban Neighbourhood Types and Participation in Formal Associations," *American Sociological Review,* Vol. 21 (1956): 25-34.

Bellin, Seymour, and Louis Kriesberg, "Informal Social Relations of Fatherless Families: A Study of Public Housing and Social Mobility," paper delivered to the 1965 Annual Meeting of the American Sociological Association, Chicago, Illinois.

Berger, Bennett, "Suburbs, Subcultures, and the Urban Future," in S. B. Warner, Jr. (ed.), *Planning for a Nature of Cities,* Cambridge: M.I.T. Press, 1966, 143-162.

_____, *Working Class Suburb: A Study of Auto-Workers in Suburbia,* Berkeley, California: University of California Press, 1960.

Beshers, James, *Urban Social Structure,* New York: Free Press of Glencoe, 1962.

Beyer, Glenn H., "Housing and Personal Values," Ithaca, New York: Cornell University Agricultural Expt. Station, New York State College of Home Economics Memoir 364, July, 1959.

_____, *Housing and Society,* New York: MacMillan, 1965.

Biderman, Albert, *et al, Historical Incidents of Extreme Overcrowding.* Washington, D.C.: Bureau of Social Science Research, Inc., 1963.

Blake, Robert R., Clifton C. Rhead, Bryant Wedge, and Jane S. Mouton, "Housing, Architecture, and Social Interaction," *Sociometry,* Vol. 19 (1956): 133-139.

Blumenfeld, Hans, "A Theory of City Form, Past and Present," *The Journal of the Society of Architectural Historians,* Vol. 8, nos. 3-4 (1949): 7-16.

Bott, Elizabeth, *Family and Social Network,* London: Tavistock Publications, 1957.

Calhoun, John B., "Population Density and Social Pathology," in Leonard Duhl (ed.), *The Urban Condition,* New York; Basic Books, Inc., 1963, 33-43.

Caplow, T., and R. Forman, "Neighbourhood Interaction in a Homogenous Community," *American Sociological Review.* Vol. 15 (1955): 357-366.

_____, et al, *The Urban Ambience,* Totawa, N.J.: Bedminster Press, 1964.

Carr, Stephen, "The City of the Mind," in William R. Ewalt, Jr., (ed.), *Environment for Man,* Bloomington: University of Indiana Press, 1967, 197-226.

Carstairs, George M., "Overcrowding and Human Aggression," in H. D. Graham and T. R. Gurr, *The History of Violence in America,* New York: Bantam Books, 1969, 751-763.

Case, Duncan F. (Jr.), "The Influence of Architecture on Patterns of Social Life," unpublished Junior Paper, Princeton University Department of Sociology, 1967.

Chapin, F. S., (Sr.), "The Effects of Slum Clearance on Family and Community Relationships in Minneapolis in 1935-36," *American Journal of Sociology,* Vol. 44 (Mar. 1938): 744-763.

Chapin, F. Stuart (Jr.), "Activity Systems and Urban Structure: A Working Schema," *Journal of the American Institute of Planners,* Vol. 34 (1968): 11-18.

_____, "The Relationship of Housing to Mental Health," working paper for the Expert Committee on the Public Health Aspects of Housing of the World Health Organization. June 1961.

_____, and Henry C. Hightower, "Household Activity Systems—A Pilot Investigation," Chapel Hill: University of North Carolina, Center for Urban and Regional Studies, 1966.

Chein, Isador, "The Environment as a Determinant of Behavior," *The Journal of Social Psychology,* Vol. 38 (1954): 115-127.

Clark, S. D., *The Suburban Society,* Toronto: University of Toronto Press, 1966.

Connor, Desmond M., "Selective Migration and Residence," *International Migration,* Vol. 2, no. 2 (1964): 97-106.

Craik, Kenneth H., "The Comprehension of the Everyday Physical Environment," *Journal of the American Institute of Planners,* Vol. 34 (1968): 29-37.

Dahir, James, *The Neighbourhood Unit Plan: Its Spread and Acceptance.* A Selected Bibliography with Interpretative Comments. New York: Russell Sage Foundation, 1947.

Dennis, Norman, "The Popularity of the Neighborhood Community Idea," in R. E. Pahl (ed.), *Readings in Urban Sociology,* London: Pergamon Press, 1968, 74-92.

Denton, Trevor, "Housing Norms," presented at the Annual Meeting of the Canadian Sociology and Anthropology Association, June 6, 1968.

Deutsch, Morton, and Collins, Mary Evans, *Inter-racial Housing: a Psychological Evaluation of a Social Experiment,* Minneapolis: University of Minnesota, 1951.

Dewey, Richard, "The Neighbourhood, Urban Ecology and City Planners," in Paul K. Hatt and Albert J. Reiss, Jr., *Cities and Society,* New York: The Free Press, 1957, 783.

Dore, Ronald Philip, *City Life in Japan,* London: Routledge and Kegan Paul, 1968.

Duhl, Leonard J., "Planning and Predicting: or What to Do When You Don't Know the Names of the Variables," *Daedalus,* (Summer 1967): 779-788.

Duncan, Otis Dudley, "From Social System to Eco-System," *Sociological Inquiry,* Vol. 31 (1961): 140-149.

_____ , "Social Organization and the Ecosystem," in Robert E. L. Faris (ed.), *Handbook of Modern Sociology,* Chicago: Rand McNally, 1964, 36-82.

Duncan, Otis Dudley, and Beverly Duncan, "Residential Distribution and Occupational Stratification," in Hatt and Reiss, *Cities and Society,* New York: The Free Press, 1957, 283-296.

_____ , and Stanley Lieberson, "Ethnic Segregation and Assimilation," *American Journal of Sociology,* Vol. 64 (1959): 364-374.

_____ , and Leo F. Schnore, "Cultural, Behavioral, and Ecological Perspections in the Study of Social Organization," *American Journal of Sociology,* Vol. 65 (1959): 132-146.

Eichler, Edward, and Marshall Kaplan, *The Community Builders,* Berkeley and Los Angeles: University of California Press, 1967.

Fanning, D. M., "Families in Flats," *British Medical Journal,* Vol. 18 (1967): 382-386.

Farr, Lee E., "Medical Consequences of Environmental Noises," *Journal of the American Medical Association,* Vol. 202 (1967): 171-174.

Faris, Robert E. L., and Warren Dunham, *Mental Disorders in Urban Areas,* Chicago: University of Chicago Press, 1939.

Fava, Sylvia F., "Suburbanism as a Way of Life," *American Sociological Review,* Vol. 21 (1956): 34-37.

Feldman, Arnold S., and Charles Tilly, "The Interaction of Social and Physical Space," *American Sociological Review,* Vol. 25 (1960): 877-884.

Festinger, Leon, Stanley Schachter, and Kurt Back, *Social Pressures in Informal Groups.* New York: Harper and Bros., 1950.

Firey, Walter, *Land Use in Central Boston.* Cambridge, Mass.: Harvard University Press, 1947, Ch. 8.

_____, "Sentiment and Symbolism as Ecological Variables," *American Sociological Review,* Vol. 10 (1945): 140-148.

Fleisher, L., "The Influence of Technology on Urban Form," *Daedalus,* (Winter 1961): 48-61.

Foley, D. L., "An Approach to Metropolitan Spatial Structure," in Melvin M. Webber *et al, Explorations into Urban Structure,* Philadelphia: University of Pennsylvania Press, 1964, 21-78.

_____, "The Use of Local Facilities in a Metropolis," in Hatt and Reiss, *Cities and Society,* New York: The Free Press, 1957, 607-616.

Form, W., "The Place of Social Structure in the Determination of Land Use," *Social Forces,* Vol. 32 (1954): 317-323.

Frankenberg, Ronald, *Communities in Britain,* Baltimore: Penguin Books, 1966.

Fried, Mark, "Functions of the Working Class Community in Modern Urban Society: Implications for Forced Relocation," *Journal of the American Institute of Planners,* Vol. 33 (1967): 90-103.

_____, "Grieving for a Lost Home," in Leonard J. Duhl (ed.), *The Urban Condition,* New York: Basic Books, 1963, 151-171.

_____, "Transitional Functions of Working-Class Communities: Implications for Forced Relocation," in Mildred B. Kantor (ed.), *Mobility and Mental Health,* Springfield, Ill.: Charles C. Thomas Publishers, 1965, 123-165.

_____, and Peggy Gleicher, "Some Sources of Residential Satisfaction in an Urban Slum," *Journal of the American Institute of Planners,* Vol. 27 (1961): 305-315.

Frieden, Elaine, "Social Differences and Their Consequences for Housing the Aged." *Journal of the American Institute of Planners,* Vol. 26 (1960): 119-124.

Gans, H. J., "The Balanced Community," *Journal of the American Institute of Planners,* Vol. 27 (1961): 176-184.

_____, "Effects of the Move from City to Suburb," in Leonard Duhl (ed.), *The Urban Condition,* New York: Basic Books, 1963, 184-198.

_____, "The Human Implications of Current Redevelopment and Relocation Planning," *Journal of American Institute of Planners,* Vol. 25 (1959): 15-25.

_____, *The Levittowners,* New York: Pantheon Books, 1967.

_____, "Planning—and City Planning—for Mental Health," in H. Wentworth Eldredge (ed.), *Taming Megalopolis,* Garden City, New York: Anchor Books, 1967, 887-916.

_____, "Planning and Social Life: Friendship and Neighbour Relations in Suburban Communities," *Journal of the American Institute of Planners,* Vol. 27 (1961): 134-140.

_____, "Urbanism and Suburbanism as Ways of Life: A Re-Evaluation of Definitions," in Arnold M. Rose (ed.), *Human Behavior and Social Processes,* Boston: Houghton Mifflin, 1962, 625-648.

_____, *The Urban Villagers,* New York: The Free Press of Glencoe, 1962.

Gillespie, Michael W., "The Effect of Residential Segregation on the Social Integration of the Aged," paper presented at the 1967 Annual Meeting of the American Sociological Association, San Francisco, California.

Glazer, Nathan, "Housing Problems and Housing Policies," in Jeffrey K. Hadden, Louis H. Masotti, and Calvin J. Larson (eds.), *Metropolis in Crisis,* Itasca, III.: F. E. Peacock Publishers, 1967, 234-265.

_____, "Slum Dwellings Do Not Make a Slum," *New York Times Magazine,* Nov. 21, 1965, 55 ff.

_____, and Daniel Patrick Moynihan, *Beyond the Melting Pot,* Cambridge, Mass.: M.I.T. Press and Harvard University Press, 1963.

Goffman, Erving, *The Presentation of Self in Everyday Life,* New York: The Free Press of Glencoe, 1959.

_____, *Behaviour in Public Places,* Garden City, N.Y.: Doubleday (Anchor Books), 1963.

_____, *Interaction Ritual,* Garden City, N.Y.: Doubleday (Anchor Books), 1967.

Goldblatt, Sylvia, "Integration or Isolation," *Habitat,* Vol. 9, nos. 1-2 (Jan.-Apr., 1966), 14-23.

Goodman, Paul, "Some Remarks on Neighbourhood Planning," *Journal of the American Institute of Planners,* Vol. 15 (Summer 1949): 40-43.

_____, and Percival Goodman, *Communitas,* New York: Vintage Books, rev. ed., 1960.

Gould, Peter R., "On Mental Maps," Ann Arbor: University of Michigan Inter-University Community of Mathematical Geographers, Discussion Paper No. 9, 1966.

Grebler, Leo, *Europe's Reborn Cities,* Washington, D. C.: Urban Land Institute Technical Bulletin No. 28, 1956.

Gutman, Robert, "Population Mobility in the American Middle Class," in Leonard Duhl (ed.), *The Urban Condition,* New York: Basic Books, 1963, 172-183.

_____, "The Questions Architects Ask," *Transactions of the Bartlett Society,* Vol. 4 (1965-66): 49-82.

_____, "Site Planning and Social Behavior," *Journal of Social Issues,* Vol. 22 (Oct. 1966): 103-115.

Hall, Edward T., *The Hidden Dimension,* Garden City, N. Y.: Doubleday, 1966.

_____, *The Silent Language,* Greenwich, Conn.: Premier Books, 1959.

Hartman, Chester, "The Housing of Relocated Families," in James Q. Wilson (ed.), *Urban Renewal: The Record and the Controversy,* Cambridge, Mass.: M.I.T. Press, 1966, 293-335.

_____ , "The Limitations of Public Housing: Relocation Choices in a Working-Class Community," *Journal of the American Institute of Planners,* Vol. 24 (1963): 283-296.

_____ , "Social Values and Housing Orientations," *The Journal of Social Issues,* Vol. 19 (April, 1963): 113-131.

Hawley, A., "Ecology and Human Ecology," *Social Forces,* Vol. 22 (1943-44): 398-405.

_____ , *Human Ecology,* New York: Ronald Press, 1950.

Hitchcock, John R., *Urbanness and Daily Activity Patterns,* Ph.D. dissertation, Department of City and Regional Planning, University of North Carolina, Chapel Hill, 1969.

Hole, Vere, "Social Effects of Planned Rehousing," *The Town Planning Review,* Vol. XXX, no. 2 (July, 1959): 161-173.

Holland, Lawrence B. (ed.), *Who Designs America?,* Garden City, N.Y.: Doubleday Anchor Books, 1966.

Hollingshead, August B., and Lloyd Rogler, "Attitudes Towards Public Housing in Puerto Rico," in Leonard Duhl (ed.), *The Urban Condition,* New York: Basic Books, 1963, 229-245.

Ingersoll, Phylliss Watt, "Concepts of Ideal Urban Form," *Master's Thesis in City Planning,* University of California at Berkeley, 1957.

Isaacs, Reginald, "The Neighbourhood Theory, An Analysis of its Adequacy," *Journal of the American Institute of Planners,* Vol. 14 (1948): 15-23.

Jackson, Brian, *Working Class Community,* London: Routledge and Kegan Paul, 1968.

Jacobs, Jane, *The Death and Life of Great American Cities,* New York: Random House, 1961.

Jonassen, C. T., "Cultural Variables in the Ecology of an Ethnic Group," *American Sociological Review,* Vol. 14 (1949): 32-41.

Kanter, Rosabeth Moss, "Commitment and Social Organization: A Study of Commitment Mechanisms in Utopian Communities," *American Sociological Review,* Vol. 33, (1968): 499-517.

Kantrowitz, Nathan, "Ethnic and Racial Segregation in the New York Metropolis, 1960," *American Journal of Sociology,* Vol. 74, (1969): 685-695.

Katz, Alvin, and Reuben Hill, "Residential Propinquity and Marriage Selection: A Review of Theory, Method and Fact," *Marriage and Family Living,* Vol. 20 (Feb. 1958): 27-35.

Katz, Robert D., *Intensity of Development and Livability of Multi-Family Housing Projects,* Washington, D.C.: U.S. Government Printing Office, 1963.

Keller, Suzanne, "Social Class in Physical Planning," *International Social Science Journal,* Vol. 18 (1966): 494-512.

———, *The Urban Neighbourhood,* New York: Random House, 1968.

Kendrick, J. D., "Human Factors Affecting Design of Physical Environments in Buildings," *The Medical Journal of Australia,* Vol. 2 (1967): 267-269.

Kerr, Madeleine, *The People of Ship Street,* New York: Humanities Press, 1958.

Kranzler, George, *Williamsburg: A Jewish Community in Transition,* New York: Philipp Feldheim Inc., 1961.

Kriesberg, Louis, "Neighborhood Setting and the Relocation of Public Housing Tenants," *Journal of the American Institute of Planners,* Vol. 34 (1968): 43-49.

Kumove, Leon, "A Preliminary Study of the Social Implications of High Density Living Conditions," Toronto: Social Planning Council of Metropolitan Toronto, 1966 (mimeo).

Kuper, Leo, "Social Science Research and the Planning of Urban Neighbourhoods," *Social Forces,* Vol. 29 (1951): 237-243.

———, *et al, Living In Towns,* London: Cresset Press, 1953.

Lamanna, R. A. "Value Consensus Among Urban Residents," *Journal of the American Institute of Planners,* Vol. 36 (1964): 317-323.

Langdon, F. J., "The Social and Physical Environment: A Social Scientist's View," *Journal of the Royal Institute of British Architects,* Vol. 73 (1966): 460-464.

Langner, Thomas S., and Stanley T. Michael, *Life Stress and Mental Health,* New York: The Free Press of Glencoe, 1963.

Lansing, John B., *Residential Location and Urban Mobility: The Second Wave of Interviews.* Prepared for U.S. Department of Commerce, Bureau of Public Roads, Jan., 1966: Survey Research Center, Institute for Social Research, The University of Michigan.

deLauwe, Paul Chambart, *L'Integration du Citadin à Sa Ville et à Son Quartier,* Montrange (Seine), France: Centre d'Etudes des Groupes Sociaux, 1961-62, Vol. 4.

Laumann, Edward O., James Beshers, and Benjamin Bradshaw, "Ethnic Congregation, Segregation, Assimilation, and Stratification," *Social Forces,* Vol. 43 (1964): 482-489.

Lee, Terence, "Urban Neighborhood as a Socio-Spatial Schema," *Human Relations,* Vol. 21, (1968): 241-267.

Leo, John, "Nearness Termed Key to Fondness," *The New York Times,* May 18, 1969: 58.

Lieberson, Stanley, "The Impact of Residential Segregation on Ethnic Assimilation," *Social Forces,* Vol. 40 (1961): 52-57.

Lindberg, Göran, *Social Omgivning: En Social-Ekologisk Undersökning av Tjugo Bostadsomradeni Malmö,* Lund: Lunds Universitet, Sociologiska Institutionen, 1967.

Lipman, Marvin, "Social Effects of the Housing Environment," in Michael Wheeler (ed.), *The Right to Housing,* Montreal: Harvest House, 1969, 171-189.

Loewy, Raymond, and William Snaith, *The Motivations Toward Homes and Housing,* New York: Raymond Loewy and William Snaith, Inc. Prepared for the Project Home Committee, 1968.

Long, N. E., "The Local Community as an Ecology of Games," *American Journal of Sociology,* Vol. 64 (1958-59): 251-261.

Loring, William C., "Housing and Social Organization," *Social Problems,* Vol. 3 (1956): 167.

Lynch, Kevin, *The Image of the City,* Cambridge, Mass.: M.I.T. Press and Harvard University Press, 1960.

———, "The Pattern of the Metropolis," *Daedalus,* (Winter 1961): 79-98.

Lynch, Kevin, and Lloyd Rodwin, "A Theory of Urban Form," *Journal of the American Institute of Planners,* Vol. 24 (1958): 201-214.

Mabry, John, "Public Housing as an Ecological Influence in three English Cities." Paper delivered to the 1965 Annual Meeting of the American Sociological Association, Chicago, Ill.

Macdonald, John Stuart, and Leatrice Macdonald, "Chain Migration, Ethnic Neighborhood Formation, and Social Networks," *Milbank Memorial Fund Quarterly,* Vol. 42 (1964): 82-97.

Marris, Peter, *Family and Social Change in an African City,* Evanston, Ill.: Northwestern University Press, 1962.

———, "A Report on Urban Renewal in the U.S.," in Duhl (ed.), *The Urban Condition,* New York: Basic Books, 1963, 113-134.

Martin, A. E., "Environment, Housing, and Health," *Urban Studies,* Vol. 4 (1967): 1-21.

Martin, Walter T., "The Structuring of Social Relationships Engendered by Suburban Residence," *American Sociological Review,* Vol. 21 (1956): 446-453.

Meier, Richard L., *A Communications Theory of Urban Growth,* Cambridge, Mass.: M.I.T. Press, 1962.

Merton, Robert K., "The Social Psychology of Housing," in Wayne Dennis (ed.), *Current Trends in Social Psychology,* Pittsburgh: University of Pittsburgh Press, 1948, 163-217.

Messer, Mark, "Engagement with Disengagement," paper presented at the 1966 Annual Meeting of the American Sociological Association, Miami Beach, Florida.

Meyerson, Martin, "National Character and Urban Development," Carl J. Friedrich and Seymour E. Harris (eds.), *Public Policy,* Vol. 12 (1963): 78-96.

——, "Utopian Traditions and the Planning of Cities," *Daedalus* (Winter 1961): 180-193.

Michelson, William, "Analytic Sampling for Design Information: A Survey of Housing Experience," a paper to be published in the proceedings of the first annual meeting of the Environmental Design Research Association, held in Chapel Hill, North Carolina, June 8-11, 1969.

——, "Ecological Thought and Its Application to School Functioning," presented at the Fourteenth Annual Eastern Research Institute of the Association for Supervision and Curriculum Development, National Education Association, Nov. 8, 1968. For publication by N.E.A.

——, "An Empirical Analysis of Urban Environmental Preferences," *Journal of the American Institute for Planners,* Vol. 32 (1966): 355-360.

——, "Potential Candidates for the Designers' Paradise: A Social Analysis From a Nationwide Survey," *Social Forces,* Vol. 46 (1967): 190-196.

——, "Social Insights to Guide the Design of Housing for Low-Income Families," in *Critical Urban Housing Issues: 1967,* Washington, D.C.: National Association of Housing and Redevelopment Officials, 1967, 60-68.

——, "Social Values, Physical Form," *Connection,* (Summer 1966): 51-54.

——, "Space as a Variable in Sociological Inquiry: Serendipitous Findings on Macro-Environment," presented at the 1969 Annual Meeting of the American Sociological Association, San Francisco, California, September 1969.

——, "Urban Sociology as an Aid to Urban Physical Development: Some Research Strategies," *Journal of the American Institute of Planners,* Vol. 34 (1968): 105-108.

——, "Value Orientations and Urban Form," unpublished doctoral dissertation, Harvard University, 1965.

——, "Value Orientations and Urban Physical Form: An Empirical Assessment," paper presented to the 1966 Annual Meeting of the Eastern Sociological Society, Philadelphia, Pa.

Mogey, J. M., *Family and Neighbourhood,* London: Oxford University Press, 1956.

Molotch, Harvey L., "Toward a More Human Ecology: An Urban Research Strategy," *Land Economics,* Vol. 43 (1967): 336-341.

Morris, R. N., and John Mogey, *The Sociology of Housing: Studies at Berinsfield,* London: Routledge and Kegan Paul, 1965.

Mumford, Lewis, "The Sky Line: Mother Jacobs' Home Remedies," *The New Yorker,* Vol. 38 (Dec. 1, 1962): 148 ff.

Musil, J., "The Development of Prague's Ecological Structure," in R. E. Pahl (ed.), *Readings in Urban Sociology,* London: Pergamon Press, 1968, 232-259.

Myers, Jerome K., "Assimilation to the Ecological and Social Systems of the Community," *American Sociological Review,* Vol. 15 (1950): 367-372.

Oeser, O. A., and S. B. Hammond, *Social Structure and Personality in a City,* New York: Macmillan, 1954.

Orleans, Peter, "Robert Park and Social Area Analysis," *Urban Affairs Quarterly,* Vol. 1, no. 4 (June 1966): 5-19.

_____ , "Sociology and Environmental Planning: A Scalar Perspective," paper presented to the 1968 Annual Meeting of the American Sociological Association, Boston, Mass.

_____ , "Urban Experimentation and Urban Sociology," paper presented to the 1967 Annual Meeting of the National Academy of Sciences, Washington, D.C.

Pahl, R.E., "A Perspective on Urban Sociology," in R. E. Pahl (ed.), *Readings in Urban Sociology,* London: Pergamon Press, 1968, 3-44.

Park, R. E., Ernest Burgess, and R. D. McKenzie, (eds.), *The City,* Chicago: University of Chicago Press, 1925.

Parr, A. E., "Environmental Design and Psychology," reprinted from *Landscape,* Vol. 14 (Winter, 1964-65): 15-18.

Parsons, Talcott, "The Principal Structures of Community: A Sociological View," in Carl J. Friedrich (ed.), *Community,* New York: The Liberal Arts Press, 1959, 152-179.

Perry, Clarence, "The Neighbourhood Unit Formula," in William L. C. Wheaton, *et al,* (eds.), *Urban Housing,* New York: The Free Press of Glencoe, 1966, 94-109.

Peterson, George L., "A Model of Preference: Qualitative Analysis of the Perception of the Visual Appearance of Residential Neighborhoods," *Journal of Regional Science,* Vol. 7 (1967): 19-32.

Pfeil, E., "The Pattern of Neighbouring Relations in Dortmund- Nordstadt" in R. E. Pahl (ed.), *Readings in Urban Sociology,* London: Pergamon Press, 1968, 136-158.

Plant, James S., "The Personality and an Urban Area," in Hatt and Reiss, *Cities and Society,* New York: The Free Press, 1957, 647-665.

Pond, M. Allen, "The Influence. of Housing on Health," *Marriage and Family Living,* Vol. XIX, no. 2 (May, 1957): 154-159.

Rainwater, Lee, "Fear and the House-as-Haven in the Lower Class," *Journal of the American Institute of Planners,* Vol. 32 (1966): 23-31.

Ramsøy, Natalie Rogoff, *"Assortive Mating and the Structure of Cities,"* American Sociological Review, Vol. 31 (1966): 773-785.

Raven, John, "Sociological Evidence on Housing (2: The Home Environment)," *The Architectural Review,* Vol. 142 (1967): 236 ff.

Reiner, Thomas A., *The Place of the Ideal Community in Urban Planning,* Philadelphia: University of Pennsylvania Press, 1963.

Reiss, Albert J., Jr., "Rural-Urban and Status Differences in Interpersonal Contacts," *American Journal of Sociology,* (1959): 182-195.

Riesman, David, "The Suburban Sadness," in Dobriner, William M. (ed.), *The Suburban Community,* New York: Putnam and Sons, 1958, 375-408.

Ripley, S. Dillon, and Helmut K. Buechner, "Ecosystem Science as a Point of Synthesis," *Daedalus,* (Fall 1967): 1192-1199.

Rose, Albert, "Housing and the Social Environment," in *Habitat 67,* collection of papers presented at the 7th Stratford (Ont.) Seminar on Civic Design, 1967, 2-19.

Rosenberg, Gerhard, "High Population Densities in Relation to Social Behaviour," *Ekistics,* Vol. 25 (1968): 425-427.

Rosow, Irving, "The Social Effects of the Physical Environment," *Journal of the American Institute of Planners,* Vol. 27 (1961): 127-133.

_____ , *Social Integration of the Aged,* New York: The Free Press of Glencoe, 1967.

Ross, H. Laurence, "The Local Community: A Survey Approach," *American Sociological Review,* Vol. 27 (1962): 75-84.

_____ , "Reasons for Moves to and from a Central City Area," *Social Forces,* Vol. 40 (1961): 261-263.

_____ , "Uptown and Downtown: A Study of Middle Class Residential Areas," *American Sociological Review,* Vol. 30 (1965): 255-259.

Rossi, Peter H., *Why Families Move,* New York: The Free Press of Glencoe, 1965.

Ryan, Edward, "Personal Identity in an Urban Slum," in Leonard J. Duhl (ed.), *The Urban Condition,* New York: Basic Books, 1963,135-150.

Schmitt, Robert C., "Implications of Density in Hong Kong," *Journal of the American Institute of Planners,* Vol. 24 (1963): 210-217.

_____ , "Density, Health, and Social Organization," *Journal of the American Institute of Planners,* Vol. 32 (1966): 38-40.

Schnore, Leo, "The Myth of Human Ecology," *Sociological Inquiry,* Vol. 31 (1961): 128-139.

_____ , "Urban Form: The Case of the Metropolitan Community," in Werner Hirsch (ed.), *Urban Life and Form,* New York: Holt, Rinehart, and Winston, 1963, 167-193.

_____ , *The Urban Scene,* New York: The Free Press of Glencoe, 1965.

Schorr, Alvin L., *Slums and Social Insecurity.* U.S. Department of Health, Education and Welfare, Social Security Administration, Division of Research and Statistics, Research Report No. 1.

Schwartz, Barry, "The Social Psychology of Privacy," *American Journal of Sociology,* Vol. 73 (1968): 741-752.

Seeley, John, "The Slum: Its Nature, Use, and Users," *Journal of the American Institute of Planners,* Vol. 25 (1959): 7-14.

_____ , R. Alexander Sim, and E. W. Loosley, *Crestwood Heights,* New York: Basic Books, 1956.

Seligman, Daniel, "The Enduring Slums," in William H. Whyte (ed.), *The Exploding Metropolis,* Garden City, N.Y.: Doubleday, 1957, 92-114.

Shanas, Ethel, "A Note on Restriction of Life Space: Attitudes of Age Cohorts," *Journal of Health and Social Behaviour,* Vol. 9, no. 1 (Mar., 1968): 86-90.

Shevky, Eshref, and Wendell Bell, *Social Area Analysis,* Stanford, Cal.: Stanford University Press, 1955.

Shulman, Norman, "Mutual Aid and Neighboring Patterns: The Lower Town Study," *Anthropologica,* Vol. 9 (1967): 51-60.

_____ , "Urban Environment and Social Interaction," unpublished term paper, Department of Sociology, University of Toronto, August 1968.

Simmel, Georg, "The Metropolis and Mental Life," in Hatt and Reiss (eds.), *Cities and Society,* New York: The Free Press of Glencoe, rev. ed., 1957, 635-646.

Smith, Robert C., "Colonial Towns of Spanish and Portuguese America," *Journal of the Society of Architectural Historians,* Vol. 14 (1955): 3-12.

Sommer, Robert, "Designed for Friendship," *Canadian Architect,* (Feb. 1961): 59-61.

_____ , "The Distance for Comfortable Conversation," *Sociometry,* Vol. 25 (1962): 111-116.

_____ , "The Ecology of Privacy," *Library Quarterly,* Vol. 6 (1966): 234-248.

_____ , "Further Studies of Small Group Ecology," *Sociometry,* Vol. 28 (1965): 337-348.

_____ , *Personal Space,* Englewood Cliffs, New Jersey: Prentice-Hall, 1969.

Spectorsky, A. C., *The Exurbanites,* Philadelphia: J. B. Lippincott Co., 1955.

Stein, Clarence S., *Towards New Towns for America,* New York: Reinhold, 1951.

Steinitz, Carl, "Meaning and the Congruence of Urban Form and Activity," *Journal of the American Institute of Planners,* Vol. 34 (1968): 233-248.

Stevenson, A., E. Martin, and J. O'Neill, *High Living: A Study of Family Life in Flats,* Melbourne: Melbourne University Press, 1967.

Strauss, A. L., *Images of the American City,* New York: The Free Press of Glencoe, 1961.

Studer, Raymond G., "Behavior-Contingent Architecture: Some Implications for Experimental Communities," paper presented at the 1966 Conference on The Experimental Community, Racine, Wisconsin December 28, 1966.

_____ , "Environmental Fit and Dynamics of Living Systems: Some Methodological Issues," paper delivered to the B.A.C. Conference on Design Methodology, Boston, May 6, 1967.

_____ , and David Stea, "Architectural Programming, Environmental Design, and Human Behavior," *Journal of Social Issues,* Vol. 22 no. 4: 127-136.

Suttles, Gerald, *The Social Order of the Slums,* Chicago: University of Chicago Press, 1968.

Sykes, Gresham, "The Differential Distribution of Community Knowledge," in Hatt and Reiss, *Cities and Society,* N.Y.: The Free Press of Glencoe, rev. ed., 1957, 711-721.

Tilly, Charles, "Anthropology on the Town," *Habitat,* Vol. 10, no. 1 (1967): 20-25.

———, "Occupational Rank and Grade of Residence in a Metropolis," *American Journal of Sociology,* Vol. 67 (1961): 323-330.

———, and Harold C. Brown, "On Uprooting, Kinship, and the Auspices of Migration," *International Journal of Comparative Sociology,* Vol. 8 (1967): 139-164.

Tomeh, Aida K., "Empirical Considerations on the Problem of Social Integration," *Sociological Inquiry,* Vol. 39 (Winter,1969): 65-76.

Toronto Real Estate Board, *A Study of Expropriation for Urban Renewal in the City of Toronto,* 1967.

Vernon, Raymond, *The Myth and Reality of Our Urban Problems,* Cambridge, Mass.: Joint Center for Urban Studies of M.I.T. and Harvard, 1962.

Wallace, Anthony F. C., "Housing and Social Structure: A Preliminary Survey with Particular Reference to Multi-Storey, Low Rent Public Housing Projects," Philadelphia: Philadelphia Housing Authority, 1952 (mimeo).

Webber, Melvin M., "Order in Diversity: Community Without Propinquity," in L. Wingo, Jr. (ed.), *Cities and Space,* Baltimore: The Johns Hopkins Press, 1963, 23-54.

———, "The Urban Place and the Non Place Urban Realm," in Webber, *et al., Explorations into Urban Structure,* Philadelphia: University of Pennsylvania Press, 1964, 79-153.

Werthman, Carl, Jerry S. Mandel, and Ted Dienstfray, *Planning and the Purchase Decision: Why People Buy in Planned Communities.* A pre-publication of the Community Development Project. University of California, Berkeley: Institute of Regional Development, Center for Planning and Development Research. Reprint No. 10, July, 1965.

Whyte, William H. (Jr.), "Cluster Development," in F. W. Eldredge (ed.), *Taming Megalopolis,* Garden City, N.Y.: Anchor Books, 1967, 462-477.

———, *The Organization Man,* Garden City, N.Y.: Anchor Books, Doubleday, 1956.

———, "The Web of Word of Mouth," *Fortune,* Vol. 50 (Nov. 1954): 140-143; 204-212.

Wiehl, Dorothy A., "Mortality and Socio-Environmental Factors," in Hatt and Reiss, *Cities and Society,* New York: The Free Press, 1957, 335-350.

Willhelm, Sidney, "The Concept of the 'Ecological Complex'," *The American Journal of Economics and Sociology,* Vol. 23 (1964): 241-248.

Willis, Margaret, *Back Gardens,* London: London County Council, Architects Department, September 1960.

———, *Environment and the Home,* London: London County Council, Architects Department, October 1954.

_____, *Living in High Flats,* London: London County Council, Architects Department, January 1955.

Willmott, Peter, *The Evolution of a Community,* London: Routledge and Kegan Paul, 1962.

_____, and M. Young, *Family and Class in a London Suburb,* London: Routledge and Kegan Paul, 1960.

Wilner, D. M., and R. P. Walkley, "Effects of Housing on Health and Performance," in Leonard J. Duhl (ed.), *The Urban Condition,* New York: Basic Books, 1962, 215-228.

_____, R. P. Walkley, and S. W. Cook, *Human Relations in Interracial Housing,* University of Minnesota Press, Minneapolis, 1955.

_____, R. P. Walkley, T. Pinkerton, and M. Tayback, *The Housing Environment and Family Life: A Longitudinal Study of the Effects of Housing on Morbidity and Mental Health,* Baltimore, Md.: The Johns Hopkins Press, 1962.

_____, R. P. Walkley, J. M. Schram, T. C. Pinkerton, and M. Tayback, "Housing as an Environmental Factor in Mental Health: The Johns Hopkins Longitudinal Study," *American Journal of Public Health,* Vol. 50 (1960): 55-63.

_____, R. P. Walkley, and M. Tayback, "How Does Quality of Housing Affect Health and Family Adjustment," *American Journal of Public Health,* Vol. 46 (1956): 736-744.

Wilson, Robert L., "Livability of the City: Attitudes and Urban Development," in F. S. Chapin, Jr., and Shirley Weiss, (ed.), *Urban Growth Dynamics,* New York: John Wiley & Sons, 1962, 359-399.

Wirth, Louis, "Human Ecology," in Richard Sennett (ed.), *Classic Essays on the Culture of Cities,* New York: Appleton-Century-Crofts, 1969, 170-179.

_____, "Urbanism as a Way of Life," *American Journal of Sociology,* Vol. 44 (1938): 1-24.

Wolf, Eleanor, and Charles W. Lebeaux, "On the Destruction of Poor Neighborhoods by Urban Renewal," paper presented to the 1966 Annual Meeting of the American Sociological Association, Miami Beach, Florida.

Wolpert, Julian, "Migration as an Adjustment to Environmental Stress," *Journal of Social Issues,* Vol. 22, no. 4 (October, 1966): 92-102.

Wood, Arthur E., *Hamtramck—Then and Now,* New Haven, Conn.: College and Universities Press, 1955.

Young, M., and P. Willmott, *Family and Kinship in East London,* London: Routledge and Kegan Paul, 1957.

Zeisel, John, "Symbolic Meaning of Space and Physical Dimension of Social Relations," Paper presented to the American Sociological Association, Annual Meeting, September 1, 1969, unpublished.

Zelan, Joseph, "Does Suburbia Make a Difference: An Exercise in Secondary Analysis," in Sylvia Fleis Fava (ed.), *Urbanism in World Perspective,* New York: Thomas Y. Crowell Co., 1968, 401-408.

index

index